FRANCIS BACON was born in London in 1561, the fifth and youngest son of Sir Nicholas Bacon, the second most important counsellor to Queen Elizabeth. After attending Trinity College Cambridge, Bacon took up a career in law, soon gaining respect as a legal adviser and becoming an MP in his twenties. He spent his whole life in public service, reaching the highest legal offices: Solicitor-General, Attorney-General, Lord Keeper, Lord Chancellor, and being created successively Baron Verulam and Viscount St Alban. In his spare time Bacon studied natural philosophy and a wide variety of other subjects, pursuing an ambitious scheme to reform the whole of human learning. His *Essays*, *Advancement of Learning*, and *New Atlantis* have assured him a distinguished place in English literature. He died in 1626.

BRIAN VICKERS, educated at St Marylebone Grammar School and Trinity College Cambridge, has been Professor of English Literature and Director of the Centre for Renaissance Studies at the ETH Zurich since 1975. He has written extensively on Francis Bacon, on Renaissance science and philosophy, and on classical rhetoric. He edited the Oxford Authors *Francis Bacon* (1996) and Bacon's *History of the Reign of King Henry VII* (1998). His other books include *Towards Greek Tragedy* (1973), *In Defence of Rhetoric* (1988), *Returning to Shakespeare* (1989), and *Appropriating Shakespeare: Contemporary Critical Quarrels* (1993). In 1996 he received the Litt.D. from Cambridge University, and in 1998 was elected a Corresponding Fellow of the British Academy.

OXFORD WORLD'S CLASSICS

*For almost 100 years Oxford World's Classics have brought
readers closer to the world's great literature. Now with over 700
titles—from the 4,000-year-old myths of Mesopotamia to the
twentieth century's greatest novels—the series makes available
lesser-known as well as celebrated writing.*

*The pocket-sized hardbacks of the early years contained
introductions by Virginia Woolf, T. S. Eliot, Graham Greene,
and other literary figures which enriched the experience of reading.
Today the series is recognized for its fine scholarship and
reliability in texts that span world literature, drama and poetry,
religion, philosophy and politics. Each edition includes perceptive
commentary and essential background information to meet the
changing needs of readers.*

OXFORD WORLD'S CLASSICS

FRANCIS BACON

The Essays or Counsels Civil and Moral

Edited with an Introduction and Notes by
BRIAN VICKERS

UNIVERSITY PRESS

OXFORD
UNIVERSITY PRESS

Great Clarendon Street, Oxford OX2 6DP

Oxford University Press is a department of the University of Oxford
and furthers the University's aim of excellence in research, scholarship,
and education by publishing worldwide in

Oxford New York

Athens Auckland Bangkok Bogotá Buenos Aires Calcutta
Cape Town Chennai Dar es Salaam Delhi Florence Hong Kong Istanbul
Karachi Kuala Lumpur Madrid Melbourne Mexico City Mumbai
Nairobi Paris São Paulo Singapore Taipei Tokyo Toronto Warsaw

and associated companies in Berlin Ibadan

Oxford is a registered trade mark of Oxford University Press
in the UK and in certain other countries

Published in the United States
by Oxford University Press Inc., New York

British Library Cataloguing Publication Data
Data available

Library of Congress Cataloging in Publication Data

Bacon, Francis, 1561–1626.
[Essays]
The essays or counsels, civil and moral / Francis Bacon;
edited by Brian Vickers.
(Oxford world's classics)
Includes bibliographical references.
1. English Essays—Early modern, 1500–1700. I. Vickers, Brian.
II. Title. III. Series: Oxford world's classics (Oxford University Press)
PR2206.V53 1999 824'.3—dc21 [b] 98–31241
ISBN 0-19-283802-4

1 3 5 7 9 10 8 6 4 2

Typeset in Ehrhardt
by Alliance Phototypesetters, Pondicherry, India
Printed in Great Britain
on acid-free paper by
Cox & Wyman Ltd., Reading, Berkshire

CONTENTS

Appendix I: Essays (1597)

Contents

ACKNOWLEDGEMENTS

THIS edition of Bacon's *Essays* is a slimmed-down version of the one given in my volume *Francis Bacon*, in the Oxford Authors series (Oxford, 1996). I have reduced the quantity of annotation, simplified the presentation, and made it easier for readers to use. Notes explaining Bacon's vocabulary—almost as rich as Shakespeare's, but far less familiar, not having been glossed in annotated editions for over three centuries—are numbered and placed at the foot of each page. Longer explanatory notes, together with the identification and translation of all foreign language quotations, are marked with an asterisk and grouped together at pp. 156–216.

The idea for producing this edition came from Judith Luna, of Oxford University Press, who was both patient and supportive of my attempts to make a compact and useful edition. She also made several shrewd suggestions about the scope and substance of the introduction.

In preparing this edition I have been much helped by my assistant, Dr Margrit Soland, who kept a keen eye on the many changes needed, and made good use of her philological training. This was the last job that we worked on before her retirement, and I would like to salute her steady control of a great variety of material over a long period. Her successors, Katherine Hahn and Annette Baertschi, have maintained the same high standards, while moving into fully electronic publishing. I am most grateful to Elizabeth Stratford and her copy-editing staff for a final meticulous scrutiny of the manuscript.

For permission to reproduce the portrait of Francis Bacon I warmly thank Sir Nicholas Bacon, Bart., of Raveningham Hall, Norfolk. According to Roy Strong, *The English Icon: Elizabethan & Jacobean Portraiture* (London and New York, 1969), the painter was perhaps William Larkin, and the work may be dated *c*.1612–19 (pp. 20–1, 329). It is inscribed top right *Moniti Meliora*, a quotation from Virgil's *Aeneid* (3. 188), where Anchises admonishes his son Aeneas to 'pursue the better course'.

I dedicate this little edition to the memory of Elizabeth Wrigley, co-editor of a concordance to the *Essays*, and for many years curator of the Francis Bacon Library of Claremont, California. Several generations of Bacon scholars had reason to be grateful for the excellence of that collection, and her readiness to answer any request, small or large. The dissolution of the Francis Bacon Foundation in 1995, and the library's absorption into the Huntington Library of San Marino, California, was a cause of great regret to scholars around the world, and of deep personal disappointment to her. She died in 1997. This book will be one of many tributes to her service to scholarship.

IN MEMORY OF

ELIZABETH WRIGLEY

INTRODUCTION

The life of Francis Bacon

FRANCIS BACON was born on 22 January 1561, at York House in the Strand, the London residence of his father Sir Nicholas Bacon (1509–79), who was Lord Keeper of the Great Seal to Queen Elizabeth I from 1558 until his death. Sir Nicholas had risen from humble origins to one of the highest offices of state, through the classic route of study at Cambridge followed by training as a lawyer at Gray's Inn, the inns of court which formed England's 'third university'. Sir Nicholas's first wife bore him six surviving children (three sons and three daughters), and after her death in 1552 he married Ann Cooke (1528–1610), who bore him two further sons, Anthony (1558–1601), and Francis. Taught at first privately, they went up to Trinity College in 1573, studying under John Whitgift, Master of Trinity and subsequently Archbishop of Canterbury. After two years at Cambridge (sons of the gentry often left without taking a degree) they were both entered at Gray's Inn, following their father and other family members. But in September 1576 a better opportunity emerged for Francis to begin the career in public service which his father had designed for him, and he joined the retinue of Sir Amyas Paulet, Queen Elizabeth's ambassador to France. Bacon worked in various diplomatic functions, and was making a good reputation for himself when, in February 1579, his father suddenly died. Returning from France the following month, he entered Gray's Inn and began his studies as a lawyer.

When Sir Nicholas died he had settled land on his first four sons, guaranteeing them a stable existence among the country gentry, where they could farm their land, enjoy hunting and other field sports, and perhaps indulge some hobbies. Left without patrimony, Francis Bacon had no option but to work for his living, depending on the products of his brain and pen, as a lawyer, counsellor, and public servant. He made rapid progress at Gray's Inn, being appointed to lectureships far earlier than was usual, and sitting on several government legal committees (see Chronology, p. xli, for details). At the same time he began a parliamentary career that was to last from 1581 to 1621, and was soon in demand on various committees, where his intellectual abilities in summarizing a debate to bring out the points at issue was widely appreciated. In the 1593 parliament, however, fulfilling his duties to his constituents by outlining the hardships that would follow if Queen Elizabeth's demands for extraordinary taxes were met, he incurred her displeasure, and was blocked from obtaining the government legal positions to which he aspired. Testing his loyalty to her, the Queen made him one of the prosecuting counsels in the two trials of his former patron, the Earl of Essex, whose reckless ignoring of the Queen's policies in Ireland and his frustrated attempt to seize power led ultimately to his execution for treason in 1601. Bacon's involvement in these trials has long been held against him as a sign of ingratitude, but with the Queen explicitly commanding his participation it is hard to know what else he could have done.

Everything in Bacon's family background and training directed him towards public service. His father had not only served the Queen for most of his life, but was actively involved in several educational reforms, including a scheme worked out in the late 1530s to found a fifth Inn of Court to provide for the systematic training of statesmen and diplomats, including proficiency in foreign languages, knowledge of the Greek and Latin classics on politics and statecraft, and practical experience as apprentices to English ambassadors abroad.[1] His uncle, William Cecil, Baron Burghley (1520–98), also a product of Cambridge and Gray's Inn, was Secretary of State 1558–72, and Lord High Treasurer 1572–98, the Queen's chief minister. He helped Bacon on a few occasions, but was more concerned to advance his son, Robert Cecil (1563–1612), Secretary of State under Elizabeth and James I, who secured the King's accession to the English throne and was rewarded with several titles, culminating as Earl of Salisbury in 1605. Bacon, lacking any powerful patrons, had to make his way by his own efforts, and eventually succeeded in becoming Solicitor-General (1607), Attorney-General (1613), Lord Keeper of the Seal (1617), and Lord Chancellor (1618)—so emulating his father—finally being elevated to the peerage as Baron Verulam (1618), and Viscount St Alban (1621).

[1] See Robert Tittler, *Nicholas Bacon. The Making of a Tudor Statesman* (London, 1976), 29–31. Bacon was involved in proposals to improve the education of the Wards of Court; he also helped to found three grammar schools, and endowed six scholarships at Corpus Christi College Cambridge. He reformed and modernized the Court of Chancery, and was one of a group of parliamentarians who produced an important 'Remembrance' advocating far-reaching social and economic reforms.

Bacon's rise to high office was merited, for his intellectual powers were exceptional, and he fulfilled his duties as counsellor, prosecutor, and finally judge with great dedication. A recent evaluation of his four years' presidency over the Court of Chancery credits him with following his father's example by clearing up a vast backlog of cases and starting some long-needed reforms.[2] But he gradually became involved in several conflicts. One involved his relationship as a political adviser to King James, who was becoming increasingly absolutist in his dealings with parliament, expecting their submissive co-operation. Bacon, already known as a supporter of parliamentary prerogative, found himself identified in the eyes of militant parliamentarians with James's autocratic rule. Secondly, being closely involved with James meant that he continually had to deal with the King's favourite, George Villiers, first Duke of Buckingham (1592–1628). Bacon gave Buckingham sound advice according to his usual high standards of responsible public service, but found himself pulled into Buckingham's corrupt and corrupting network of gifts and favours, and unwillingly granted some of his dubious suits. Since Buckingham was the most despised man in England, Bacon's association with him was another source of annoyance. Thirdly, since Chancery was a court of equity, to which alleged cases of injustice from other courts were referred, Bacon found himself in conflict with judges presiding over other courts, notably his old rival Sir Edward Coke. And the fact that cases referred to Chancery suspended legal action until a decision was made (which often took years) meant that many bankrupts were able to postpone settlement, to the irritation of their debtors, powerful city merchants.

All these conflicts came together in the 1621 parliament, focused on the fourth and most serious conflict involving Bacon, that concerning monopolies. These patents gave their possessors the exclusive right to import or exploit a commodity (copper; gold and silver thread), or to issue the licences controlling a commercial activity (inns, for example). The power to award monopolies lay with the sovereign, and represented both a useful way of rewarding loyal servants and of producing income for the crown. But the execution of these rights was often tainted with bribery and corruption, and it included the particularly contentious feature that patentees could enforce their monopolies by private actions of seizure or distraint, outside the common law. Bacon

[2] See Daniel R. Coquillette, *Francis Bacon* (Edinburgh, 1992), in the series 'Jurists: Profiles in Legal Theory'.

had attacked the monopoly system in parliamentary debate several times, and had even advised James, before the 1621 parliament sat, to suspend the most unpopular monopolies. But the King refused, and a few weeks later found himself, his favourite, and his government officials being attacked by a concerted movement in parliament.[3] Unable to prosecute the King, who also protected Buckingham, the parliamentary opposition attacked the referees who had signed the monopolies—high legal officials merely endorsing the King's wishes—who included Bacon.

As a kind of witch-hunt built up, with accused parties being put into the Tower without trial, the opposition group learned of two cases where Bacon, in his office as Judge of Chancery, had accepted presents from litigants who had not won their legal action. (In the Jacobean court, where officials received only nominal salaries, and had to exist by selling offices and favours, the distinction between gifts from suitors and bribes intended to influence the outcome of a case, was often lost, and there were several notorious instances of corruption.)[4] Dropping their attack on monopolies, the anti-government party made an intensive examination of Bacon's four years in office, and found some twenty-odd instances of his having accepted gifts from litigants. But in nearly every case this was after the trial had been completed; in no case has it been shown to have affected his verdict; and none of his judgements was ever reversed. It was wrong of him not to have taken greater care in this matter, and he paid dearly for it: as he said in extenuation, 'howsoever I may be frail, and partake of the abuse of the times'.[5] Pleading guilty, he was convicted by the House of Lords of bribery, expelled from office, fined £40,000, sentenced to several days' imprisonment in the Tower, and forbidden to come within twelve miles of the King. By sacrificing Bacon James preserved his favourite, and placated parliament for the time being. But the monopolies system continued, with the most notorious profiteer, Sir Giles

[3] See Robert Zaller, *The Parliament of 1621. A Study in Constitutional Conflict* (Berkeley, Los Angeles, London, 1971); Conrad Russell, *Parliament and English Politics 1621–1629* (Oxford, 1979).

[4] See Joel Hurstfield, *Freedom, Corruption and Government in Elizabethan England* (London, 1973); Linda L. Peck, *Court Patronage and Corruption in Early Stuart England* (London, 1990).

[5] Letter to King James, March 1621, in *Francis Bacon*, ed. Brian Vickers (The Oxford Authors; Oxford, 1996), 326. Future references to this edition will be in the form TOA 326.

Mompesson, soon back in business, together with Buckingham, while those who had led the parliamentary attack on Bacon—Sir Edward Coke and Sir Lionel Cranfield—themselves fell into royal disfavour shortly afterwards. Coke suffered a long imprisonment in the Tower, and Cranfield was deprived of all offices, heavily fined, and forced into exile. Just to complete this sad story of royal opportunism, James ensured that Bacon was spared the real effects of his severe-sounding punishments. He spent only a few hours in the Tower; his fine was transferred to his creditors; and he was allowed back into London—at a price, namely that of selling to Buckingham, against his deepest wishes, York House, which, as he put it in one of several pathetically powerless letters, was 'the house where my father died, and where I first breathed, and there will I yield my last breath, if it so please God'.[6] As we review this tragic end to a lifetime's devoted public service, we see an especially poignant irony in his observation that

The rising unto place is laborious; and by pains men come to greater pains; and it is sometimes base; and by indignities men come to dignities. The standing is slippery, and the regress is either a downfall, or at least an eclipse, which is a melancholy thing.[7]

Bacon's fall from office, although it cost him untold personal anguish, and has provided uninformed or malicious detractors, from that day to this, with material to vilify him,[8] was in many ways a blessing in disguise. It freed him to return to the numerous literary, historical, and scientific projects that had occupied him in his little spare time over the previous decade. The first fruit, which appeared in March 1622, was a history of Henry VII, a monarch whose reign had long fascinated him for the great variety of events it contained, domestic and foreign. He used this opportunity of writing a full account to demonstrate his own theory of history writing, based on Tacitus and Machiavelli and their concern with cause and effect, the psychological motives governing political action.[9] Then in November of that year he continued publication of his *Instauratio Magna*, of which the first, incomplete

---

[6] *The Works of Francis Bacon*, ed. J. Spedding, R. L. Ellis, and D. D. Heath, 14 vols. (London, 1857–74), xiv. 327. Future references to this edition will be in the form *Works*, xiv. 327.

[7] Essay 'Of Great Place', p. 24 below.

[8] See the admirable study by Nieves Mathews, *Francis Bacon. The History of a Character Assassination* (New Haven and London, 1996).

[9] See *The History of the Reign of King Henry VII*, ed. Brian Vickers (Cambridge, 1998), pp. xv–xxxi.

instalment, consisting of the *Novum Organum* (a 'New Instrument' of scientific method) had appeared in 1620, by issuing the first part of his 'Natural and Experimental History', the second part appearing in January 1623. In that year he issued a Latin version of the *Advancement of Learning* (1605), its two books expanded to nine, to be followed in 1624 by two lesser works, his collection of *Apophthegms* and his verse translation of selected psalms. The last work published in his lifetime was the *Essays or Counsels, Civil and Moral* (1625), his devoted chaplain William Rawley bringing out the *Sylva Sylvarum* and *New Atlantis* posthumously (1627).

The *Essays: composition*

The *Essays* have proved to be Bacon's most popular work, and have probably never been out of print.[10] Whereas many of his works were quickly sketched in, often left unfinished, surviving manuscripts even bearing Bacon's own description, 'Several fragments of discourses',[11] the *Essays* were revised not once but twice. They first appeared in 1597, published by Bacon in some haste, to forestall a pirated edition. In January 1597 one Richard Serger obtained a manuscript copy of the *Essays* (no doubt one of several circulating among Bacon's friends and acquaintances, in the common practice of those days) and announced that he intended to print 'a book entitled *ESSAYES of M.F.B. with the prayers of his Sovereigne*' (that is, Queen Elizabeth), a completely spurious publication. Within a few days Bacon had negotiated with another printer to produce an authorized edition, which was published a week later.[12] Dedicating this work to his older brother Anthony, Bacon wrote that he was now publishing 'these fragments of my conceit' which had 'passed long ago from my pen', in order 'to prevent stealing', and to avoid the distortion created by 'untrue copies'. But he did so reluctantly, 'because they will be like the late new half-pence, which though the silver were good, yet the pieces were small'. And indeed

---

[10] See Brian Vickers, *Francis Bacon and Renaissance Prose* (Cambridge, 1968), 264, 303 n. 2, on the publishing history of Bacon's works.

[11] See ibid. 202–4. For Bacon's surviving manuscripts, many of them identified for the first time, see Peter Beal's epoch-making *Index of English Literary Manuscripts, i/I, 1450–1625: Andrewes–Donne* (London and New York, 1980), 17–52.

[12] For the publishing details of this attempted piracy see W. W. Greg, *Some Aspects and Problems of London Publishing between 1550 and 1650* (Oxford, 1956), 56–8, and TOA 545–6.

they were: in order to produce a saleable book Bacon added to the ten essays (which total only 3,400 words) two other short works, the *Meditationes Sacrae* ('Religious Meditations'), and the 'Places of perswasion and disswasion' (title-page), or 'Of the Colours of good and evil, a fragment' (subtitle). Even with these additions, it was a tiny volume, 'a little booke no bigger than a Primer', as John Aubrey described it.[13]

This first recension is notable for its extreme bareness of style. Individual sentences are often printed separately, and marked with a paragraph sign to signal their status as aphorisms, discrete observations embodying wisdom drawn from experience. It is important to realize that the bareness of style was a deliberate, sought-after factor, the corollary of Bacon's choosing the aphoristic form, not a proof that he was somehow lacking in eloquence or unable to write a coherent argument. Although critics unfamiliar with Bacon's writings as a whole describe his style as 'aphoristic', in fact it follows the principles laid down by rhetorical theory, varying according to the subject-matter treated and the audience addressed. As we can see from other works written in the 1590s, Bacon had already mastered a great range of expressive resources. But the issue of style is secondary here, since the aphorism is a distinct form or genre which Bacon only used when his subject-matter demanded it.

The prime quality for which Bacon valued the aphorism was not the pithiness commonly associated with it but its unsystematic quality, which allowed its user to set down separate observations without implying any firm connections between them. The advantage of aphorisms was that they would neither foreclose inquiry nor give a premature and spurious coherence to discussions which were not yet definitive and complete.[14] In many ways the best comment on the form of the 1597 *Essays* is a passage in Bacon's Preface to a professional treatise that he composed in that same year, the *Maxims of the Law* (not published until 1859), a collection of legal maxims which he had deliberately not arranged in the sequential form of a treatise. As he explained,

whereas I could have digested these rules into a certain method or order, which, I know, would have been more admired, as that which would have made every particular rule, through his coherence and relation unto other rules, seem more cunning and more deep; yet I have avoided so to do,

[13] *Brief Lives*, ed. O. L. Dick (Harmondsworth, 1962), 120.
[14] See Vickers, *Francis Bacon and Renaissance Prose*, ch. 3, pp. 60–95.

because this delivering of knowledge in distinct and disjoined aphorisms doth leave the wit of man more free to turn and toss, and to make use of that which is so delivered to more several purposes and applications. For we see all the ancient wisdom and science was wont to be delivered in that form; as may be seen by the parables of Solomon, and by the aphorisms of Hippocrates, and the moral verses of Theognis and Phocylides: but chiefly the precedent of the civil law, which hath taken the same course with their rules, did conform in my opinion.[15]

This combination of pregnant utterance and free form meant that the aphorism could be an appropriate vehicle for quite different areas of knowledge, from Bacon's works in natural philosophy to his treatment of politics and ethics, subjects where it was vital to preserve detail of observation without subsuming it into restricting categories. The *Advancement of Learning* contains several important discussions of the aphorism, showing Bacon's constant awareness of the need to find the most suitable vehicle for the communication of knowledge.[16]

The 1597 *Essays* are Bacon's first attempt to systematize his observations on human behaviour, especially the interplay between private life and the political arena. They evidently belong to the literature of advice, the so-called 'conduct-books' whose vogue in the Renaissance attracted many readers bent on self-improvement, from courtiers to citizens. The subject-matter of Bacon's collection similarly concerns the training and self-preparation needed by a man entering public life, and although presented separately the topics overlap, to form a miniature treatise. The first essay, on education, also deals with discourse, treated more fully in the second essay. The fourth, on followers and friends, also deals with suitors and expense, which become the subjects of the fifth and sixth essays. A continuity of attitude can be traced, too, in Bacon's constant emphasis on what is 'honourable', a fundamental ethical alignment that many commentators have missed. Bacon's laconic definitions, with the simplest verb-forms of 'to be' ('is' and 'are' recur most frequently), his curt imperatives ('Discern', 'Beware'), and his baldly stated preferences ('It is better') all convey his observations from experience in the plainest and most functional form.

This first edition enjoyed a modest success, being reprinted in 1597, 1598, 1606, and 1612.[17] At some time following the publication of *The*

---

[15] TOA 544; *Works*, vii. 321. [16] See TOA 145–6, 234–5, 270–1.

[17] For details of publication see R. W. Gibson, *Francis Bacon: A Bibliography of his Works and of Baconiana to the year 1750* (Oxford, 1950); supplement (Oxford, 1959).

*Twoo Bookes of Francis Bacon. Of the proficience and aduancement of
Learning, diuine and humane* (London, 1605) Bacon began work on a
new and enlarged edition, which appeared in 1612. Evidence of his revisions, not all of which were included in that volume, can be found in
a manuscript preserved in the British Library, MS Harleian 5106,
which contains 34 essays, including all but six of the 38 essays printed
in 1612, and two not included in that collection: 'Of Seditions and
Troubles', and an enlarged version of the 1597 'Of Honour and
Reputation'. This manuscript, transcribed some time between 1607,
when Bacon became Solicitor-General, and 1612, when the new edition appeared, is in the handwriting of one of Bacon's secretaries, and
contains interlineations in Bacon's own hand.[18] Of particular signific-
ance for his conception of the essay as a form is the title that this manuscript bears: *The writings of Sr Francis Bacon Knt, the King's Sollicitor
Generall: in Moralitie, Policie, and Historie.*

   This triple focus on the ethical, political, and historical constraints
and influences on human behaviour give the *Essays* their unique quality. In terms of content they are serious contributions to knowledge,
drawn from Bacon's own experience and reading; but in form they
continue to eschew system, adding to the aphoristic utterance of the
1597 version a new loose, discursive structure. Further indication of
how Bacon conceived the *Essays* is provided by the dedication to
Prince Henry, which had been due to appear in the printed volume.
The Prince's sudden and tragic death on 6 November 1612 foiled this
plan, but a copy of Bacon's dedication has survived in the British
Library, and is very revealing:

It may please your Highness:

Having divided my life into the contemplative and active part, I am desirous to give his Majesty and your Highness of the fruits of both, simple
though they be.

To write just treatises requireth leisure in the writer and leisure in the
reader, and therefore are not so fit, neither in regard of your Highness'
princely affairs, nor in regard of my continual services; which is the cause
that hath made me choose to write certain brief notes, set down rather
significantly than curiously, which I have called *Essays*. The word is late, but
the thing is ancient, for Seneca's *Epistles to Lucilius*, if one mark them well,

---

[18] For a full description of this manuscript see Michael Kiernan (ed.), *Sir Francis
Bacon: The Essayes or Counsels, Civill and Morall* (Oxford, 1985), lxxi ff.; and *Works*, vi.
35–6.

are but *Essays*, that is, dispersed meditations, though conveyed in the form of Epistles. These labours of mine I know cannot be worthy of your Highness, for what can be worthy of you? But my hope is, they may be as grains of salt, that will rather give you an appetite than offend you with satiety. And although they handle those things wherein both men's lives and their pens are most conversant, yet (what I have attained, I know not), but I have endeavoured to make them not vulgar, but of a nature whereof a man shall find much in experience, and little in books; so as they are neither repetitions nor fancies. . . .[19]

Bacon's conception of the *Essays* as 'brief notes, set down rather significantly than curiously'—that is, concerned with pregnancy of meaning rather than nicety of form—and as 'dispersed meditations', well describes their unsystematic nature ('dispersed' implying their not being organized around a single argument). But he also describes them as 'meditations', a word which (like 'contemplation' or 'contemplative') had for him secular connotations, implying prolonged study, rather than the religious associations held by other writers of this period. Their substance, further, is of a kind found 'much in experience, little in books', which makes them neither 'repetitions', reworkings of *topoi* within a literary tradition, nor 'fancies', purely imaginary constructs unanchored in social reality, but observations drawn from life.

The principles on which Bacon enlarged the 1597 Essays in 1612, and added new ones, can be found clearly stated in the *Advancement of Learning*. As R. S. Crane first pointed out,[20] Bacon used his *Essays* to fill the lacunae in knowledge, those areas yet to be properly discussed, which he had identified in Book Two of that work. In particular, these involved lacunae in 'moral' and 'civil' knowledge, that is 'The Regiment or Culture of the Mind', a discipline which should prescribe 'rules how to subdue, apply [adapt], and accommodate the will of man' to 'the nature of good'—so uniting psychology and ethics. In this connection Bacon noted the lack of any systematic 'descriptions of the several characters and tempers of man's natures and dispositions', including

those impressions of nature, which are imposed upon the mind by the sex, by the age, by the region, by health and sickness, by beauty and deformity,

---

[19] TOA 677–8; *Works*, xi. 340.
[20] 'The Relation of Bacon's *Essays* to his Program for the Advancement of Learning', in Brian Vickers (ed.), *Essential Articles for the Study of Francis Bacon* (Hamden, Conn., 1968; London, 1972), 272–92.

and the like, which are inherent and not extern; as sovereignty, nobility, obscure birth, riches, want, magistracy, privateness, prosperity, adversity, constant fortune, variable fortune, rising *per saltum, per gradus* and the like. . . .[21]

As Crane argued, it was to fulfil these desiderata that (already in 1612) Bacon wrote the essays 'Of Youth and Age', 'Of Beauty', 'Of Deformity', 'Of Nobility', 'Of Great Place', 'Of Riches', and 'Of Fortune', expanding them all in 1625 and adding a new essay for this group, 'Of Adversity'. Bacon's diagnosis of the absence of 'active and ample observations' concerning 'the diseases and infirmities of the mind, . . . the perturbations and distempers of the passions' (TOA 259), gave rise to the essays 'Of Love', 'Of Envy', and 'Of Anger', as well as to many incidental comments in other essays on the effect that the passions have on human affairs.

Turning from the formative influences of nature and external fortune to 'those points which are within our own command, and have force and operation upon the mind to affect the will and to alter manners', the topics which Bacon listed as deficient included 'custom, exercise, habit, education, example, imitation, emulation, company, friends, praise, reproof, exhortation, fame, laws, books, studies'. Correspondingly, the *Essays* provided discussions 'Of Custom and Education', 'Of Praise', 'Of Nature in Men', 'Of Friendship', and 'Of Fame' (unfinished). These links reveal that, at the time when he was writing the *Advancement of Learning* (*c.*1603–5), Bacon was already planning an expanded edition of the *Essays* in order to cultivate those 'parts' of learning which he had identified as lying 'fresh and waste, and not improved by the industry of man'. Under the heading 'civil knowledge' Bacon included three topics: 'wisdom of the behaviour', or conversation, in the wider sense of social intercourse; 'wisdom of business', or negotiation; and 'wisdom of state', or government. It is significant that five of the essays first published in 1597—'Of Discourse', 'Of Ceremonies and Respects', 'Of Negotiating', 'Of Followers and Friends', and 'Of Faction'—already dealt with topics that Bacon subsequently noted in the *Advancement* as needing discussion, suggesting that his plan for a coherent and systematic treatment of this area of human affairs already existed before the turn of the century. All these essays were enlarged in 1612, while the new ones written for that volume and for 1625 fulfil the desiderata Bacon had noted for treatises

[21] TOA 258.

on the 'doctrine of advancement in life' (the essays 'Of Vain-Glory', 'Of Dispatch', 'Of Boldness', 'Of Delays', and 'Of Simulation and Dissimulation'), and for discussions of the art of government (the essays 'Of Seditions and Troubles', 'Of the True Greatness of Kingdoms and Estates', 'Of Empire', and 'Of Plantations'). The fact that, as Crane also showed,[22] many of these essays absorb material first published either in the *Advancement of Learning* or as occasional papers in Bacon's political career, helps us to see the *Essays* as forming an integral part of Bacon's overall scheme for the reform and improvement of knowledge concerning individual and social life.

Although continuing the scope of inquiry established in 1597, the 1612 volume differs in form, the separated aphorisms being surrounded by more sustained discursive passages. Perhaps the best way of understanding this change is provided, once again, by Bacon's Preface to the *Maxims of the Law* (1597). Having grouped those maxims at the beginning of his treatise as separate aphorisms, he explained why he had added to them a commentary:

Lastly, there is one point above all the rest I account the most material for making these rules indeed profitable and instructing; which is, that they be not set down alone, like short dark oracles, which every man will be content still to allow to be true, but in the meantime they give little light or direction; but I have attended them (a matter not practised, no not in the civil law to any purpose, and for want whereof, indeed, the rules are but as proverbs, and many times plain fallacies), with a clear and perspicuous exposition; breaking them into cases, and opening their sense and use and limiting them with distinctions; and sometimes showing the reasons above whereupon they depend, and the affinity they have with other rules.[23]

If the aphorisms in the 1597 edition are 'like short dark oracles', the *Essays* of 1612 add to them 'a clear and perspicuous exposition', a kind of running commentary, 'opening their sense and use' by explanatory passages, 'and limiting them with distinctions' so as to achieve a more exact differentiation of the issues discussed.

The 1612 collection was also successful, being reprinted in 1612 (twice), 1613 (twice), 1614, and 1624, but Bacon evidently felt unsatisfied with its coverage and in 1625 he published the third and final version. In dedicating it to Buckingham, Bacon wrote:

[22] 'Relation', 276–8.   [23] *Works*, vii. 323.

I do now publish my *Essays*; which, of all my other works, have been most current; for that, as it seems, they come home to men's business and bosoms. I have enlarged them both in number and weight; so that they are indeed a new work.[24]

By 'most current' he meant 'most in circulation', for to the earlier editions of 1597 and 1612 he could list the (anonymous) Italian translation, *Saggi Morali* (including also the *De Sapientia Veterum*), which was published in London in 1617 and reprinted both in England and Italy during his lifetime; a different Italian translation, by Andrea Cioli, which first appeared in 1619; and a French translation, which appeared in 1619 and was reprinted three times before his death.[25] As for the English version of the *Essays*, Gibson records some 30 editions by 1706, and there have been several hundred since then. By 'bosoms' Bacon implies that his work affects the individual reader in the privacy of his or her room. So his friend Lancelot Andrewes said in one of his sermons that recognition of human responsibility for the sufferings of Christ 'bringeth home this text to us, even into our own bosoms; and applieth it most effectually, to me that speak, and to you that hear, to every one of us'.[26]

Bacon had obviously enlarged them 'in number', for while the 1597 volume had contained 10 essays that of 1612 contained 38, of which 29 were new, and the rest corrected or enlarged in varying degrees. The 1625 volume, finally, contains 58 essays, of which 20 are new, the remainder being further enlarged and corrected.[27] The *Essays* of 1597, being essentially aphoristic, resisted expansion: their average length in 1597 is 325 words; as revised in 1612, 400 words; as further revised in 1625, 550 words. Those of 1612, by contrast, being already more discursive, and making more use of the opening division of topics (the rhetorical technique of *partitio*), averaged 490 words originally, rising to 980 in 1625. The new essays in 1625, by contrast, average 950 words: like other writers, Bacon found the alteration of an already extant text a greater invitation to expansiveness.

---

[24] TOA 711–12; *Works*, vi. 373.

[25] For these editions see Gibson, *Francis Bacon: A Bibliography*, items 33–47.

[26] *XCVI. Sermons by the Right Honourable and Reverend Father in God, Lancelot Andrewes*, 5th edn. (London, 1661), 232.

[27] The best way to follow this double enlargement is provided by Edward Arber, *A Harmony of the Essays* (London, 1871), which prints the three published texts in parallel columns, together with the manuscript version preceding the 1612 volume. See also Vickers, *Francis Bacon and Renaissance Prose*, ch. 7, 'Literary Revisions', pp. 217–31, 298–9.

Rewriting a book, although unusual today, was quite common in the Renaissance. Sir Philip Sidney rewrote his *Arcadia* on a wholly new plan, unfortunately left unfinished at his death. Montaigne's *Essais* appeared in 1580 (divided into two books), and were enlarged in 1588 (now in three books, with over six hundred additions to books I and II). At his death Montaigne left behind a copy of the 1588 edition which included profuse marginal additions, amounting to about a quarter of the work's total length. Erasmus' *Praise of Folly* (*Moriae Encomium*) went through no less than seven revisions of one kind or another, not all of them beneficial to its overall coherence (or so it seems to me). But Bacon's revisions of his book were unusual in that he claimed to have also enlarged them 'in weight', that is, seriousness. Writing to the Italian scholar Fulgentio in the autumn of 1625, and describing his current publishing projects, Bacon announced that he was having not only his scientific but also his 'moral and political writings' translated into Latin, including 'the little book which in your language you have called *Saggi Morali*. But I give it a weightier name, entitling it "Faithful Discourses—or the Inwards of things" ' (*Sermones Fideles, sive Interiora rerum*) (*Works*, xiv. 531–3). Archbishop Tenison, in the collection of minor works that he edited in 1679, noted that Bacon gave to the Latin edition

the Title of *Sermones Fideles* after the manner of the Jews, who call'd the words Adagies, or Observations of the Wise, Faithfull Sayings; that is, credible Propositions worthy of Firm Assent and ready Acceptance. And (as I think) he alluded more particularly, in this title, to a passage in Ecclesiastes [12: 10, 11], where the Preacher saith that he sought to find out *Verba Delectabilia* (as Tremellius rendreth the Hebrew), 'pleasant Words' (that is, perhaps, his Book of Canticles); and *Verba Fidelia* (as the same Tremellius), 'Faithful sayings'; meaning it may be, his Collection of Proverbs. In the next Verse, he calls them 'Words of the Wise', and so many Goads and Nails given *ab eodem Pastore*, from the same Shepherd [of the flock of Israel].[28]

This concern to address serious issues is announced in the new title, *Essays or Counsels, Civil and Moral*, and is explicitly commented on in the dismissive opening of Essay 37, 'Of Masques and Triumphs':

---

[28] *Baconiana* (London, 1679), 60–1. The Tremellius referred to is the Protestant theologian Emmanuel Tremellius, who, together with Franciscus Junius, produced a Latin translation of the Bible for a scholarly Protestant readership, in competition with the Catholic Vulgate text. Their edition was reissued some 18 times in England between 1579 and 1640, as against the single, incomplete edition of the Vulgate which appeared in 1535.

'These things are but toys, to come amongst such serious observations'. By describing them as 'Counsels', writings giving advice, Bacon openly aligned himself with the 'Advice to Princes' genre, which includes what we would today call political science. The projects described in 'Of Building' and 'Of Gardens', for instance, are certainly conceived on a grand scale, some truly forming (as Bacon says of Essay 29, 'Of the True Greatness of Kingdoms and Estates') 'an argument fit for great and mighty princes to have in their hand' (p. 67). The dedication to Buckingham was appropriate in that, as the courtier closest to the monarch, he was in the best position to influence James towards responsible government, and it is no accident that several precepts from the *Essays* appear in the 'Letter of Advice' to Villiers that Bacon had addressed to him in 1616, when he had just been made Duke of Buckingham and publicly declared the King's favourite (*Works*, xiii. 27–56). Other essays, such as 'Of Great Place', 'Of Nobility', similarly address issues that largely concern those living at the upper levels of society. Here Bacon was able to draw on his vast experience of forty years' public service in both Houses of Parliament, and his first-hand knowledge of power structures, recently from the inside, at the very top. A modern historian, describing the advices he prepared for King James on the eve of the fateful 1621 parliament, judges that 'Bacon, with his omnibus mind, had a remarkably clear and broad overview of the problems of governing England. Nothing escaped his interest . . .'.[29] Another recent historian ascribes the appeal of the *Essays* to 'the pragmatic intelligence and knowledge informing its observations', and praises the 'trenchant political analyses' they contain, 'which in their incisiveness and clarity are like little works of political art'.[30] Yet at the same time, the reason Bacon gave for the *Essays* being his most popular work, that 'they come home to men's business and bosoms', describes their dual appeal, explicitly recognized in the new subtitle, 'Civil and Moral', that is involving both the *civitas* or public life and the *mores* or behaviour of the private individual.

The Essays: *structure*

It is important to recognize the *Essays*' functional role in relation to the 'small Globe of the Intellectual World' which Bacon made in the

[29] Zaller, *The Parliament of 1621*, 20.
[30] Perez Zagorin, *Francis Bacon* (Princeton, 1998), 141, 153.

Advancement of Learning, in order to promote 'amendment and proficience' (TOA 299). However, this does not mean that they have a unitary form or style. Indeed, they fascinate by their very diversity. As Anne Righter [Barton] put it, 'the 1625 edition . . . is an accumulation of disparate pieces as difficult to generalize about, or to connect internally, as Donne's *Songs and Sonets*, and it is to be read in a not dissimilar fashion'.[31] Some essays are organized systematically, with an opening *partitio* (division into topics) that sets out the heads of the argument, a technique that Bacon used more frequently in the 1625 volume.[32] Such are 'Of Counsel', 'Of Great Place', 'Of Seditions and Troubles', and 'Of Judicature', among others. But announcing the topics does not tie Bacon down to a tidily sequential treatment of them, and even in these systematic essays the reader will meet several surprising developments of the argument. Other essays are constructed rather by the association or juxtaposition of ideas and metaphors, such as 'Of Fortune', 'Of Revenge', or 'Of Delays',[33] or demand to be read as a 'metaphysical' poem is read. 'Of Truth' begins with one of Bacon's most striking quotations. ' "What is Truth?" said jesting Pilate; and would not stay for an answer.' As Anne Righter comments:

The rifle-shot of this opening, the little imaginative explosion, is a familiar Bacon technique and frequently imitated. Less imitable, however, is the curious configuration of the space which separates this first sentence from the one which follows. 'Certainly there be, that delight in Giddinesse; And count it a Bondage, to fix a Beleefe; Affecting Free-Will in Thinking, as well as in Acting'. It is not merely that these two sentences are of a markedly different kind: the second simply does not move forward from the first in any fashion which we normally associate with the logic of prose. The movement performed is deliberately oblique in a way that forces the reader in part to create the link himself. A passive attitude here, or even a very rapid perusal of the page, is fatal to the essay.[34]

Some modern critics, expecting the straightforward movement of expository prose as practised in undergraduate composition, have complained that the *Essays* contradict or 'subvert' themselves; others, expecting a strict logical structure, complain that they do not function rationally by appealing to recognized conventions of argument. But this is to bring inappropriate, anachronistic expectations to bear. The

[31] 'Francis Bacon', in Vickers (ed.), *Essential Articles*, 300–21, at 317–18.
[32] Vickers, *Francis Bacon and Renaissance Prose*, 219–20.
[33] Ibid. 228–31.   [34] 'Francis Bacon', 319.

very title, *Essays*, with its homage to Montaigne, announces that Bacon was disclaiming any systematic treatment, and all of Bacon's descriptions of them, as aphorisms or 'dispersed meditations', imply that the onus is on the reader to respond to their individual and varying structures, using them for insight and for stimulus to further thought. One of the best accounts of their oblique movement was given by John Aubrey, recording their formative influence on him in his teens:

I met accidentally a booke of my Mothers, Lord Bacon's *Essaies*, which first opened my Understanding as to Moralls (for Tullies *Offices* was too crabbed for my young yeares) and the excellency of the Style, or Hints and transitions.[35]

That Aubrey should rank the *Essays* with Cicero's *De officiis*, for centuries one of the key texts for ethics in school and university education, is not surprising, but the really striking phrase there is the description of Bacon's style as consisting of 'Hints and transitions'. (Aubrey, reminiscing at this point about his entry to Blandford School in Dorset, in 1638, is probably referring to the 1625 edition: his other comment on the tiny size of the 1597 volume referred to a copy 'which I have seen in the Bodlyan Library'.)

The non-linear nature of the *Essays* should be evident to any sensitive reader. But fascinating evidence that this was a deliberate authorial creation is provided by the *Antitheta rerum*, one of several aids in acquiring argumentative skills that Bacon had originally developed for his own use. These 'antitheses of things', sketched out in the *Promus of Formularies and Elegancies*, a collection of *sententiae* and sayings that he set down from memory in the Christmas vacation of 1594–5 (*Works*, vii. 207–10), are briefly mentioned and illustrated in the *Advancement of Learning* (TOA 240–1), and were finally published in the *De Augmentis Scientiarum* (1623). Commenting there on Cicero's recommendation that the orator should 'have commonplaces ready at hand, in which the question is argued and handled on either side', Bacon urged that all topics which a writer would frequently discuss should be

studied and prepared beforehand; and not only so, but the case exaggerated both ways with the utmost force of the wit, and urged unfairly, as it were, and quite beyond the truth. And the best way of making such a collection, with a view to use as well as brevity, would be to contract those commonplaces into certain acute and concise sentences; to be as skeins or bottoms of thread which may be unwinded at large when they are wanted.[36]

[35] *Brief Lives*, 15. [36] *Works*, iv. 472; trans. Spedding.

Bacon modestly offers 'a few instances of the thing, having a great many by me'. In fact, his inclusion of some 47 topics amounts to quite a substantial treatise (iv. 473–92), and he concludes, rather self-ironically, that 'these Antitheses (which I have here set down) are perhaps of no great value; but as I had long ago prepared and collected them, I was loth to let the fruit of my youthful industry perish—the rather because (if they be carefully examined) they are *seeds* only, not *flowers*' (492). Of the 47 titles, no fewer than 26 correspond to titles of the *Essays*, the first six being: 'Nobility; Beauty; Youth; Health; Riches; Honours'.

In Appendix III I have given a selection of 24 titles, including some that were treated in the *Essays*, but where Bacon's notebooks contained additional material, which he had not used. More interesting, no doubt, are the topics which he had noted but which were never treated in essay form, and which represent, so to speak, essays that remained unwritten.

Under each topic brief sentences are arranged for and against, as here:

RICHES

For	*Against*
They despise riches who despair of them.	Of great riches you may have either the keeping, or the giving away, or the fame, but no use.
It is envy of riches that has made virtue a goddess.	Do you not see what feigned prices are set upon little stones and such rarities, only that there may be some use of great riches?
While philosophers are disputing whether virtue or pleasure be the proper aim of life, do you provide yourself with the instruments of both.	
Virtue is turned by riches into a common good.	Many men while they have thought to buy everything with their riches, have been first sold themselves.
Other goods have but a provincial command; only riches have a general one.	I cannot call riches better than the baggage of virtue; for they are both necessary to virtue and cumbersome.
	Riches are a good handmaid but the worst mistress.[37]

That collection of 'acute and concise sentences' looks like the raw material for Essay 34, 'Of Riches', and comparison will show that Bacon indeed used some of them for that essay, but without arranging them into a continuous flow of argument. The apparent continuity given by the essay as a whole is in fact deceptive, for in reading it the reader's mind needs to be able to shift ground, to see the topic from different sides in rapid succession. To think of these constituent arguments as being arranged into opposed poles is actually too simple, for the finished essays deal with considerations that are complementary rather than opposed. But seeing them set out in this antithetical form helps make us aware of the unpredictable, constantly suggestive effect that Bacon's *Essays* have, existing as 'skeins or bottoms of thread' to be unwound by the reader's mind in a variety of directions and lengths, according to each person's age and experience of life. In this respect the *Essays* fulfil Bacon's own ideal for the communication of knowledge, which ought to be 'delivered to others as a thread to be spun on' (*Works*, iv. 449), stimulating the receiver to examination and inquiry, a dynamic process intended to provoke thought but not exhaust it. For that reason their endings are often abrupt: the last word is not, cannot be, spoken.

The *Essays*: style

The style of the *Essays* is equally varied, responding to the great range of material and to the varying emphases Bacon gives to it. Many essays begin with a sudden attack on the subject, startling the reader into attention:

The greatest trust between man and man is the trust of giving counsel. ('Of Counsel', p. 46)

That opening definition challenges our preconceived ideas about trust, and at once justifies its claim:

For in other confidences men commit the parts of life; their lands, their goods, their children, their credit, some particular affair; but to such as they make their counsellors, they commit the whole: by how much the more they are obliged to all faith and integrity.

That is, the trusted adviser exceeds in power and responsibility all other officers of trust—estate manager, housekeeper, teacher, banker,

reminding us again of the high status enjoyed by the counsellor in
Renaissance political theory and practice. From this point the essay
develops through the twin realms of ethics and politics, with many
penetrating observations. Other essays arrest the reader's attention
with an analogy:

Suspicions amongst thoughts are like bats among birds, they ever fly by
twilight.   ('Of Suspicion', p. 75)

Instead of explaining his metaphor, Bacon presses on to give the necessary counsel, warning of the destructive social and psychological
effects of mistrust:

Certainly they [suspicions] are to be repressed, or at the least well guarded:
for they cloud the mind; they leese friends; and they check with business, . . .
They dispose kings to tyranny, husbands to jealousy, wise men to irresolution and melancholy. They are defects, not in the heart, but in the brain . . .

From psychological and moral analysis of the corroding effects of mistrust (seen, finally, as an intellectual weakness) Bacon moves on to the
practical consequences, offering a remedy: 'Certainly, the best mean to
clear the way in this same wood of suspicions, is frankly to communicate them with the party that he suspects . . .', so establishing the open
and plain dealing which best manages human affairs. Bacon's practic-
ality, appropriate to the advice tradition, accounts for several long sequences couched in the imperative voice, the simplest and most direct
linguistic form, such as the sequence in 'Of Great Place', with its
fifteen consecutive injunctions: 'Neglect not . . . Reform therefore . . .
Reduce . . . Seek . . . Preserve . . .' (p. 25), or a similar sequence in 'Of
Travel' addressed to the conscientious traveller (pp. 41–2).

   The essay openings also use the simplest means, often the verb 'to
be' in the present tense. Yet this plainest of linguistic forms none the
less enables a great variety of utterances, as can be seen from this sequence of five consecutive essays:

A man that is young in years may be old in hours, if he have lost no time. But
that happeneth rarely.   ('Of Youth and Age', p. 96)

Virtue is like a rich stone, best plain set; and surely virtue is best in a body
that is comely, though not of delicate features; and that hath rather dignity
of presence, than beauty of aspect.   ('Of Beauty', p. 98)

Deformed persons are commonly even with nature; for as nature hath done
ill by them, so do they by nature; being for the most part (as the Scripture

saith), 'void of natural affection'; and so they have their revenge of nature. ('Of Deformity', p. 99)

Houses are built to live in, and not to look on; therefore let use be preferred before uniformity, except where both may be had.   ('Of Building', p. 100)

God Almighty first planted a Garden. And indeed it is the purest of human pleasures. It is the greatest refreshment to the spirits of man; without which, buildings and palaces are but gross handy-works ... ('Of Gardens', p. 104)

The opening defines one aspect of the topic, but Bacon's thought at once sets off in other directions, as can be seen from the conjunctions that follow: 'But'; 'and surely'; 'for, as'; 'therefore'; 'And indeed'. The paths of his thought are unpredictable, and the reader must learn how to read the *Essays*, and to follow a thread of argument that moves at varying speeds from the outside to the inside of each topic, now obliquely, now directly.

   As well as varying the trajectories of thought, Bacon could vary the tempo of argument in order to highlight important aspects. Some essays give an even-paced treatment of their subject, moving systematically through each of its stages, such as the two related accounts 'Of Building' (p. 100), and 'Of Gardens' (p. 104), or the discussion of civic and political topics, such as 'Of Plantations' (p. 78), and 'Of the True Greatness of Kingdoms and Estates' (p. 66). But in 'Of Youth and Age' Bacon uses a most effective variation in tempo, now slowing down, now speeding up, together with syntactical parallelism, in order to characterize the two opposed stages of life. 'Youth makes decision quickly, and if they are wrong ones they can have disastrous effects; old age tends to hesitate in making decisions, to procrastinate, and to take half-hearted courses.' That is a rather laboured attempt to restate what Bacon says much more expressively by making the first clause of the sentence swift and direct, the second more of an afterthought:

The errors of young men are the ruin of business; but
the errors of aged men amount but to this, that more might have been done,
                              or sooner.   (p. 97)

   In the following sentence Bacon immediately expands that juxtaposition, evoking the precipitancy of youth by a series of eight main verbs (here italicized), animating each clause with a fresh access of energy, albeit unfocused:

> Young men, in the conduct and manage of actions,
>> *embrace* more than they can hold;
>>
>> *stir* more than they can quiet;
>>
>> *fly* to the end, without consideration of
>>> the means and degrees;
>>
>> *pursue* some few principles which they have chanced
>>> upon absurdly;
>>
>> *care not to innovate*, which draws unknown
>>> inconveniences;
>>
>> *use* extreme remedies at first;
>>
>> and that which doubleth all errors,
>>
>> *will not acknowledge or retract* them;
>>
>> like an unready horse, that will neither stop
>>> nor *turn*.

That long, apparently sprawling sentence, has a pattern in it, one of repeated rushing into inadequately prepared actions, unable to draw back or redirect energies, a headlong process mirrored in the sentence's own syntax. Bacon uses exactly the same technique, mirroring human behaviour in the movement of language, to describe the vices of old age—but in what different terms:

> Men of age object too much,
>> consult too long,
>>
>> adventure too little,
>>
>> repent too soon,
>
> and seldom drive business home to the full period,
>
> but   content themselves with a mediocrity of success. (p. 97)

There the symmetries evoke a vacillating state of mind, fearful of risk, turning back before anything worthwhile has been accomplished, lower energies expiring in a longer, unpatterned sequence, expressing the pleasure of safety. It is hard to imagine a more brilliant analysis of the faults of both extremes.

This analytical, or perhaps diagnostic element—rather like a doctor's case-studies—is central to the *Essays*' treatment of human life in its civic and moral aspects. But Bacon's intention is also persuasive: he wishes to communicate not just a series of detailed and carefully differentiated observations, but also the ethical evaluations that a responsible observer would make at any one point. Persuasion was a skill taught by rhetoric, an art that Bacon both valued and excelled in,[38] and

---

[38] See Brian Vickers, *In Defence of Rhetoric* (Oxford, 1988), and 'Bacon and rhetoric', in Markku Peltonen (ed.), *The Cambridge Companion to Bacon* (Cambridge, 1996), 200–31.

to which (unlike many writers) he gave an unmistakably ethical function: 'The duty and office of Rhetoric is to apply Reason to Imagination for the better moving of the will' (TOA 238)—that is, to good ends, as defined by reason, not by the passions or affections. Rightly used, the 'Eloquence of Persuasions will contract a confederacy between the Reason and Imagination against the Affections' (TOA 239). Bacon applied to his own purposes the traditional division of rhetoric into three processes, *docere*, to teach or inform, *delectare*, to stimulate or delight, and *movere*, to arouse the emotions so as to reinforce good attitudes, transform bad.

The stylistic resources of rhetoric are many and varied, but Bacon used two in particular, one involving the 'figures' of rhetoric (which disposed words in regular sequences, such as having the same word begin, or end, a series of clauses and sentences), the other involving its 'tropes' (which 'turned' or re-adapted the meaning of words, as in metaphor, metonymy, allegory, irony). The basic function of syntactical symmetry, as we have seen from that passage in 'Of Youth and Age', is to give statements or arguments the maximum clarity by making the balance of style parallel the balance of thought. For instance, take the most balanced essay in the earliest version, 'Of Studies':

> Studies serve for pastimes,
>   for ornaments,
>   and for abilities.
> Their chief use for pastime, is in privateness and retiring;
>   for ornament is in discourse;
>   and for ability is in judgment. (p. 134)

The equality of linguistic structure (conjunction corresponding to conjunction, noun to noun, verb to verb), created by using the rhetorical figures *parison* and *isocolon*, does not, however, imply that the individual parts are of equal value. Indeed, to a Renaissance reader sharing the values of the *vita activa*, convinced of the need to apply all knowledge and experience to the benefit of our fellow human beings, and of the corresponding superiority of virtue (*arete, virtus*) over mere pleasure (*hedone, voluptas*), it would be immediately apparent that the combination 'delight . . . privateness and retiring' was not to be indulged in too often. In case we missed that point, Bacon adds a matching triplicity:

To spend too much time in them is sloth;
to use them too much for ornament is affectation;
to make judgment wholly by their rules is the humour [whimsy] of a scholar.

This sequence of symmetrical clauses existed already in the 1597 version and was retained in 1612, with a few alterations: 'pastimes' is replaced by 'delight', and 'judgment' is more fully defined as 'the judgment and disposition of business' (cf. pp. 114 and 134). When expanding the *Essays* in 1612 and 1625 Bacon sometimes added more symmetries, clarifying an argument by making the addition correspond, point for point; in other cases the added material gave the argument more detail and precision, overriding the symmetries.[39] For an example of the first process we could take 'Of Counsel', first appearing in the manuscript collection (*c*.1607–12),[40] and a passage which carefully balances the respective advantages to a prince of advice given in public and in private. In the 1612 printed text Bacon retained the balance but added to it two final clauses (here italicized) which expand the sense while retaining the symmetrical opposition between public and private counsel:

> therefore it is good to take both;
> and of the inferior sort rather in private, *to preserve freedom*;
>   of the greater rather in consort, *to preserve respect*.

For an example of the reverse process, discarding a careful pattern, we can take 'Of Followers and Friends', where both 1597 and 1612 versions include this balanced distinction:

> to be governed by one is not good, and
> to be distracted with many is worse;
> but to take advice of friends is ever honourable . . .   (p. 136)

In 1625 Bacon kept the outline of the distinction but added so much new material that its structure is obscured:

To be governed (as we call it) by one, is not safe; for it shews softness, and gives a freedom to scandal and disreputation; for those that would not censure or speak ill of a man immediately, will talk more boldly of those that are so great with them, and thereby wound their honour. Yet to be distracted with many is worse; for it makes men to be of the last impression, and full of change. To take advice of some few friends is ever honourable . . . (pp. 111–12)

[39] For specimen analyses see Vickers, *Francis Bacon and Renaissance Prose*, 132–40, 219–24.

[40] This collection was reprinted in Arber's parallel-column version (above, n. 27), not always accurately. The forthcoming edition of the *Essays* by Michael Kiernan in *The Oxford Francis Bacon* will include all three versions.

Bacon's willingness to jettison a neat structure in favour of an exten-sion of meaning shows the priority that he—together with most Renaissance writers—gave to thought or subject-matter (*res*) over words (*verba*).

Drawing attention to this way of writing might suggest that Bacon was a self-conscious stylist, who allowed patterns of style to dominate his thought. This is far from the truth. Bacon was certainly a self-aware writer, balancing clarity of exposition against fullness of treat-ment and the careful nuancing of thought. But unlike some of his contemporaries (such as Nicholas Breton or John Lyly), who allowed patterning to dominate their style, for Bacon symmetrical syntax, like *partitio*, could set up the framework for an ordered treatment, should he wish, but did not commit him to any predictable utterance. In 'Of Simulation and Dissimulation', for instance, he begins by brusquely rejecting the use of pretence in political life as a sign of weakness, not strength: 'Dissimulation is but a faint kind of policy or wisdom; for it asketh a strong wit and a strong heart to know when to tell truth, and to do it' (p. 12). Bacon contrasts this feeble evasiveness with a more valuable mental faculty, arguing that a wise politician should develop

> that penetration of judgment as he can discern
> what things are to be laid open,
> and what to be secreted,
> and what to be shewed at half lights,
> and to whom
> and when . . . (p. 12–13)

There the unpredictable reduction in the mass or volume of each clause forces the reader to go more slowly, leaving a pause so as to grasp the importance of the considerations governing this choice, ending with the most important. In 'Of Friendship', which Bacon totally rewrote from the 1612 version (p. 144) as a present to his friend Tobie Matthew (see p. 180), the friendship between two individuals is seen as a microcosm of society, to be set against solitude, with all its connota-tions of wilderness and savagery. That evaluation is familiar, memor-ably expressed in Aristotle's *Politics*, but no one could have predicted the symmetrical sequence which Bacon used to make a further dis-tinction within the category of 'society': it is not just the *presence* of other people that makes for fellowship:

> But little do men perceive what solitude is,
>   and how far it extendeth.
> For a crowd is not company;
> and faces are   but a gallery of pictures;
> and talk   but a tinkling cymbal,
> where there is no love.   (p. 59)

That memorable distinction between mere company and the necessary precondition for friendship was expressed in the simplest verb-forms, 'is' and 'are', which are among the most frequently used words in the 1625 *Essays*.[41] Many of Bacon's most deeply held beliefs are uttered in this direct manner, in particular the moral superiority of giving love or help to other people over selfishly gratifying the ego. In 'Of Great Place' he justifies holding of high office solely for the power it gives to benefit others:

In place there is licence to do good and evil; whereof the latter is a curse: for in evil the best condition is not to will; the second not to can. But power to do good is the true and lawful end of aspiring.   (p. 24)

(Here the unexpected juxtaposition of the unusual verb-forms, 'not to will . . . not to can', uses syntactical symmetry to enforce an important point in the most economical manner.) In 'Of Goodness and Goodness of Nature' Bacon both praises *Philanthropia* ('affecting of the weal of men', caring for others' welfare), in the highest possible terms and denounces its absence:

This of all virtues and dignities of the mind is the greatest; being the character of the Deity: and without it man is a busy, mischievous, wretched thing; no better than a kind of vermin.   (p. 28)

His ethical disgust regularly finds utterance in metaphors of unpleasant insects, as again later in the essay, describing those people who do not simply lack goodness but have a 'natural malignity' towards their fellow human beings:

Such men in other men's calamities are, as it were, in season, and are ever on the loading part: not so good as the dogs that licked Lazarus' sores; but like flies that are still buzzing upon any thing that is raw.   (p. 29)

In 'Of Wisdom for a Man's Self' human egoism is seen as destructive of society, like the ant that destroys fruit and plants: 'An ant is a wise

[41] From the useful work by D. W. Davies and E. Wrigley (eds.), *A Concordance to the Essays of Francis Bacon* (Detroit, 1973), we derive the following figures: 'is', 1,115 instances; 'be', 746; and 'are', 500.

creature for itself, but it is a shrewd [destructive] thing in an orchard or garden. And certainly men that are great lovers of themselves waste the public' (p. 54). To develop his attack on self-centredness Bacon then shifts to a metaphor from cosmology:

It is a poor centre of a man's actions, *himself.* It is right earth. For that only stands fast upon his own centre; whereas all things that have affinity with the heavens, move upon the centre of another, which they benefit.   (p. 54)

In that sequence Bacon plays simultaneously on two ancient ideas, the earth as the centre of the universe, and earth as the lowest of the four elements, below water, air, and fire. Both analogies use imaginative means to express a moral evaluation persuasively.

Traditionally speeches (and, by extension, other literary compositions) were divided into three genres: deliberative, for political assemblies; forensic, for the courts of law; and epideictic, the related techniques of praise and blame, used to celebrate virtue and attack vice. As Bacon well knew, every human being reveals his or her moral values by the attitudes or behaviour they cherish or dislike. We value his *Essays* for many reasons, not least for their combination of a dispassionate observation of human life with powerfully expressed moral judgements. This combination was recognized by a kindred spirit, Samuel Johnson, who said that 'their excellence and their value consisted in being the observations of a strong mind operating upon life; and in consequence you find what you seldom find in other books'.[42]

---

[42] *Johnsonian Miscellanies*, ed. G. B. Hill (Oxford, 1897), ii. 229.

NOTE ON THE TEXT

THE fundamental source for the *Essays* remains the edition of Bacon's *Works* by James Spedding, R. L. Ellis, and D. D. Heath, 14 vols. (London, 1857–74; repr. New York, 1968; London, 1996), which is still the only edition to print the complete texts of the 1597, 1612, and 1625 versions. Spedding also collates the manuscript text of thirty-four essays which (in the handwriting of one of Bacon's secretaries, with Bacon's autograph correction and revisions) has survived in the British Library (Harley MS 5106), entitled 'The Writings of Sr Francis Bacon Knt.: the Kinges Sollicitor Generall: in Moralitie, Policie, and Historie', and gives occasional references to it. He reprints the essay 'Of Seditions and Troubles' (vi. 589–91) from this source, which I include in Appendix II. It was for some reason omitted from the 1612 volume, and first appeared in a much enlarged form in 1625 (cf. p. 31). I have based my text on Spedding's, correcting a few errors.

SELECT BIBLIOGRAPHY

1. Editions

The Works of Francis Bacon, ed. J. Spedding, R. L. Ellis, and D. D. Heath, 14 vols. (London, 1857–74; repr. New York, 1968, London, 1996): contains all three versions of the *Essays*: vol. vi, pp. 367–591.

Francis Bacon, ed. Brian Vickers (The Oxford Authors; Oxford, 1996): contains the 1625 text, with full annotation; the 1597 text and selections from *The Colours of Good and Evil*, together with the other major works in English: *The Advancement of Learning*, *New Atlantis*, the early 'Devices', selected letters and speeches.

Bacon's Essays and Colours of Good and Evil, ed. W. A. Wright (London, 1862).

Bacon's Essays, ed. E. A. Abbott, 2 vols. (London, 1876).

The Promus of Formularies and Elegancies by Francis Bacon, ed. Mrs H. Pott (London, 1883).

The Essays or Counsels, Civil and Moral, ed. S. H. Reynolds (Oxford, 1890).

A Harmony of the Essays of Francis Bacon, ed. E. Arber (London, 1871; repr. 1895): parallel-text edition, but with errors.

Gli 'Essayes' di Francis Bacon. Studio Introduttivo, Testo Critico e Commento, ed. Mario Melchionda (Florence, 1979).

Sir Francis Bacon, The Essayes or Counsels, Civill and Morall, ed. Michael Kiernan (Oxford, 1985); revised edition in preparation for *The Oxford Francis Bacon*, vol. xv, to include the text of all three versions.

2. Critical studies

R. S. Crane, 'The Relation of Bacon's *Essays* to his Program for the Advancement of Learning', in *Schelling Anniversary Papers* (New York, 1923), 87–105; reprinted in Brian Vickers (ed.), *Essential Articles for the Study of Francis Bacon* (Hamden, Conn., 1968; London, 1972), 272–92.

Brian Vickers, *Francis Bacon and Renaissance Prose* (Cambridge, 1968).

Anne Righter [Barton], 'Francis Bacon', in Vickers (ed.), *Essential Articles*, 300–21.

William A. Sessions (ed.), *Francis Bacon's Legacy of Texts* (New York, 1990).

Markku Peltonen (ed.), *The Cambridge Companion to Bacon* (Cambridge, 1996): Brian Vickers, 'Bacon and rhetoric' (pp. 200–31); Ian Box, 'Bacon's moral philosophy' (pp. 260–82).

William A. Sessions, *Francis Bacon Revisited* (New York, 1996).

Perez Zagorin, *Francis Bacon* (Princeton, 1998).

Studies of individual essays are cited in the headnote to the essay concerned.

3. General background

T. W. Baldwin, *William Shakspere's 'Small Latine & Lesse Greeke'*, 2 vols. (Urbana, Il., 1944, 1966): on the Renaissance grammar school and its training in logic and rhetoric.

R. R. Bolgar, *The Classical Heritage and its Beneficiaries* (Cambridge, 1954): on the importance of the notebook in Renaissance educational theory, and the practice of *imitatio*.

Ann Moss, *Printed Commonplace-books and the Structuring of Renaissance Thought* (Oxford, 1996).

4. Further reading in Oxford World's Classics

Aristotle, *Nicomachean Ethics*, trans. and ed. Sir David Ross.
—— *Politics*, trans. Sir Ernest Barker, rev. and ed. Richard Stalley.
The Meditations of Marcus Aurelius, trans. A. S. L. Farquharson and R. B. Rutherford.
Hobbes, Thomas, *Human Nature and De Corpore*, ed. J. C. A. Gaskin.
—— *Leviathan*, ed. J. C. A. Gaskin.
Machiavelli, Niccolò, *Discourses on Livy*, trans. and ed. Peter and Julia Bondanella.
—— *The Prince*, trans. Peter Bondanella and Mark Musa, introduction by Peter Bondanella.
Pascal, Blaise, *Pensées and Other Writings*, trans. Honor Levi and Anthony Levi.
Plutarch, *Selected Essays and Dialogues*, trans. and ed. Donald Russell.
Shakespeare, William, *Hamlet*, ed. G. R. Hibbard.
Sidney, Sir Philip, *The Countess of Pembroke's Arcadia* (*The Old Arcadia*), ed. Katherine Duncan-Jones.

A CHRONOLOGY OF FRANCIS BACON

1561   (22 Jan.) Born at York House, the Strand, the youngest of Sir Nicholas Bacon's two sons by his marriage to Lady Ann (née Cooke), his second wife (there being three sons from the first marriage).

1573   (5 Apr.) Goes up to Trinity College Cambridge with his elder brother Anthony; matriculates 10 June.

1575   (Dec.) Leaves Cambridge.

1576   (27 June) Is entered at Gray's Inn (admitted 21 Nov.), but in Sept. accompanies Sir Amias Paulet, English ambassador to France.

1579   (22 Feb.) Death of his father; (20 Mar.) returns from France; Trinity Term, admitted to Gray's Inn.

1581   Elected to Parliament as member for Bossiney, Cornwall.

1582   (27 June) Admitted as Utter Barrister of Gray's Inn.

1584   (23 Nov.) MP for Weymouth and Melcombe Regis.

1586   (29 Oct.) MP for Taunton; becomes a Bencher of Gray's Inn.

1587   Lent Term, elected Reader at Gray's Inn; Privy Council consults him on legal matters.

1588   (Aug.) Appointed to government committee examining recusants; (Dec.) appointed to select committee of 16 lawyers (4 from each Inn of Court) to review parliamentary statutes.

1589   (4 Feb.) MP for Liverpool; asked to prepare official document justifying the Queen's religious policies; (29 Oct.) granted reversion of Clerkship of Star Chamber.

1591   Easter Term, first appearance as pleader in court.

1593   (19 Feb.) MP for Middlesex; (2 and 8 Mar.) speaks in a Commons debate against the Queen's demand for additional taxes, and loses royal favour.

1594   (25 Jan.) Argument in Chudleigh's case; Michaelmas Term, appointed Queen's Counsel Extraordinary (honorific title).

1597   (Feb.) First edition of *Essays* (10 essays, with *Colours of Good and Evil*, and *Religious Meditations*), reprinted 1597, 1598, 1606, 1612; (18 Oct.) MP for Ipswich; speaks against enclosures.

1599   (Mar.) Queen Elizabeth appoints him prosecuting counsel in trial of Essex for the Irish débâcle.

1600   (24 Oct.) Double Reader at Gray's Inn.

1601   (19 Feb.) The Queen appoints him one of the state prosecutors in trial of Essex for rebellion; at the Queen's command, writes *A Declaration of the Practises & Treasons attempted and committed by Robert late Earle of Essex . . .*; (May) death of his brother Anthony;

(27 Oct.) MP for Ipswich; (Nov.) introduces bill for repealing superfluous laws.

1603 (24 Mar.) Death of Queen Elizabeth; accession of King James I; (23 July) Bacon knighted by James, along with 300 others; publishes (anonymously) *A Brief Discourse, touching the Happie Union of the Kingdomes of England, and Scotland*; member of the ecclesiastical commission.

1604 (Mar.) MP for Ipswich; (June) publishes *Sir Francis Bacon His Apologie, in certaine imputations concerning the late Earl of Essex*, and (anonymously) *Certain Considerations touching the better Pacification and Edification of the Church of England*, which is suppressed by the Bishop of London; (18 Aug.) appointed King's Counsel.

1605 (Oct.) Publishes *The Twoo Bookes of Francis Bacon. Of the proficience and aduancement of Learning, diuine and humane*; reprinted 1629.

1606 (10 May) Marries Alice Barnham, 14-year-old daughter of wealthy London alderman.

1607 (17 Feb.) Makes important speeches in Parliament supporting union of the kingdoms and naturalization of Scottish citizens; (25 June) appointed Solicitor-General.

1608 Becomes Clerk of the Star Chamber; appointed Treasurer of Gray's Inn; argument in Calvin's case, concerning the Postnati.

1609 Publishes *De Sapientia Veterum*; English trans. by Sir Arthur Gorges, 1619.

1610 (Feb.) MP for Ipswich; (June) speaks in defence of the royal prerogative; (Aug.) death of his mother, Lady Ann Bacon.

1612 (Nov.) Publishes enlarged edition of the *Essays* (38 essays); reprinted 1612, 1613 (three editions so dated), 1614, 1624.

1613 (26 Oct.) Appointed Attorney-General.

1614 (Jan.) Publishes *The Charge of Sir Francis Bacon, Knight, His Majesties Attourney-generall, touching Duells . . .*; (Apr.) MP for Cambridge University.

1616 (25 May) Is appointed one of the state prosecutors in the trial of the Earl and Countess of Somerset for the poisoning of Sir Thomas Overbury; (9 June) appointed Privy Counsellor.

1617 (7 Mar.) Appointed Lord Keeper of the Seal; reforms workings of Chancery.

1618 (Jan.) Granted the title of Lord Chancellor; (12 July) created Baron Verulam.

1619 (Oct.) Involved in prosecution of the Earl of Suffolk for illegal exaction.

1620   (12 Oct.) Publishes in part *Instauratio Magna*: Preface, 'Plan of the Work', and part II, *Novum Organum* (two books only); this volume includes *Parasceve ad Historiam Naturalem et Experimentalem*; (Nov.) involved in prosecution of Sir Henry Yelverton, Attorney-General, for unlawfully amending the charter of the City of London.

1621   (27 Jan.) Created Viscount St Alban; (3 May) sentenced by the House of Lords on charge of taking bribes; dismissed from office as Lord Chancellor, fined £40,000, and temporarily imprisoned, but retains other titles and is given a limited pardon; retires to Gorhambury.

1622   (Mar.) Publishes *The Historie of the Raigne of King Henry the Seuenth*; (Nov.) publishes *Historia Naturalis et Experimentalis ad condendam Philosophiam*, part I: *Historia Ventorum*.

1623   (Jan.) Publishes part II: *Historia Vitae et Mortis*; (Oct.) publishes *De Dignitate & Augmentis Scientiarum Libri IX*.

1624   (Dec.) Publishes *Apophthegms New and Old*, and *The Translation of Certaine Psalmes into English verse*.

1625   (27 Mar.) Death of King James; accession of King Charles I; (Apr.) publishes third edition of the *Essayes or Counsels, Civill and Morall . . . Newly enlarged* (58 essays), reprinted 1625, 1629, 1632, etc.; (Dec.) makes last will and testament.

1626   (9 Apr.) Dies at Highgate of a cold.

1627   *Sylva Sylvarum* and *New Atlantis* published posthumously.

BACON'S ESSAYS

THE ESSAYS OR COUNSELS
CIVIL AND MORAL (1625)
NEWLY ENLARGED

1. OF TRUTH

'What is Truth?'* said jesting[1] Pilate; and would not stay for an answer.
Certainly there be that[2] delight in giddiness,[3] and count it a bondage to
fix a belief; affecting[4] free-will in thinking, as well as in acting. And
though the sects of philosophers of that kind* be gone, yet there remain certain discoursing wits* which are of the same veins,[5] though
there be not so much blood in them as was in those of the ancients. But
it is not only the difficulty and labour which men take in finding out
of truth; nor again that when it is found it imposeth[6] upon men's
thoughts; that doth bring lies in favour; but a natural though corrupt
love of the lie itself. One of the latter school of the Grecians* exam-
ineth the matter, and is at a stand[7] to think what should be in it, that
men should love lies, where neither they make for[8] pleasure, as with
poets, nor for advantage, as with the merchant; but for the lie's sake.
But I cannot tell: this same truth is a naked and open day-light,[9] that
doth not shew the masks and mummeries[10] and triumphs[11] of the
world, half so stately and daintily[12] as candle-lights. Truth may perhaps come to the price of a pearl, that sheweth[13] best by day; but it will
not rise to the price of a diamond or carbuncle,* that sheweth best in
varied lights. A mixture of a lie doth ever add pleasure.

Doth any man doubt, that if there were taken out of men's minds
vain opinions, flattering hopes, false valuations, imaginations as one
would,[14] and the like, but it would leave the minds of a number of men
poor shrunken things, full of melancholy and indisposition, and unpleasing to themselves? One of the Fathers, in great severity, called
poesy *vinum daemonum** because it filleth the imagination; and yet it is
but with the shadow of a lie. But it is not the lie that passeth through

---

1 scoffing   2 there are some who   3 constantly changing opinions   4 liking
5 inclination   6 lays restraints on   7 at a loss   8 conduce to   9 window
10 splendour, shows   11 triumphant processions   12 elegantly   13 looks
14 wishful fantasies

the mind, but the lie that sinketh in and settleth in it, that doth the hurt; such as we spake of before. But howsoever[1] these things are thus in men's depraved judgments[2] and affections,[3] yet truth,* which only doth judge itself, teacheth that the inquiry of truth, which is the love-making or wooing of it, the knowledge of truth, which is the presence of it, and the belief* of truth, which is the enjoying of it, is the sovereign good of human nature.

The first creature[5] of God, in the works of the days,* was the light of the sense; the last was the light of reason; and his sabbath[6] work ever since, is the illumination of his Spirit.* First he breathed light upon the face of the matter or chaos; then he breathed light into the face of man; and still[7] he breatheth and inspireth light into the face of his chosen. The poet that beautified the sect* that was otherwise inferior to the rest, saith yet* excellently well: 'It is a pleasure to stand upon the shore, and to see ships tossed upon the sea; a pleasure to stand in the window of a castle, and to see a battle and the adventures[8] thereof below: but no pleasure is comparable to the standing upon the vantage ground of Truth' (a hill not to be commanded,[9] and where the air is always clear and serene), 'and to see the errors, and wanderings, and mists, and tempests, in the vale below'; so[10] always that this prospect[11] be with pity,[12] and not with swelling[13] or pride. Certainly, it is heaven upon earth, to have a man's mind move in charity, rest[14] in providence, and turn upon the poles* of truth.

To pass from theological and philosophical truth, to the truth of civil business;[15] it will be acknowledged even by those that practise it not, that clear and round[16] dealing is the honour of man's nature; and that mixture of falsehood is like allay[17] in coin of gold and silver, which may make the metal work the better, but it embaseth[18] it. For these winding and crooked courses are the goings of the serpent; which goeth basely upon the belly, and not upon the feet. There is no vice that doth so cover a man with shame as to be found false and perfidious. And therefore Montaigne* saith prettily, when he inquired the reason, why the word of the lie should be such a disgrace and such an odious charge? Saith he, 'If it be well weighed, to say that a man lieth, is as

1 although   2 perceptions   3 passions   4 trust in   5 thing created
6 time of rest, cessation of labour   7 always, ever since   8 alternating fortunes
9 overgone   10 provided   11 observing the spectacle   12 also meant 'piety'
13 arrogance   14 enjoy peace   15 politics, public affairs
16 straightforward, honest   17 alloy (mixture of base metal in coinage, allowed by law)
18 the metal is easier to work with, but loses value

much to say, as that he is brave towards God and a coward towards men'. For a lie faces God, and shrinks from man. Surely the wickedness of falsehood and breach of faith cannot possibly be so highly[1] expressed, as in that it shall be the last peal* to call the judgments of God upon the generations of men; it being foretold,* that when Christ cometh, 'he shall not find faith upon the earth'.

2. OF DEATH

Men fear Death, as children fear to go in the dark;* and as that natural fear in children is increased with tales, so is the other. Certainly, the contemplation[2] of death, as the wages of sin* and passage to another world, is holy and religious; but the fear of it, as a tribute[3] due unto nature, is weak.[4] Yet in religious meditations there is sometimes mixture of vanity[5] and of superstition. You shall read in some of the friars' books of mortification,* that a man should think with himself what the pain is if he have but his finger's end pressed or tortured, and thereby imagine what the pains of death are, when the whole body is corrupted and dissolved;[6] when many times death passeth with less pain than the torture of a limb: for the most vital parts[7] are not the quickest of sense.[8] And by him that spake only as a philosopher and natural* man, it was well said, *Pompa mortis magis terret, quam mors ipsa.** Groans and convulsions, and a discoloured face, and friends weeping, and blacks,[9] and obsequies,[10] and the like, shew[11] death terrible.

It is worthy the observing, that there is no passion in the mind of man so weak, but it mates[12] and masters the fear of death; and therefore death is no such terrible enemy when a man hath so many attendants about him that can win the combat of him. Revenge triumphs over death; Love slights it; Honour aspireth to it;* Grief flieth to it; Fear pre-occupateth* it. Nay we read, after Otho* the emperor had slain himself, Pity (which is the tenderest[13] of affections) provoked many to die, out of mere compassion to their sovereign, and as the truest sort of followers. Nay Seneca adds niceness[14] and satiety: *Cogita quamdiu eadem feceris; mori velle, non tantum fortis, aut miser, sed etiam fastidiosus*

---

1 solemnly   2 consideration   3 something owing; levy; payment by subject people   4 inconsistent (since it is natural)   5 futility   6 disintegrating 7 organs   8 most sensitive   9 mourning clothes   10 funeral rites 11 make it seem   12 overpowers   13 weakest, most delicate   14 fastidiousness

potest.* A man would[1] die, though he were neither valiant nor miserable, only upon a weariness to do the same thing so oft over and over.

It is no less worthy to observe, how little alteration in good spirits[2] the approaches of death make; for they appear to be the same men till the last instant. Augustus Caesar died in a compliment; *Livia, conjugii nostri memor, vive et vale.** Tiberius in dissimulation; as Tacitus saith of him, *Iam Tiberium vires et corpus, non dissimulatio, deserebant.** Vespasian in a jest; sitting upon the stool,[3] *Ut puto Deus fio.** Galba with a sentence; *Feri, si ex re sit populi Romani,** holding forth his neck. Septimius Severus in despatch;[4] *Adeste si quid mihi restat agendum.** And the like. Certainly the Stoics bestowed too much cost* upon death, and by their great preparations made it appear more fearful. Better saith he, *qui finem vitae extremum inter munera ponat naturae.** It is as natural to die as to be born; and to a little infant, perhaps, the one is as painful as the other. He that dies in an earnest pursuit[5] is like one that is wounded in hot blood;[6] who, for the time, scarce feels the hurt; and therefore a mind fixed and bent upon somewhat that is good doth avert the dolours of death. But above all, believe it, the sweetest canticle is, *Nunc dimittis*;* when a man hath obtained[7] worthy ends and expectations. Death hath this also; that it openeth the gate to good fame, and extinguisheth envy. *Extinctus amabitur idem.**

3. Of Unity in Religion

Religion being the chief band[8] of human society, it is a happy thing when itself is well contained[9] within the true band of Unity. The quarrels and divisions about religion were evils unknown to the heathen. The reason was, because the religion of the heathen consisted rather in rites and ceremonies, than in any constant belief.[10] For you may imagine what kind of faith theirs was, when the chief doctors[11] and fathers of their church were the poets. But the true God hath this attribute, that he is a 'jealous God';* and therefore his worship and religion will endure no mixture[12] nor partner. We shall therefore speak a few words concerning the Unity of the Church; what are the Fruits thereof; what the Bounds;[13] and what the Means.[14]

1 wishes to   2 men of courage   3 toilet   4 speed in settling business
5 pursuing some great cause   6 in the heat of combat   7 attained   8 bond
9 held together   10 coherent system of beliefs   11 teachers   12 dilution
13 limits   14 ways of attaining

The Fruits of Unity (next unto the well pleasing of God, which is all in all) are two; the one towards those that are without[1] the church, the other towards those that are within. For the former; it is certain that heresies and schisms* are of all others the greatest scandals;* yea, more than corruption of manners.[2] For as in the natural body a wound or so-lution of continuity* is worse than a corrupt humour;* so in the spir-itual. So that nothing doth so much keep men out of the church, and drive men out of the church, as breach of unity. And therefore, when-soever it cometh to that pass,[3] that one saith *Ecce in deserto*, another saith *Ecce in penetralibus*;* that is, when some men seek Christ in the conventicles* of heretics, and others in an outward face of a church, that voice[4] had need continually to sound in men's ears, *Nolite exire*,— 'Go not out'. The Doctor of the Gentiles* (the propriety[5] of whose vocation drew him to have a special care of those without) saith, 'If an heathen come in, and hear you speak with several tongues,[6] will he not say that you are mad?'* And certainly it is little better, when atheists and profane persons do hear of so many discordant and contrary opin-ions in religion; it doth avert them from the church, and maketh them 'to sit down in the chair of the scorners'.* It is but a light thing to be vouched[7] in so serious a matter, but yet it expresseth well the deform-ity: there is a master of scoffing,* that in his catalogue of books of a feigned library sets down this title of a book, 'The morris-dance* of Heretics'. For indeed every sect of them hath a diverse posture[8] or cringe* by themselves, which cannot but move derision in worldlings and depraved politiques,[9] who are apt to contemn[10] holy things.

As for the fruit towards those that are within; it is peace; which con-taineth infinite blessings. It establisheth[11] faith. It kindleth charity. The outward peace of the church distilleth[12] into peace of conscience. And it turneth the labours of writing and reading of controversies into treatises of mortification and devotion.

Concerning the Bounds of Unity; the true placing of them im-porteth exceedingly.[13] There appear to be two extremes. For to certain zelants[14] all speech of pacification is odious. 'Is it peace, Jehu? What hast thou to do with peace? turn thee behind me'.* Peace is not the matter, but following and party.* Contrariwise,[15] certain Laodiceans*

---

1 outside   2 behaviours   3 point, stage   4 saying   5 special nature
6 in several languages   7 appealed to as an authority   8 attitude
9 corrupt politicians, schemers   10 despise   11 fortifies   12 yields
13 is very important   14 zealots   15 on the contrary

and lukewarm persons think they may accommodate[1] points of religion by middle ways, and taking part of[2] both, and witty[3] reconcile-
ments;[4] as if they would make an arbitrement[5] between God and man.
Both these extremes are to be avoided; which will be done, if the
league[6] of Christians penned[7] by our Saviour himself were in the two
cross[8] clauses thereof soundly and plainly expounded: 'He that is not
with us is against us';* and again, 'He that is not against us is with us';*
that is, if the points fundamental and of substance in religion were
truly discerned and distinguished from points not merely[9] of faith, but
of opinion, order,[10] or good intention.[11] This is a thing may seem to
many a matter trivial, and done already. But if it were done less par-
tially,[12] it would be embraced more generally.

Of this I may give only this advice, according to my small model.[13]
Men ought to take heed of rending God's church by two kinds of controversies. The one is, when the matter of the point controverted is too
small and light, not worth the heat and strife about it, kindled only by
contradiction. For as it is noted by one of the fathers, 'Christ's coat indeed had no seam, but the church's vesture[14] was of divers colours';
whereupon he saith, *In veste varietas sit, scissura non sit*:* they be two
things, Unity and Uniformity. The other is, when the matter of the
point controverted is great, but it is driven to an over-great subtilty[15]
and obscurity; so that it becometh a thing rather ingenious[16] than substantial. A man that is of judgment and understanding shall sometimes
hear ignorant men differ,[17] and know well within himself that those
which so differ mean one thing,[18] and yet they themselves would never
agree. And if it come so to pass in that distance of judgment which is
between man and man, shall we not think that God above, that knows
the heart, doth not discern that frail men* in some of their contradic-
tions intend[19] the same thing; and accepteth of both? The nature of
such controversies is excellently expressed by St Paul in the warning
and precept that he giveth concerning the same, *Devita profanas vocum
novitates, et oppositiones falsi nominis scientiae*.* Men create oppositions
which are not;[20] and put them into new terms* so fixed, as whereas the
meaning ought to govern the term, the term in effect governeth the

1 compromise, settle disputed issues   2 siding with   3 ingenious
4 reconciliations   5 arbitration   6 covenant, alliance   7 set out
8 contradictory   9 wholly, altogether   10 discipline   11 goodwill
12 in a partisan manner   13 limited outline, scheme   14 garments
15 excessive refinement in argument   16 clever, insubstantial   17 disagree
18 the same thing   19 mean   20 do not exist

meaning. There be also two false peaces or unities: the one, when the peace is grounded but upon an implicit[1] ignorance; for all colours will agree in the dark:* the other, when it is pieced up[2] upon a direct admission of contraries in fundamental points. For truth and falsehood, in such things, are like the iron and clay in the toes of Nebuchadnezzar's image;* they may cleave,[3] but they will not incorporate.[4]

Concerning the Means of procuring Unity; men must beware, that in the procuring or muniting[5] of religious unity they do not dissolve* and deface the laws of charity and of human society. There be two swords* amongst Christians, the spiritual and temporal; and both have their due office and place in the maintenance of religion. But we may not take up the third sword, which is Mahomet's* sword, or like unto it; that is, to propagate religion by wars or by sanguinary[6] persecutions to force consciences; except it be in cases of overt scandal, blasphemy, or intermixture of practice[7] against the state; much less to nourish seditions; to authorise[8] conspiracies and rebellions; to put the sword into the people's hands; and the like; tending to the subversion of all government, which is the ordinance[9] of God. For this is but to dash the first table against the second;* and so to consider men as Christians, as we forget that they are men. Lucretius the poet, when he beheld the act of Agamemnon, that could endure the sacrificing of his own daughter, exclaimed:

*Tantum religio potuit suadere malorum.**

What would he have said, if he had known of the massacre in France,* or the powder treason of England?* He would have been seven times more Epicure and atheist* than he was. For as the temporal sword is to be drawn with great circumspection in cases of religion; so it is a thing monstrous to put it into the hands of the common people. Let that be left unto the Anabaptists,* and other furies. It was great blasphemy when the devil said, 'I will ascend and be like the Highest';* but it is greater blasphemy to personate[10] God, and bring him in[11] saying, 'I will descend, and be like the prince of darkness': and what is it better, to make the cause of religion to descend to the cruel and execrable actions of murthering princes, butchery of people, and subversion of

1 entangled   2 put together   3 adhere, cling to   4 unite into one body
5 fortifying   6 bloody   7 scheming, conspiracy   8 legitimize   9 command
10 impersonate, act the part of   11 bring on to the stage

states and governments? Surely this is to bring down the Holy Ghost, instead of the likeness of a dove,* in the shape of a vulture or raven; and set out of the bark* of a Christian church a flag of a bark of pirates and Assassins.* Therefore it is most necessary that the church by doctrine[1] and decree, princes by their sword, and all learnings,[2] both Christian and moral, as[3] by their Mercury rod, do damn and send to hell for ever those facts[4] and opinions tending to the support of the same;* as hath been already in good part done. Surely in counsels[5] concerning religion, that counsel of the apostle would[6] be prefixed, *Ira hominis non implet justitiam Dei*.* And it was a notable observation of a wise father,* and no less ingenuously[7] confessed; that 'those which held and persuaded[8] pressure of consciences, were commonly interested[9] therein themselves for their own ends'.

4. OF REVENGE*

Revenge is a kind of wild* justice; which the more man's nature runs to, the more ought law to weed it out. For as for the first wrong, it doth but[10] offend the law; but the revenge of that wrong putteth the law out of office.[11] Certainly, in taking revenge, a man is but even with his enemy; but in passing it over, he is superior; for it is a prince's part[12] to pardon. And Salomon, I am sure, saith, 'It is the glory of a man to pass by an offence'.* That which is past is gone, and irrevocable; and wise men have enough to do with things present and to come; therefore they do but trifle with themselves, that labour in past matters. There is no man doth a wrong for the wrong's sake; but thereby to purchase[13] himself profit, or pleasure, or honour, or the like. Therefore why should I be angry with a man for loving himself better than me? And if any man should do wrong merely[14] out of ill-nature, why, yet it is but like the thorn or briar, which prick and scratch, because they can do no other. The most tolerable sort of revenge is for those wrongs which there is no law to remedy; but then let a man take heed the revenge be such as there is no law to punish; else a man's enemy is still before hand,[15] and it is two for one.*

1 teaching	2 sciences	3 as though	4 deeds (Lat. *facta*)
5 considerations, advice	6 should, ought	7 candidly	
8 urged, recommended	9 personally involved, for their own advantage		
10 merely	11 use, function	12 role	13 obtain 14 altogether
15 in the advantage			

Some, when they take revenge, are desirous the party[1] should know whence it cometh.* This the more generous. For the delight seemeth to be not so much in doing the hurt as in making the party repent. But base and crafty cowards are like the arrow that flieth in the dark.* Cosmus,* duke of Florence, had a desperate[2] saying against perfidious or neglecting[3] friends, as if those wrongs were unpardonable; 'You shall read' (saith he) 'that we are commanded to forgive our enemies; but you never read that we are commanded to forgive our friends'. But yet the spirit of Job was in a better tune: 'Shall we' (saith he) 'take good at God's hands, and not be content to take evil also?'* And so of friends in a proportion.[4] This is certain, that a man that studieth revenge keeps his own wounds green, which otherwise would heal and do well. Public revenges are for the most part fortunate;[5] as that for the death of Caesar; for the death of Pertinax; for the death of Henry the Third* of France; and many more. But in private revenges it is not so. Nay rather, vindictive persons live the life of witches; who, as they are mischievous,[6] so end they infortunate.

5. OF ADVERSITY

It was a high[7] speech of Seneca* (after[8] the manner of the Stoics), that 'the good things which belong to prosperity are to be wished; but the good things that belong to adversity are to be admired'.[9] *Bona rerum secundarum optabilia; adversarum mirabilia.* Certainly if miracles be the command over nature,* they appear most in adversity. It is yet a higher[10] speech of his than the other* (much too high for a heathen), 'It is true greatness to have in one[11] the frailty of a man, and the security[12] of a God'. *Vere magnum habere fragilitatem hominis, securitatem Dei.* This would have done better in poesy, where transcendences[13] are more allowed. And the poets indeed have been busy with it; for it is in effect the thing which is figured[14] in that strange fiction* of the ancient poets, which seemeth not to be without mystery; nay, and to have some approach to the state of a Christian; that 'Hercules, when he went to unbind Prometheus' (by whom human nature is represented), 'sailed

1 the adversary   2 disconsolate   3 negligent   4 proportionately
5 bringing good fortune   6 malicious, destructive   7 proud   8 according to
9 i.e. as extraordinary   10 more exalted   11 at the same time
12 freedom from care   13 exaggerations, hyperboles   14 represented

the length of the great ocean in an earthen pot or pitcher'; lively describing Christian resolution, that saileth in the frail bark of the flesh thorough[1] the waves of the world.

But to speak in a mean.[2] The virtue of Prosperity is temperance, the virtue of Adversity is fortitude; which in morals[3] is the more heroical virtue. Prosperity is the blessing of the Old Testament; Adversity is the blessing of the New; which carrieth the greater benediction,[4] and the clearer revelation of God's favour. Yet even in the Old Testament, if you listen to David's harp, you shall hear as many hearse-like airs as carols;[5] and the pencil of the Holy Ghost hath laboured more in describing the afflictions of Job than the felicities[6] of Salomon. Prosperity is not without many fears and distastes;[7] and Adversity is not without comforts and hopes. We see in needle-works and embroideries, it is more pleasing to have a lively work* upon a sad[8] and solemn ground, than to have a dark and melancholy work upon a lightsome ground: judge therefore of the pleasure of the heart by the pleasure of the eye. Certainly virtue is like precious odours, most fragrant when they are incensed[9] or crushed:[10] for Prosperity doth best discover* vice, but Adversity doth best discover virtue.

6. OF SIMULATION AND DISSIMULATION

Dissimulation* is but a faint kind of policy[11] or wisdom; for it asketh a strong wit[12] and a strong heart to know when to tell truth, and to do it. Therefore it is the weaker sort of politiques[13] that are the great dissemblers.

Tacitus* saith, 'Livia sorted[14] well with the arts[15] of her husband and dissimulation of her son'; attributing arts or policy to Augustus, and dissimulation to Tiberius. And again, when Mucianus* encourageth Vespasian to take arms against Vitellius, he saith, 'We rise not against the piercing judgment of Augustus, nor the extreme caution or closeness[16] of Tiberius'. These properties, of arts or policy and dissimulation or closeness, are indeed habits and faculties several,[17] and to be distinguished. For if a man have that penetration of judgment as he

---

1 through   2 in moderate language   3 ethics   4 blessedness
5 joyous dance-songs   6 good fortune   7 discomforts, annoyances
8 sober, dark-coloured   9 set on fire (as incense is)   10 compressed, squeezed
11 sagacity in public affairs   12 understanding   13 men in public life
14 adapted herself to   15 devices   16 secrecy   17 different

can discern what things are to be laid open, and what to be secreted, and what to be shewed at half lights,* and to whom and when (which indeed are arts of state¹ and arts of life, as Tacitus* well calleth them), to him a habit of dissimulation is a hinderance and a poorness. But if a man cannot obtain to² that judgment, then it is left to him generally to be close,³ and a dissembler. For where a man cannot choose or vary in particulars,⁴ there it is good to take the safest and wariest way in general; like the going softly,⁵ by one that cannot well see. Certainly the ablest men that ever were have had all an openness⁶ and frankness of dealing; and a name of certainty⁷ and veracity; but then they were like horses well managed; for they could tell passing well when to stop or turn; and at such times when they thought the case indeed required dissimulation, if then they used it, it came to pass that the former opinion⁸ spread abroad of their good faith and clearness of dealing made them almost invisible.

There be three degrees of this hiding and veiling of a man's self. The first, Closeness,⁹ Reservation,¹⁰ and Secrecy; when a man leaveth himself without observation, or without hold to be taken, what he is.* The second, Dissimulation, in the negative; when a man lets fall signs and arguments,¹¹ that he is not that he is. And the third, Simulation, in the affirmative; when a man industriously and expressly feigns and pretends to be that he is not.

For the first of these, Secrecy; it is indeed the virtue of a confessor. And assuredly the secret man heareth many confessions. For who will open himself to a blab or babbler? But if a man be thought secret, it inviteth discovery;¹² as the more close air sucketh in the more open;* and as in confession the revealing is not for worldly use, but for the ease of a man's heart, so secret men come to the knowledge of many things in that kind;* while men rather discharge¹³ their minds than impart¹⁴ their minds. In few words, mysteries are due to secrecy.* Besides (to say truth) nakedness is uncomely,¹⁵ as well in mind as body; and it addeth no small reverence to men's manners and actions, if they be not altogether open. As for talkers and futile* persons, they are commonly vain¹⁶ and credulous withal.¹⁷ For he that talketh what he knoweth, will also talk what he knoweth not. Therefore set it down,* that an habit of

1 statesmanship, government   2 attain   3 secretive   4 individual cases
5 treading warily   6 sincerity   7 reputation for reliability   8 good reputation
9 secrecy   10 reservedness   11 tokens, proofs   12 disclosure   13 relieve
14 share with, communicate   15 improper, unseemly   16 lightminded
17 in addition

secrecy is both politic and moral. And in this part,[1] it is good that a man's face give his tongue leave* to speak. For the discovery[2] of a man's self by the tracts[3] of his countenance is a great weakness and betraying; by how much it is many times more marked[4] and believed than a man's words.

For the second, which is Dissimulation; it followeth many times upon secrecy by a necessity; so that he that will be secret must be a dissembler in some degree. For men are too cunning to suffer a man to keep an indifferent carriage[5] between both, and to be secret, without swaying the balance on either side. They will so beset a man with questions, and draw him on, and pick it out of him, that, without an absurd[6] silence, he must shew an inclination one way; or if he do not, they will gather as much by his silence as by his speech. As for equivocations,* or oraculous speeches,* they cannot hold out long. So that no man can be secret, except he give himself a little scope[7] of dissimulation; which is, as it were, but the skirts or train[8] of secrecy.

But for the third degree, which is Simulation and false profession;[9] that I hold more culpable, and less politic; except it be in great and rare matters. And therefore a general custom of simulation (which is this last degree) is a vice, rising either of a natural falseness or fearfulness, or of a mind that hath some main faults, which because a man must needs disguise, it maketh him practise simulation in other things, lest his hand should be out of ure.[10]

The great advantages of simulation and dissimulation are three. First, to lay asleep opposition, and to surprise. For where a man's intentions are published, it is an alarum[11] to call up all that are against them. The second is, to reserve to a man's self a fair[12] retreat. For if a man engage himself by a manifest declaration, he must go through or take a fall.* The third is, the better to discover the mind of another. For to him that opens himself men will hardly shew themselves adverse; but will (fair)[13] let him go on, and turn their freedom of speech to freedom of thought.* And therefore it is a good shrewd proverb of the Spaniard, 'Tell a lie and find a truth.' As if there were no way of discovery but by simulation. There be also three disadvantages, to set it

1 point   2 revealing   3 traits, features   4 noticed
5 maintain an impartial bearing   6 deaf to reason, unreasonable
7 space for free movement   8 subordinate, attending circumstances
9 declaration, pretence   10 use, practice   11 signal calling men to arms
12 honourable   13 just, probably

even. The first, that simulation and dissimulation commonly carry with them a shew[1] of fearfulness, which in any business doth spoil the feathers of round flying up to the mark.* The second, that it puzzleth and perplexeth the conceits[2] of many, that perhaps would otherwise co-operate with him; and makes a man walk almost alone to his own ends. The third and greatest, is, that it depriveth a man of one of the most principal instruments for action; which is trust and belief.[3] The best composition[4] and temperature* is to have openness in fame and opinion;* secrecy in habit;[5] dissimulation in seasonable use;[6] and a power to feign, if there be no remedy.

7. OF PARENTS AND CHILDREN

The joys of parents are secret; and so are their griefs and fears. They cannot utter[7] the one; nor they will not utter the other. Children sweeten labours; but they make misfortunes more bitter. They increase the cares of life; but they mitigate[8] the remembrance[9] of death. The perpetuity by generation[10] is common to beasts; but memory,* merit, and noble works, are proper[11] to men. And surely a man shall see the noblest works and foundations[12] have proceeded from childless men; which have sought to express[13] the images of their minds, where those of their bodies have failed.* So the care of[14] posterity is most in them that have no posterity. They that are the first raisers of their houses* are most indulgent towards their children; beholding them as the continuance not only of their kind[15] but of their work;* and so both children and creatures.*

The difference in affection[16] of parents towards their several children is many times unequal;[17] and sometimes unworthy; especially in the mother; as Salomon saith, 'A wise son rejoiceth the father, but an ungracious son shames the mother'.* A man shall see, where there is a house full of children, one or two of the eldest respected, and the youngest made wantons;[18] but in the midst some that are as it were forgotten, who many times nevertheless prove the best. The illiberality of parents in allowance[19] towards their children is an harmful[20] error;

1 token, sign 2 thoughts 3 credit 4 constitution 5 in practice
6 at the opportune moment 7 reveal 8 reduce, render less painful
9 thought 10 procreation 11 peculiar 12 charitable institutions
13 give shape to 14 concern for 15 kin, family 16 regard 17 unfair
18 spoiled, dissolute 19 financial support 20 pernicious

makes them base;[1] acquaints them with shifts;[2] makes them sort with[3] mean company; and makes them surfeit[4] more when they come to plenty. And therefore the proof[5] is best, when men keep their authority towards their children, but not their purse.* Men have a foolish manner (both parents and schoolmasters and servants) in creating and breeding an emulation[6] between brothers during childhood, which many times sorteth to[7] discord when they are men, and disturbeth families. The Italians make little difference between children and nephews or near kinsfolks;[8] but so they be of the lump,* they care not though they pass not through their own body. And, to say truth, in nature it is much a like matter; insomuch that we see a nephew sometimes resembleth an uncle or a kinsman more than his own parent; as the blood happens.*

Let parents choose betimes[9] the vocations and courses[10] they mean their children should take; for then they are most flexible; and let them not too much apply[11] themselves to the disposition of their children, as thinking they will take best to that which they have most mind to. It is true, that if the affection or aptness[12] of the children be extraordinary, then it is good not to cross[13] it; but generally the precept is good, *optimum elige, suave et facile illud faciet consuetudo*.* Younger brothers are commonly fortunate, but seldom or never where the elder are disinherited.

8. Of Marriage and Single Life

He that hath wife and children hath given hostages* to fortune; for they are impediments[14] to great enterprises, either of virtue or mischief. Certainly the best works, and of greatest merit for the public, have proceeded from the unmarried or childless men; which* both in affection[15] and means[16] have married and endowed the public. Yet it were great reason[17] that those that have children should have greatest care of future times; unto which they know they must transmit their dearest pledges. Some there are, who though they lead a single life, yet their thoughts do end with themselves, and account future times im-

---

1 bad   2 subterfuges (to get money)   3 associate with   4 gorge themselves
5 result of experience   6 strife, contention   7 results in   8 relatives
9 in good time   10 ways of life   11 bend, conform   12 attitude or inclination
13 thwart   14 obstacles   15 love   16 generosity   17 reasonable

pertinences.[1] Nay, there are some other that account wife and children but as bills of charges.[2] Nay more, there are some foolish rich covetous men, that take a pride in having no children, because[3] they may be thought so much the richer. For perhaps they have heard some talk, 'Such an one is a great rich man,' and another except[4] to it, 'Yea, but he hath a great charge[5] of children'; as if it were an abatement[6] to his riches. But the most ordinary cause of a single life is liberty, especially in certain self-pleasing and humorous[7] minds, which are so sensible of[8] every restraint, as they will go near to think their girdles[9] and garters to be bonds and shackles.[10]

Unmarried men are best friends, best masters, best servants; but not always best subjects; for they are light to[11] run away; and almost all fugitives[12] are of that condition. A single life doth well with[13] churchmen;[14] for charity will hardly water the ground where it must first fill a pool. It is indifferent[15] for judges and magistrates; for if they be facile[16] and corrupt, you shall have a servant five times worse than a wife. For soldiers, I find the generals commonly in their hortatives[17] put men in mind of their wives and children; and I think the despising of marriage amongst the Turks maketh the vulgar[18] soldier more base. Certainly wife and children are a kind of discipline[19] of humanity; and single men, though they may be many times more charitable, because their means are less exhaust, yet, on the other side, they are more cruel and hardhearted (good to make severe inquisitors),[20] because their tenderness is not so oft called upon. Grave natures, led by custom, and therefore constant, are commonly loving husbands; as was said of Ulysses, *vetulam suam praetulit immortalitati.** Chaste women are often proud and froward,[21] as presuming upon the merit of their chastity. It is one of the best bonds[22] both of chastity and obedience in the wife, if she think her husband wise;[23] which she will never do if she find him jealous. Wives are young men's mistresses; companions for middle age; and old men's nurses. So as a man may have a quarrel* to marry when he will. But yet he was reputed one of the wise men, that made answer* to the question, when a man should marry?—'A young man not yet, an elder man not at all'. It is often seen that bad husbands have very good

1 irrelevances　　2 expenses　　3 in order that　　4 object
5 burden, responsibility　　6 reduction　　7 whimsical　　8 sensitive to
9 belts　　10 chains　　11 quick, prone to　　12 outlaws　　13 is proper for
14 ecclesiastics　　15 neutral　　16 easily swayed, fickle　　17 exhortations
18 common　　19 training　　20 legal officers charged with cross-examinations
21 bad-tempered, contrary　　22 guarantees　　23 of sound judgement

wives; whether it be that it raiseth the price[1] of their husband's kindness when it comes; or that the wives take a pride in their patience. But this never fails, if the bad husbands were of their own choosing, against their friends' consent; for then they will be sure to make good their own folly.

9. OF ENVY

There be none of the affections[2] which have been noted to fascinate* or bewitch, but love and envy. They both have vehement wishes; they frame themselves readily into imaginations[3] and suggestions;[4] and they come easily into the eye,* especially upon the presence of the objects; which are the points[5] that conduce to fascination, if any such thing there be. We see likewise the Scripture* calleth envy an 'evil eye'; and the astrologers call the evil influences* of the stars 'evil aspects';* so that still[6] there seemeth to be acknowledged, in the act of envy, an ejaculation or irradiation of the eye.* Nay some have been so curious[7] as to note, that the times when the stroke or percussion of an envious eye doth most hurt, are when the party envied is beheld in glory[8] or triumph; for that sets an edge[9] upon envy: and besides, at such times the spirits* of the person envied do come forth most into the outward parts, and so meet the blow.

But leaving these curiosities[10] (though not unworthy to be thought on in fit place), we will handle,[11] what persons are apt[12] to envy others; what persons are most subject to be envied themselves; and what is the difference between public and private envy.

A man that hath no virtue* in himself, ever envieth virtue in others. For men's minds will either feed upon their own good or upon others' evil; and who wanteth[13] the one will prey upon the other; and whoso is out of hope to attain to another's virtue, will seek to come at even hand[14] by depressing[15] another's fortune.

A man that is busy[16] and inquisitive[17] is commonly envious. For to know much of other men's matters cannot be because all that ado[18] may

---

1 value   2 passions   3 fantasies   4 temptations   5 characteristics
6 always   7 careful, meticulous   8 display (of success or potency)
9 sharpens   10 fruitless questions   11 discuss   12 prone to   13 lacks
14 get even with   15 bringing low   16 meddlesome, prying
17 unduly curious   18 fuss, activity

concern his own estate;[1] therefore it must needs[2] be that he taketh a kind of play-pleasure[3] in looking upon the fortunes of others. Neither can he that mindeth but[4] his own business find much matter for envy. For envy is a gadding[5] passion, and walketh the streets, and doth not keep home: *Non est curiosus, quin idem sit malevolus.**

Men of noble birth are noted to be envious towards new men* when they rise. For the distance is altered; and it is like a deceit of the eye,* that when others come on they think themselves go back.

Deformed persons, and eunuchs, and old men,* and bastards, are envious. For he that cannot possibly mend[6] his own case will do what he can to impair another's; except these defects light upon[7] a very brave and heroical nature, which thinketh to make his natural wants[8] part of his honour; in that it should be said that an eunuch, or a lame man, did such great matters; affecting[9] the honour of a miracle; as it was in Narses the eunuch, and Agesilaus and Tamberlanes,* that were lame men.

The same is the case of men that rise after calamities and misfortunes. For they are as men fallen out with the times; and think other men's harms a redemption of their own sufferings.

They that desire to excel in too many matters, out of levity[10] and vain-glory,* are ever envious. For they cannot want work;* it being impossible but many in some one of those things should surpass them. Which was the character of Hadrian* the Emperor; that mortally envied poets and painters and artificers, in works wherein he had a vein[11] to excel.

Lastly, near kinsfolks,* and fellows in office,* and those that have been bred together, are more apt to envy their equals when they are raised.[12] For it doth upbraid unto them their own fortunes, and pointeth at* them, and cometh oftener into their remembrance, and incurreth likewise more into the note of others; and envy ever redoubleth[13] from speech and fame. Cain's envy was the more vile and malignant towards his brother Abel, because when his sacrifice* was better accepted there was nobody to look on.* Thus much for those that are apt to envy.

Concerning those that are more or less subject to envy: First, persons of eminent virtue, when they are advanced,[14] are less envied. For

1 interests, affairs   2 of necessity   3 vicarious pleasure, as when watching a play
4 only   5 restless, rushing hither and thither   6 improve   7 happen to
8 disadvantages   9 aiming at   10 instability   11 inclination
12 promoted   13 echoes, increases   14 promoted, awarded distinctions

their fortune seemeth but due unto them; and no man envieth the payment of a debt, but rewards and liberality rather. Again, envy is ever joined with the comparing of a man's self; and where there is no comparison, no envy; and therefore kings are not envied but by kings.* Nevertheless it is to be noted that unworthy persons are most envied at their first coming in,[1] and afterwards overcome it better; whereas contrariwise,[2] persons of worth and merit are most envied when their fortune continueth long. For by that time, though their virtue be the same, yet it hath not the same lustre; for fresh men grow up that darken it.

Persons of noble blood are less envied in their rising. For it seemeth but right done to their birth. Besides, there seemeth not much added to their fortune; and envy is as the sunbeams, that beat hotter upon a bank or steep rising ground, than upon a flat. And for the same reason those that are advanced by degrees are less envied than those that are advanced suddenly and *per saltum*.*

Those that have joined with their honour great travels,* cares, or perils, are less subject to envy. For men think that they earn their honours hardly,[3] and pity them sometimes; and pity ever healeth envy. Wherefore you shall observe that the more deep and sober[4] sort of politique persons, in their greatness, are ever bemoaning themselves, what a life they lead; chanting a *quanta patimur*.* Not that they feel it so, but only to abate[5] the edge of envy. But this is to be understood of business that is laid upon men, and not such as they call unto themselves. For nothing increaseth envy more than an unnecessary and ambitious engrossing[6] of business. And nothing doth extinguish envy more than for a great person to preserve all other inferior officers in their full rights and pre-eminences of their places. For by that means there be so many screens between him and envy.

Above all, those are most subject to envy, which carry the greatness of their fortunes in an insolent and proud manner; being never well[7] but while they are shewing how great they are, either by outward pomp, or by triumphing over all opposition or competition; whereas wise men will rather do sacrifice to envy, in suffering themselves sometimes of purpose to be crossed[8] and overborne in things that do not much concern them. Notwithstanding so much is true, that the carriage[9] of greatness in a plain and open manner (so it be without

1 prominence   2 on the contrary   3 with difficulty   4 serious-seeming
5 beat down, blunt   6 monopolizing, acquiring   7 satisfied   8 thwarted
9 bearing, reaction to

arrogancy and vain-glory) doth draw less envy than if it be in a more crafty and cunning fashion. For in that* course a man doth but disavow fortune;* and seemeth to be conscious of his own want[1] in worth; and doth but teach others to envy him.

Lastly, to conclude this part; as we said in the beginning that the act of envy had somewhat in it of witchcraft, so there is no other cure of envy but the cure of witchcraft; and that is, to remove the 'lot'* (as they call it) and to lay it upon another. For which purpose, the wiser sort of great persons bring in ever upon the stage somebody upon whom to derive[2] the envy that would come upon themselves; sometimes upon ministers and servants; sometimes upon colleagues and associates; and the like; and for that turn[3] there are never wanting some persons of violent and undertaking[4] natures, who, so they may have power and business, will take it at any cost.

Now, to speak of public envy. There is yet some good in public envy, whereas in private there is none. For public envy is as an ostracism,[5] that eclipseth[6] men when they grow too great. And therefore it is a bridle also to great ones, to keep them within bounds.

This envy, being in the Latin word *invidia*, goeth in the modern languages by the name of 'discontentment'; of which we shall speak in handling Sedition.* It is a disease in a state like to infection. For as infection spreadeth upon that which is sound, and tainteth[7] it; so when envy is gotten[8] once into a state, it traduceth[9] even the best actions thereof, and turneth them into an ill odour.[10] And therefore there is little won by intermingling of plausible[11] actions. For that doth argue but a weakness and fear of envy, which hurteth so much the more; as it is likewise usual in infections; which if you fear them, you call them upon you.

This public envy seemeth to beat chiefly upon principal officers or ministers, rather than upon kings and estates[12] themselves. But this is a sure rule, that if the envy upon the minister be great, when the cause of it in him is small; or if the envy be general[13] in a manner upon all the ministers of an estate;[14] then the envy (though hidden) is truly upon the state itself. And so much of public envy or discontentment, and the difference thereof from private envy, which was handled* in the first place.

---

1 lack of   2 transfer   3 trick, purpose   4 impetuous, enterprising
5 temporary banishment   6 makes disappear   7 corrupts   8 begotten
9 slanders   10 bad reputation   11 praiseworthy, deserving applause
12 states, republics   13 widespread   14 state

We will add this in general, touching[1] the affection of envy; that of all other affections it is the most importune[2] and continual. For of other affections there is occasion given but now and then; and therefore it was well said, *Invidia festos dies non agit*:* for it is ever working upon some or other. And it is also noted that love and envy do make a man pine,[3] which other affections do not, because they are not so continual. It is also the vilest affection, and the most depraved; for which cause it is the proper attribute of the devil,* who is called 'The envious man, that soweth tares[4] amongst the wheat by night';* as it always cometh to pass, that envy worketh subtilly,[5] and in the dark; and to the prejudice[6] of good things, such as is the wheat.

10. OF LOVE

The stage is more beholding[7] to Love, than the life of man. For as to the stage, love is ever matter of comedies, and now and then of tragedies; but in life it doth much mischief; sometimes like a syren,* sometimes like a fury.* You may observe, that amongst all the great and worthy persons whereof the memory remaineth, either ancient or recent, there is not one that hath been transported to the mad degree of love: which shews that great spirits* and great business[8] do keep out this weak[9] passion. You must except nevertheless Marcus Antonius,* the half-partner* of the empire of Rome, and Appius Claudius,* the decemvir and lawgiver; whereof the former was indeed a voluptuous man, and inordinate;[10] but the latter was an austere and wise man: and therefore it seems (though rarely) that love can find entrance not only into an open heart, but also into a heart well fortified, if watch be not well kept. It is a poor saying of Epicurus, *Satis magnum alter alteri theatrum sumus*;* as if man, made for the contemplation of heaven and all noble objects, should do nothing but kneel before a little idol,[11] and make himself a subject, though not of the mouth (as beasts are), yet of the eye; which was given him for higher purposes.

It is a strange[12] thing to note the excess of this passion, and how it braves[13] the nature and value of things, by this; that the speaking in a

---

1 concerning 2 pressing, insistent 3 long for 4 weeds in a cornfield
5 'subtly', often in the pejorative sense of 'craftily, cunningly' 6 harm
7 indebted, obliged 8 employments, tasks 9 inconstant 10 ungovernable
11 image or puppet 12 remarkable 13 distorts by exaggeration

perpetual hyperbole is comely in nothing but in love. Neither is it merely in the phrase;* for whereas it hath been well said* that the arch-flatterer, with whom all the petty flatterers have intelligence,* is a man's self; certainly the lover is more. For there was never proud man thought so absurdly well of himself as the lover doth of the person loved; and therefore it was well said, that 'it is impossible to love and to be wise'.* Neither doth this weakness appear to others only, and not to the party loved; but to the loved most of all, except the love be reciproque.[1] For it is a true rule, that love is ever rewarded either with the reciproque or with an inward and secret contempt. By how much the more men ought to beware of this passion, which loseth not only other things, but itself. As for the other losses, the poet's relation* doth well figure[2] them; That he that preferred Helena, quitted the gifts of Juno and Pallas. For whosoever esteemeth too much of amorous affection quitteth both riches and wisdom.

This passion hath his floods[3] in the very times of weakness; which are great prosperity and great adversity; though this latter hath been less observed: both which times kindle love, and make it more fervent, and therefore shew it to be the child of folly. They do best, who if they cannot but admit love, yet make it keep quarter;[4] and sever[5] it wholly from their serious affairs and actions of life; for if it check[6] once with business, it troubleth men's fortunes, and maketh men that they can no ways be true to their own ends.* I know not how, but martial men* are given to love: I think it is but as they are given to wine; for perils commonly ask to be paid in pleasures. There is in man's nature a secret inclination and motion[7] towards love of others, which if it be not spent upon some one or a few, doth naturally spread itself towards many, and maketh men become humane and charitable; as it is seen sometime in friars. Nuptial love maketh[8] mankind; friendly love perfecteth it; but wanton love corrupteth and embaseth[9] it.

11. Of Great Place

Men in great place* are thrice servants: servants of the sovereign or state;[10] servants of fame;[11] and servants of business. So as they have no

---

1 return, reciprocity   2 describe   3 overwhelming power
4 stay in its proper place   5 keep apart   6 interfere   7 impulse   8 creates
9 degrades   10 republic   11 reputation

freedom; neither in their persons,[1] nor in their actions, nor in their times. It is a strange desire, to seek power and to lose liberty: or to seek power over others and to lose power over a man's self. The rising unto place[2] is laborious; and by pains men come to greater pains; and it is sometimes base;[3] and by indignities[4] men come to dignities. The standing is slippery, and the regress is either a downfall, or at least an eclipse, which is a melancholy thing. *Cum non sis qui fueris, non esse cur velis vivere.** Nay, retire men cannot when they would, neither will they when it were reason;[5] but are impatient of privateness,[6] even in age and sickness, which require the shadow;* like old townsmen, that will be still sitting at their street door, though thereby they offer age to scorn.

Certainly great persons had need to borrow other men's opinions, to think themselves happy; for if they judge by their own feeling, they cannot find it: but if they think with themselves what other men think of them, and that other men would fain[7] be as they are, then they are happy as it were by report; when perhaps they find the contrary within. For they are the first that find their own griefs, though they be the last that find their own faults. Certainly men in great fortunes are strangers to themselves, and while they are in the puzzle of business* they have no time to tend[8] their health either of body or mind. *Illi mors gravis incubat, qui notus nimis omnibus, ignotus moritur sibi.**

In place[9] there is licence[10] to do good and evil; whereof the latter is a curse: for in evil the best condition is not to will;[11] the second not to can.* But power to do good is the true and lawful end of aspiring.[12] For good thoughts[13] (though God accept them) yet towards men are little better than good dreams, except they be put in act; and that cannot be without power and place, as the vantage and commanding ground.* Merit and good works is the end[14] of man's motion;[15] and conscience[16] of the same is the accomplishment of man's rest. For if a man can be partaker of God's theatre,* he shall likewise be partaker of God's rest.* *Et conversus Deus, ut aspiceret opera quae fecerunt manus suae, vidit quod omnia essent bona nimis;** and then the sabbath.

In the discharge[17] of thy place set before thee the best examples; for imitation is a globe[18] of precepts. And after a time set before thee thine

---

1 body, self　　2 high position　　3 despicable　　4 dishonourable acts
5 appropriate　　6 private or retired life　　7 gladly　　8 attend to
9 in a position of power　　10 opportunity　　11 desire　　12 ambition
13 good intentions　　14 aim　　15 activity　　16 consciousness
17 carrying out　　18 'a complete or perfect body' (*SOED*)

own example; and examine thyself strictly whether thou didst not best at first. Neglect not also the examples of those that have carried themselves ill[1] in the same place; not to set off thyself[2] by taxing[3] their memory, but to direct thyself what to avoid. Reform therefore, without bravery[4] or scandal of former times and persons; but yet set it down to thyself as well to create good precedents as to follow them. Reduce[5] things to the first institution,* and observe wherein and how they have degenerate; but yet ask counsel of both times; of the ancient time, what is best; and of the latter time, what is fittest. Seek to make thy course regular, that men may know beforehand what they may expect; but be not too positive[6] and peremptory;[7] and express[8] thyself well when thou digressest from thy rule. Preserve the right of thy place; but stir not questions of jurisdiction: and rather assume thy right in silence and *de facto*, than voice it with claims and challenges. Preserve likewise the rights of inferior places; and think it more honour to direct in chief* than to be busy in all. Embrace and invite helps and advices touching[9] the execution[10] of thy place; and do not drive away such as bring thee information, as meddlers; but accept of them in good part.

The vices of authority are chiefly four: delays, corruption, roughness, and facility.[11] For delays: give easy access; keep times appointed; go through with that which is in hand, and interlace[12] not business but of necessity. For corruption: do not only bind thine own hands or thy servants' hands from taking, but bind the hands of suitors also from offering.* For integrity used[13] doth the one; but integrity professed,[14] and with a manifest detestation of bribery, doth the other. And avoid not only the fault, but the suspicion. Whosoever is found variable, and changeth manifestly without manifest cause, giveth suspicion of corruption. Therefore always when thou changest thine opinion or course, profess it plainly, and declare it, together with the reasons that move thee to change; and do not think to steal[15] it. A servant or a favourite, if he be inward,[16] and no other apparent cause of esteem, is commonly thought but a by-way[17] to close[18] corruption. For roughness:[19] it is a needless cause of discontent; severity breedeth fear, but roughness breedeth hate. Even reproofs from authority ought to be

---

1 behaved badly 2 elevate, distinguish yourself 3 censuring 4 ostentation
5 bring back 6 self-assured 7 autocratic 8 explain 9 concerning
10 carrying out of duties 11 pliancy, being over-ready to yield
12 intersperse, mix up together 13 practised 14 displayed, declared
15 perform secretly 16 familiar, intimate 17 indirect path 18 secret
19 coarse or brutal treatment

grave, and not taunting.[1] As for facility: it is worse than bribery. For bribes come but now and then; but if importunity* or idle respects* lead a man, he shall never be without. As Salomon saith, 'To respect persons is not good; for such a man will transgress for a piece of bread'.* It is most true that was anciently* spoken, 'A place sheweth the man'. And it sheweth some to the better, and some to the worse. *Omnium consensu capax imperii, nisi imperasset,* saith Tacitus of Galba; but of Vespasian he saith, *Solus imperantium, Vespasianus mutatus in melius**: though the one was meant of sufficiency,* the other of manners and affection.[2] It is an assured[3] sign of a worthy and generous spirit, whom honour* amends. For honour is, or should be, the place of virtue; and as in nature things move violently to their place and calmly in their place,* so virtue in ambition is violent, in authority settled and calm.

All rising to great place is by a winding stair; and if there be factions, it is good to side a man's self[4] whilst he is in the rising, and to balance himself when he is placed.[5] Use the memory of thy predecessor fairly and tenderly;[6] for if thou dost not, it is a debt will sure be paid when thou art gone. If thou have colleagues, respect them, and rather call them when they look not for it, than exclude them when they have reason to look to be called.[7] Be not too sensible[8] or too remembering of thy place[9] in conversation and private answers to suitors; but let it rather be said, 'When he sits in place he is another man'.

12. OF BOLDNESS

It is a trivial grammar-school text,* but yet worthy a wise man's consideration. Question was asked of Demosthenes,* 'what was the chief part of an orator?' he answered, 'action': what next? 'action': what next again? 'action'.* He said it that knew it best, and had by nature himself no advantage in that* he commended. A strange thing, that that part of an orator which is but superficial, and rather the virtue of a player,[10] should be placed so high, above those other noble* parts of invention, elocution, and the rest; nay almost alone, as if it were all in all. But the reason is plain. There is in human nature generally more of the fool

---

1 mocking   2 benevolence   3 sure   4 to take sides
5 put in place or position   6 carefully   7 consulted   8 sensitive
9 do not stand on your dignity   10 actor

than of the wise; and therefore those faculties by which the foolish part of men's minds is taken* are most potent. Wonderful like is the case of Boldness, in civil business;[1] what first? Boldness: what second and third? Boldness. And yet boldness is a child of ignorance and baseness, far inferior to other parts. But nevertheless it doth fascinate and bind hand and foot those that are either shallow in judgment or weak in courage, which are the greatest part; yea and prevaileth with wise men at weak times. Therefore we see it hath done wonders in popular* states; but with senates and princes less; and more ever upon the first entrance of bold persons into action than soon after; for boldness is an ill keeper of promise. Surely as there are mountebanks[2] for the natural body, so are there mountebanks for the politic body;[3] men that under-take[4] great cures, and perhaps have been lucky in two or three experiments, but want the grounds of science, and therefore cannot hold out.

Nay you shall see a bold fellow many times do Mahomet's miracle.* Mahomet made the people believe that he would call an hill to him, and from the top of it offer up his prayers for the observers of his law. The people assembled; Mahomet called the hill to come to him, again and again; and when the hill stood still, he was never a whit abashed, but said, 'If the hill will not come to Mahomet, Mahomet will go to the hill.' So these men, when they have promised great matters and failed most shamefully, yet (if they have the perfection of boldness) they will but slight it over,[5] and make a turn, and no more ado.[6] Certainly to men of great judgment, bold persons are a sport[7] to behold; nay and to the vulgar also, boldness has somewhat of the ridiculous. For if absurdity be the subject of laughter, doubt you not but great boldness is seldom without some absurdity. Especially it is a sport to see, when a bold fellow is out of countenance; for that puts his face into a most shrunken and wooden posture; as needs it must; for in bashfulness the spirits do a little go and come; but with bold men, upon like occasion, they stand at a stay;* like a stale[8] at chess, where it is no mate, but yet the game cannot stir. But this last were fitter for a satire than for a serious observation.

This is well to be weighed; that boldness is ever blind; for it seeth not dangers and inconveniences. Therefore it is ill in counsel,[9] good in execution; so that the right use of bold persons is, that they never

1 politics, public life   2 spurious healers or quacks   3 'the nation in its corporate character; the State' (*SOED*)   4 promise   5 dismiss, make light of   6 fuss
7 source of laughter   8 stalemate   9 deliberation

command in chief, but be seconds, and under the direction of others. For in counsel it is good to see dangers; and in execution not to see them, except they be very great.

13. OF GOODNESS AND GOODNESS OF NATURE

I take Goodness in this sense, the affecting[1] of the weal[2] of men, which is that the Grecians call *Philanthropia*;* and the word 'humanity'* (as it is used) is a little too light to express it. Goodness I call the habit, and Goodness of Nature the inclination.* This of all virtues and dignities of the mind is the greatest; being the character[3] of the Deity: and without it man is a busy,[4] mischievous, wretched thing; no better than a kind of vermin. Goodness answers to the theological virtue Charity, and admits no excess,* but[5] error. The desire of power in excess caused the angels to fall; the desire of knowledge in excess caused man to fall: but in charity there is no excess; neither can angel or man come in danger by it. The inclination to goodness is imprinted deeply in the nature of man; insomuch that if it issue[6] not towards men, it will take unto other living creatures; as it is seen in the Turks,* a cruel people, who nevertheless are kind to beasts, and give alms to dogs and birds; insomuch as Busbechius* reporteth, a Christian boy in Constantinople had like[7] to have been stoned for gagging in a waggishness[8] a long-billed fowl.[9]

Errors* indeed in this virtue of goodness or charity may be committed. The Italians have an ungracious proverb, *Tanto buon che val niente*; 'So good, that he is good for nothing'. And one of the doctors[10] of Italy, Nicholas Machiavel,* had the confidence[11] to put in writing, almost in plain terms, that 'the Christian faith had given up good men in prey to those that are tyrannical and unjust'. Which he spake, because indeed there was never law, or sect, or opinion, did so much magnify goodness, as the Christian religion doth. Therefore, to avoid the scandal[12] and the danger both, it is good to take knowledge of the errors of an habit so excellent.

Seek the good of other men, but be not in bondage to their faces or fancies;* for that is but facility or softness; which taketh an honest

1 desiring, having a love for   2 well-being   3 expression   4 meddlesome
5 only   6 manifest itself   7 was nearly   8 mischievous game
9 bird (of any kind)   10 learned men, teachers   11 boldness
12 discredit to religion

mind prisoner. Neither give thou Aesop's cock* a gem, who would be better pleased and happier if he had a barley-corn. The example of God teacheth the lesson truly; 'He sendeth his rain, and maketh his sun to shine, upon the just and unjust';* but he doth not rain wealth, nor shine honour and virtues, upon men equally. Common benefits are to be communicate with all; but peculiar benefits with choice. And beware how in making the portraiture[1] thou breakest the pattern. For divinity maketh the love of ourselves the pattern; the love of our neighbours but the portraiture. 'Sell all thou hast, and give it to the poor, and follow me':* but sell not all thou hast, except thou come and follow me; that is, except thou have a vocation wherein thou mayest do as much good with little means as with great; for otherwise in feeding the streams thou driest the fountain.

Neither is there only a habit of goodness,* directed by right reason;* but there is in some men, even in nature, a disposition towards it; as on the other side there is a natural malignity. For there be[2] that in their nature do not affect[3] the good of others. The lighter sort of malignity turneth but to a crossness,[4] or frowardness,[5] or aptness to oppose, or difficilness,[6] or the like; but the deeper sort to envy and mere[7] mischief. Such men in other men's calamities are, as it were, in season,[8] and are ever on the loading part:* not so good as the dogs that licked Lazarus' sores;* but like flies that are still[9] buzzing upon any thing that is raw; *misanthropi*, that make it their practice to bring men to the bough, and yet have never a tree for the purpose in their gardens, as Timon* had. Such dispositions are the very errors* of human nature; and yet they are the fittest timber[10] to make great politiques[11] of; like to knee timber,* that is good for ships, that are ordained to be tossed; but not for building houses, that shall stand firm.

The parts and signs of goodness are many. If a man be gracious and courteous to strangers, it shews he is a citizen of the world,* and that his heart is no island cut off from other lands,* but a continent that joins to them. If he be compassionate towards the afflictions of others, it shews that his heart is like the noble tree* that is wounded itself when it gives the balm. If he easily pardons and remits offences, it shews that his mind is planted above injuries; so that he cannot be shot.[12] If he be thankful for small benefits, it shews that he weighs men's minds,[13] and

---

1 portrait　　2 are　　3 desire　　4 contrariness　　5 stubbornness
6 awkwardness　　7 real　　8 flourishing　　9 always　　10 material
11 politicians　　12 hurt　　13 intentions

not their trash.[1] But above all, if he have St Paul's perfection,* that he would wish to be an *anathema*[2] from Christ for the salvation of his brethren, it shews much of a divine nature, and a kind of conformity with Christ himself.

14. OF NOBILITY

We will speak of Nobility first as a portion of an estate;[3] then as a condition of particular[4] persons. A monarchy where there is no nobility at all, is ever a pure[5] and absolute tyranny; as that of the Turks. For nobility attempers[6] sovereignty, and draws the eyes of the people somewhat aside from the line royal.[7] But for democracies, they need it not; and they are commonly more quiet and less subject to sedition, than where there are stirps of nobles.[8] For men's eyes are upon the business,[9] and not upon the persons; or if upon the persons, it is for the business' sake, as fittest, and not for flags[10] and pedigree.[11] We see the Switzers* last well, notwithstanding their diversity of religion and of cantons. For utility[12] is their bond, and not respects.[13] The united provinces* of the Low Countries in their government excel; for where there is an equality, the consultations[14] are more indifferent,[15] and the payments and tributes more cheerful. A great and potent nobility addeth majesty to a monarch, but diminisheth power; and putteth life and spirit into the people, but presseth* their fortune. It is well when nobles are not too great for sovereignty nor for justice;* and yet maintained in that height, as the insolency of inferiors may be broken upon them before it come on too fast[16] upon the majesty of kings. A numerous nobility causeth poverty and inconvenience in a state; for it is a surcharge of expense; and besides, it being of necessity that many of the nobility fall[17] in time[18] to be weak in fortune, it maketh a kind of disproportion between honour and means.[19]

As for nobility in particular persons; it is a reverend[20] thing to see an ancient castle or building not in decay; or to see a fair[21] timber tree[22]

---

1 anything worthless; a cant word for money   2 a person or thing formally cursed by a church authority   3 state   4 individual   5 mere   6 moderates
7 royal family, descendants   8 stems of noble families   9 management of public affairs   10 insignia (as coats of arms)   11 genealogy of nobility
12 mutual benefit   13 respecting of persons (rank, nobility)   14 considerations
15 impartial   16 close   17 chance, happen   18 sooner or later   19 riches
20 worthy of respect   21 handsome   22 useful, not ornamental

sound and perfect. How much more to behold an ancient noble family, which hath stood against the waves and weathers of time. For new nobility is but the act of power,* but ancient nobility is the act of time. Those that are first raised to nobility are commonly more virtuous,[1] but less innocent, than their descendants; for there is rarely any rising[2] but by a commixture of good and evil arts. But it is reason[3] the memory of their virtues remain to their posterity, and their faults die with themselves. Nobility of birth commonly abateth industry;[4] and he that is not industrious, envieth him that is. Besides, noble persons cannot go much higher: and he that standeth at a stay[5] when others rise, can hardly avoid motions[6] of envy. On the other side, nobility extinguisheth the passive envy[7] from others towards them; because they are in possession of honour. Certainly, kings that have able men of[8] their nobility shall find ease in employing them, and a better slide[9] into their business; for people naturally bend to them, as born in some sort to command.

15. OF SEDITIONS AND TROUBLES

Shepherds* of people had need know the calendars of tempests in state; which are commonly greatest when things grow to equality;* as natural tempests are greatest about the *Equinoctia.** And as there are certain hollow blasts of wind and secret swellings of seas before a tempest, so are there in states:

> *Ille etiam caecos instare tumultus*
> *Saepe monet, fraudesque et operta tumescere bella.**

Libels and licentious discourses against the state, when they are frequent and open; and in like sort, false news often running up and down to the disadvantage of the state, and hastily embraced; are amongst the signs of troubles. Virgil giving the pedigree of Fame, saith she was sister to the Giants:

> *Illam Terra parens, ira irritata Deorum,*
> *Extremam (ut perhibent) Cœo Enceladoque sororem*
> *Progenuit.**

---

1 strong, resourceful (cf. Italian *virtù*)   2 social advancement   3 it is right
4 blunts initiative   5 in the same place   6 emotions   7 being envied
8 among   9 access (business will flow more smoothly)

As if fames[1] were the relics of seditions past; but they are no less indeed the preludes of seditions to come. Howsoever he noteth it right, that seditious tumults and seditious fames differ no more but as brother and sister, masculine and feminine; especially if it come to that, that the best actions of a state, and the most plausible,[2] and which ought to give greatest contentment, are taken in ill sense, and traduced:[3] for that shews the envy[4] great, as Tacitus saith, *conflata magna invidia, seu bene seu male gesta premunt.** Neither doth it follow, that because these fames are a sign of troubles, that the suppressing of them with too much severity should be a remedy of troubles. For the despising of them many times checks them best; and the going about to stop them doth but make a wonder long-lived. Also that kind of obedience which Tacitus speaketh of, is to be held suspected: *Erant in officio, sed tamen qui mallent mandata imperantium interpretari quam exequi;** disputing, excusing, cavilling[5] upon mandates[6] and directions,[7] is a kind of shaking off the yoke, and assay of disobedience; especially if in those disputings they which are for the direction speak fearfully[8] and tenderly,[9] and those that are against it audaciously.

Also, as Machiavel* noteth well, when princes, that ought to be common parents,* make themselves as a party,[10] and lean to a side, it is as a boat that is overthrown by uneven weight on the one side; as was well seen in the time of Henry the Third of France; for first himself entered league* for the extirpation of the Protestants; and presently after[11] the same league was turned upon himself. For when the authority of princes is made but an accessary to a cause,* and that there be other bands[12] that tie faster[13] than the band of sovereignty, kings begin to be put almost out of possession.[14]

Also, when discords, and quarrels, and factions, are carried* openly and audaciously, it is a sign the reverence of government is lost. For the motions of the greatest persons in a government ought to be as the motions of the planets under *primum mobile** (according to the old opinion),* which is, that every of them is carried swiftly by the highest motion, and softly in their own motion. And therefore, when great ones in their own particular* motion move violently, and, as Tacitus expresseth it well, *liberius quam ut imperantium meminissent,** it is a sign

1 rumours   2 deserving applause   3 misrepresented   4 discontent
5 making trivial objections   6 commands   7 orders   8 hesitatingly
9 cautiously   10 political group, faction   11 immediately afterwards
12 links   13 more closely   14 office

the orbs are out of frame.* For reverence is that wherewith princes are girt[1] from God; who threateneth the dissolving thereof: *Solvam cingula regum.**

So when any of the four pillars of government are mainly[2] shaken or weakened (which are Religion, Justice, Counsel,[3] and Treasure), men had need to pray for fair weather. But let us pass from this part[4] of predictions (concerning which, nevertheless, more light may be taken from that which followeth); and let us speak first of the Materials of seditions; then of the Motives* of them; and thirdly of the Remedies.

Concerning the Materials of seditions. It is a thing well to be considered; for the surest way to prevent seditions (if the times do bear it) is to take away the matter of them. For if there be fuel prepared, it is hard to tell whence the spark shall come that shall set it on fire. The matter[5] of seditions is of two kinds; much poverty and much discontentment.[6] It is certain, so many overthrown estates,[7] so many votes for troubles. Lucan noteth well the state[8] of Rome before the civil war,

> *Hinc usura vorax, rapidumque in tempore foenus,*
> *Hinc concussa fides, et multis utile bellum.**

This same *multis utile bellum*, is an assured and infallible sign of a state disposed to seditions and troubles. And if this poverty and broken estate in the better sort be joined with a want and necessity in the mean people, the danger is imminent and great. For the rebellions of the belly* are the worst. As for discontentments, they are in the politic body[9] like to humours[10] in the natural, which are apt to gather a preternatural heat and to inflame. And let no prince measure the danger of them by this, whether they be just or unjust: for that were to imagine people to be too reasonable; who do often spurn at their own good: nor yet by this, whether the griefs[11] whereupon they rise be in fact great or small: for they are the most dangerous discontentments where the fear is greater than the feeling: *Dolendi modus, timendi non item.** Besides, in great oppressions, the same things that provoke the patience, do withal mate[12] the courage; but in fears it is not so. Neither let any prince or state be secure[13] concerning discontentments, because they have been often,[14] or have been long, and yet no peril hath

1 fitted out   2 violently   3 advisory and consultative functions, as in the Privy Council   4 of the discussion   5 cause   6 public envy   7 ruined fortunes; bankrupts   8 condition   9 the state; civil society   10 the four fluids whose proper balance maintained health   11 grievances   12 beat down, overpower   13 without care, complacent   14 frequently occurring

ensued: for as it is true that every vapour or fume[1] doth not turn into a storm; so it is nevertheless true that storms, though they blow over divers times, yet may fall at last; and, as the Spanish proverb noteth well, 'The cord breaketh at the last by the weakest pull'.

The Causes and Motives* of seditions are, innovation* in religion; taxes; alteration of laws and customs; breaking of privileges; general oppression; advancement of unworthy persons; strangers;* dearths; disbanded soldiers; factions grown desperate; and whatsoever, in offending people, joineth and knitteth[2] them in a common cause.

For the Remedies; there may be some general preservatives,[3] whereof we will speak: as for the just cure, it must answer to the particular disease; and so be left to counsel rather than rule.*

The first remedy or prevention is to remove by all means possible that material cause of sedition whereof we spake; which is, want and poverty in the estate.[4] To which purpose serveth, the opening and well-balancing of trade; the cherishing of manufactures; the banishing of idleness; the repressing of waste and excess by sumptuary laws;* the improvement and husbanding[5] of the soil; the regulating of prices of things vendible;[6] the moderating of taxes and tributes,[7] and the like. Generally, it is to be foreseen[8] that the population of a kingdom (especially if it be not mown down by wars) do not exceed the stock[9] of the kingdom which should maintain them. Neither is the population to be reckoned only by number; for a smaller number that spend more and earn less, do wear out an estate[10] sooner than a greater number that live lower and gather more.* Therefore the multiplying of nobility* and other degrees of quality[11] in an over-proportion to the common people, doth speedily bring a state to necessity; and so doth likewise an overgrown clergy; for they bring nothing to the stock; and in like manner, when more are bred[12] scholars than preferments[13] can take off.[14]

It is likewise to be remembered, that forasmuch as the increase of any estate must be upon the foreigner* (for whatsoever is somewhere gotten is somewhere lost),* there be but three things which one nation selleth unto another: the commodity[15] as nature yieldeth it; the manufacture; and the vecture,[16] or carriage. So that if these three wheels[17]

---

1 mist or damp cloud arising from the earth or sea   2 unites   3 safeguards
4 state, country   5 careful agricultural treatment   6 for sale   7 payments by
subject people   8 provided   9 available wealth, resources   10 state, country
11 rank   12 educated   13 appointments, positions   14 absorb
15 raw materials, natural produce   16 transportation   17 sources of trade

go, wealth will flow as in a spring tide.* And it cometh many times to pass, that *materiam superabit opus*;* that the work and carriage is more worth than the material, and enricheth a state more; as is notably seen in the Low-Countrymen, who have the best mines above ground* in the world.

Above all things, good policy is to be used that the treasure and monies in a state be not gathered into few hands. For otherwise a state may have a great stock, and yet starve. And money is like muck,[1] not good except it be spread. This is done chiefly by suppressing, or at the least keeping a strait hand[2] upon the devouring trades of usury, ingrossing,* great pasturages,* and the like.

For removing discontentments, or at least the danger of them; there is in every state (as we know) two portions of subjects; the nobless[3] and the commonalty. When one of these is discontent,[4] the danger is not great; for common people are of slow motion, if they be not excited by the greater sort; and the greater sort are of small strength, except the multitude be apt and ready to move of themselves. Then is the danger, when the greater sort do but wait for the troubling of the waters* amongst the meaner, that then they may declare themselves.[5] The poets* feign, that the rest of the gods would have bound Jupiter; which he hearing of, by the counsel of Pallas, sent for Briareus, with his hundred hands, to come in to his aid. An emblem, no doubt, to show how safe[6] it is for monarchs to make sure of the good will of common people.

To give moderate liberty for griefs and discontentments to evaporate (so it be without too great insolency or bravery),[7] is a safe way. For he that turneth the humours back,* and maketh the wound bleed inwards, endangereth* malign ulcers and pernicious imposthumations.

The part[8] of Epimetheus* might well become[9] Prometheus, in the case of discontentments; for there is not a better provision[10] against them. Epimetheus, when griefs and evils flew abroad, at last shut the lid, and kept hope in the bottom of the vessel. Certainly, the politic[11] and artificial[12] nourishing and entertaining[13] of hopes, and carrying men from hopes to hopes, is one of the best antidotes against the poison of discontentments. And it is a certain sign of a wise government and

---

1 manure, fertilizer   2 strict control   3 nobility   4 discontented
5 disclose their grievances   6 salutary, tending to safety   7 boastful defiance
8 role, action   9 suit   10 precaution   11 artful   12 skilful
13 encouraging

proceeding,[1] when it can hold men's hearts by hopes, when it cannot by satisfaction; and when it can handle things in such manner, as no evil shall appear so peremptory[2] but that it hath some outlet of hope: which is the less hard to do, because both particular persons and factions are apt[3] enough to flatter themselves, or at least to brave[4] that, which they believe not.

Also the foresight and prevention, that there be no likely or fit head[5] whereunto discontented persons may resort, and under whom they may join, is a known, but an excellent point of caution. I understand a fit head to be one that hath greatness* and reputation; that hath confidence with the discontented party, and upon whom they turn their eyes; and that is thought discontented in his own particular:[6] which kind of persons are either to be won and reconciled to the state, and that in a fast[7] and true manner; or to be fronted[8] with some other of the same party, that may oppose them, and so divide the reputation. Generally, the dividing and breaking of all factions and combinations[9] that are adverse to the state, and setting them at distance,[10] or at least distrust, amongst themselves, is not one of the worst remedies. For it is a desperate case, if those that hold with the proceeding of the state be full of discord and faction, and those that are against it be entire and united.

I have noted that some witty and sharp[11] speeches which have fallen from princes have given fire to seditions. Caesar did himself infinite hurt in that speech, *Sulla nescivit literas, non potuit dictare*:* for it did utterly cut off that hope which men had entertained, that he would at one time or other give over his dictatorship. Galba undid himself by that speech, *legi a se militem, non emi*;* for it put the soldiers out of hope of the donative.[12] Probus likewise, by that speech, *si vixero, non opus erit amplius Romano imperio militibus*;* a speech of great despair for the soldiers. And many the like. Surely princes had need, in tender[13] matters and ticklish[14] times, to beware what they say; especially in these short speeches, which fly abroad like darts,[15] and are thought to be shot out of their secret intentions. For as for large discourses, they are flat[16] things, and not so much noted.

1 policy   2 destructive, irremediable   3 willing   4 boastfully pretend
5 leader   6 personal concerns   7 firm, binding   8 confronted, opposed by
9 alliances   10 against each other   11 sarcastic   12 a gift of money; a bonus
13 delicate, needing tact   14 tricky, unstable   15 arrows
16 dull, uninteresting

Lastly, let princes, against all events, not be without some great person, one or rather more, of military valour, near unto them, for the repressing of seditions in their beginnings. For without that, there useth to be more trepidation[1] in court upon the first breaking out of troubles than were fit. And the state runneth the danger of that which Tacitus saith; *Atque is habitus animorum fuit, ut pessimum facinus auderent pauci, plures vellent, omnes paterentur.** But let such military persons be assured,[2] and well reputed of, rather than factious and popular;[3] holding also good correspondence* with the other great men in the state; or else the remedy is worse than the disease.

16. OF ATHEISM

I had rather believe all the fables in the Legend,* and the Talmud,* and the Alcoran,* than that this universal frame* is without a mind. And therefore God never wrought miracle to convince[4] atheism, because his ordinary works convince it. It is true, that a little philosophy inclineth man's mind to atheism; but depth in philosophy bringeth men's minds about to religion. For while the mind of man looketh upon second causes scattered,* it may sometimes rest[5] in them, and go no further; but when it beholdeth the chain of them, confederate[6] and linked together, it must needs fly to Providence and Deity. Nay, even that school which is most accused of atheism doth most demonstrate religion; that is, the school* of Leucippus and Democritus and Epicurus. For it is a thousand times more credible, that four mutable elements,* and one immutable fifth essence, duly and eternally placed,[7] need no God, than that an army of infinite small portions[8] or seeds unplaced, should have produced this order and beauty without a divine marshal.[9] The Scripture saith, 'The fool hath said in his heart, there is no God';* it is not said, 'The fool hath thought in his heart'; so as he rather saith it by rote[10] to himself as that he would have,[11] than that he can throughly[12] believe it or be persuaded of it. For none deny there is a God, but[13] those for whom it maketh* that there were no God.

1 trembling, alarm   2 trustworthy   3 relying on popular support (likely to be subversive)   4 refute, overcome in argument   5 remain contented with
6 leagued, united   7 fixed for ever in their correct position   8 particles
9 commander   10 mechanically   11 wants to believe   12 wholly
13 except

It appeareth in nothing more,* that atheism is rather in the lip than in the heart of man, than by this; that atheists will ever be talking of that their opinion, as if they fainted[1] in it within themselves, and would be glad to be strengthened by the consent of others. Nay more, you shall have atheists strive to get disciples, as it fareth with other sects. And, which is most of all,[2] you shall have of them that will suffer for atheism, and not recant; whereas if they did truly think that there were no such thing as God, why should they trouble themselves? Epicurus is charged* that he did but dissemble for his credit's sake, when he affirmed there were blessed natures,* but such as enjoyed themselves without having respect to the government of the world. Wherein they say he did temporize;[3] though in secret he thought there was no God. But certainly he is traduced;[4] for his words are noble and divine: *Non Deos vulgi negare profanum; sed vulgi opiniones Diis applicare profanum.** Plato could have said no more. And although he* had the confidence to deny the administration, he had not the power to deny the nature.

The Indians of the west* have names for their particular gods, though they have no name for God: as if the heathens should have had the names Jupiter, Apollo, Mars, &c. but not the word *Deus*; which shews that even those barbarous people have the notion, though they have not the latitude and extent of it. So that against atheists the very savages[5] take part[6] with the very subtlest[7] philosophers. The contemplative[8] atheist is rare: a Diagoras, a Bion,* a Lucian* perhaps, and some others; and yet they seem to be more than they are; for that all that impugn[9] a received[10] religion or superstition are by the adverse part branded with the name of atheists. But the great atheists indeed are hypocrites; which are ever handling[11] holy things, but without feeling; so as they must needs be cauterized[12] in the end.

The causes of atheism are: divisions in religion, if they be many; for any one main division addeth zeal to both sides; but many divisions introduce atheism. Another is, scandal[13] of priests; when it is come to that which St Bernard saith, *Non est jam dicere, ut populus sic sacerdos; quia nec sic populus ut sacerdos.** A third is, custom of profane scoffing[14] in holy matters; which doth by little and little deface the reverence of religion. And lastly, learned times, specially with peace and prosperity;

---

1 became feeble, doubted   2 most significant   3 conform to time and circumstances   4 misrepresented, maligned   5 Indians   6 agree   7 most acute   8 speculative   9 oppose   10 accepted, established   11 discussing, having to do with   12 burned, branded   13 discredit (to religion)   14 mockery

for troubles and adversities do more bow men's minds to religion. They that deny a God destroy man's nobility; for certainly man is of kin[1] to the beasts by his body; and, if he be not of kin to God by his spirit, he is a base and ignoble creature. It destroys likewise magnanimity,[2] and the raising* of human nature; for take an example of a dog, and mark[3] what a generosity and courage he will put on when he finds himself maintained[4] by a man; who to him is instead of a god, or *melior natura;** which courage is manifestly such as that creature, without that confidence of a better nature than his own, could never attain. So man, when he resteth[5] and assureth[6] himself upon divine protection and favour, gathereth a force and faith which human nature in itself could not obtain.

Therefore, as atheism is in all respects hateful, so in this, that it depriveth human nature of the means to exalt itself above human frailty. As it is in particular persons, so it is in nations. Never was there such a state for magnanimity as Rome. Of this state hear what Cicero saith: *Quam volumus licet, patres conscripti, nos amemus, tamen nec numero Hispanos, nec robore Gallos, nec calliditate Poenos, nec artibus Graecos, nec denique hoc ipso hujus gentis et terrae domestico nativoque sensu Italos ipsos et Latinos; sed pietate, ac religione, atque hac una sapientia, quod Deorum immortalium numine omnia regi gubernarique perspeximus, omnes gentes nationesque superavimus.**

17. Of Superstition

It were better to have no opinion[7] of God at all, than such an opinion as is unworthy of him. For the one is unbelief, the other is contumely:[8] and certainly superstition is the reproach of the Deity.* Plutarch* saith well to that purpose: 'Surely' (saith he) 'I had rather a great deal men should say there was no such man at all as Plutarch, than that they should say that there was one Plutarch that would eat his children as soon as they were born'; as the poets speak of Saturn.* And as the contumely is greater towards God, so the danger is greater towards men. Atheism leaves[9] a man to sense,[10] to philosophy, to natural piety,* to laws, to reputation; all which may be guides to an outward moral

1 akin   2 noble, generous feelings   3 observe   4 supported, looked after
5 relies   6 trusts   7 conception   8 insolent abuse   9 directs
10 experience through the senses

virtue, though religion were not; but superstition dismounts[1] all these, and erecteth an absolute monarchy in the minds of men. Therefore atheism did never perturb states; for it makes men wary of themselves, as looking no further: and we see the times inclined to atheism (as the time of Augustus Caesar)* were civil times. But superstition hath been the confusion[2] of many states, and bringeth in a new *primum mobile*,* that ravisheth[3] all the spheres of government. The master of superstition is the people; and in all superstition wise men follow fools; and arguments are fitted to practice,* in a reversed order. It was gravely* said by some of the prelates in the council of Trent,* where the doctrine of the schoolmen[4] bare great sway, that 'the schoolmen were like astronomers, which did feign eccentrics and epicycles, and such engines of orbs,* to save the phaenomena;* though they knew there were no such things'; and in like manner, that the schoolmen had framed a number of subtle and intricate axioms and theorems,* to save the practice of the church.

The causes of superstition are: pleasing and sensual[5] rites and ceremonies; excess of outward and pharisaical[6] holiness; over-great reverence of traditions, which cannot but load the church; the stratagems of prelates for their own ambition and lucre;[7] the favouring too much of good intentions, which openeth the gate to conceits[8] and novelties;[9] the taking an aim at divine matters by human,* which cannot but breed mixture of imaginations;[10] and, lastly, barbarous times, especially joined with calamities and disasters. Superstition, without a veil, is a deformed thing; for as it addeth deformity to an ape to be so like a man, so the similitude[11] of superstition to religion makes it the more deformed. And as wholesome meat corrupteth to little worms, so good forms and orders corrupt into a number of petty[12] observances. There is a superstition in avoiding superstition, when men think to do best if they go furthest from the superstition formerly received; therefore care would be had that (as it fareth in ill purgings)[13] the good be not taken away with the bad; which commonly is done when the people is the reformer.

1 dethrones, disqualifies   2 cause of chaos   3 hurries away, disturbs
4 medieval scholastic philosophers   5 appealing to the senses
6 self-righteous, hypocritical   7 profit   8 fantastic conceptions
9 innovations (in belief)   10 confused, fantastic theories   11 comparison
12 trivial   13 medical treatment, emptying the bowels

18. OF TRAVEL

Travel, in the younger sort, is a part of education; in the elder, a part of experience. He that travelleth into a country before he hath some entrance into the language, goeth to school, and not to travel. That young men travel under some tutor, or grave[1] servant, I allow well; so[2] he be such a one that hath the language, and hath been in the country before; whereby he may be able to tell them what things are worthy to be seen in the country where they go; what acquaintances they are to seek; what exercises or discipline* the place yieldeth.[3] For else young men shall go hooded,* and look abroad[4] little. It is a strange thing, that in sea voyages, where there is nothing to be seen but sky and sea, men should make diaries; but in land-travel, wherein so much is to be observed, for the most part they omit it; as if chance were fitter to be registered than observation. Let diaries therefore be brought in use.

The things to be seen and observed are: the courts of princes, specially when they give audience to ambassadors; the courts of justice, while they sit[5] and hear causes;[6] and so of consistories[7] ecclesiastic; the churches and monasteries, with the monuments which are therein extant; the walls and fortifications of cities and towns, and so the havens and harbours; antiquities and ruins; libraries; colleges, disputations,[8] and lectures, where any are; shipping and navies; houses and gardens of state and pleasure, near great cities; armories;* arsenals; magazines;* exchanges; burses;* warehouses; exercises of horsemanship, fencing, training of soldiers, and the like; comedies, such whereunto the better sort of persons do resort; treasuries of jewels and robes; cabinets and rarities;* and, to conclude, whatsoever is memorable in the places where they go. After all which the tutors or servants ought to make diligent inquiry. As for triumphs,[9] masks, feasts, weddings, funerals, capital executions, and such shows, men need not to be put in mind of them; yet are they not to be neglected.

If you will have a young man to put his travel into a little room,* and in short time to gather much, this you must do. First as was said, he must have some entrance into the language before he goeth. Then he must have such a servant or tutor as knoweth the country, as was likewise said. Let him carry with him also some card[10] or book describing

---

1 reliable   2 provided   3 offers   4 around   5 are in session   6 cases
7 ecclesiastical courts of justice   8 formal university debates
9 triumphant processions   10 map, itinerary

the country where he travelleth; which will be a good key[1] to his inquiry. Let him keep also a diary. Let him not stay long in one city or town; more or less as the place deserveth, but not long; nay, when he stayeth in one city or town, let him change his lodging from one end and part of the town to another; which is a great adamant[2] of acquaintance. Let him sequester himself from the company of his countrymen, and diet[3] in such places where there is good company of the nation where he travelleth. Let him upon his removes[4] from one place to another, procure recommendation[5] to some person of quality[6] residing in the place whither he removeth; that he may use his favour in those things he desireth to see or know. Thus he may abridge[7] his travel with much profit.

As for the acquaintance which is to be sought in travel; that which is most of all profitable, is acquaintance with the secretaries and employed men[8] of ambassadors: for so in travelling in one country he shall suck[9] the experience of many. Let him also see and visit eminent persons in all kinds, which are of great name abroad; that he may be able to tell[10] how the life* agreeth with the fame. For quarrels, they are with care and discretion[11] to be avoided. They are commonly for mistresses, healths,* place,[12] and words.[13] And let a man beware how he keepeth company with choleric and quarrelsome persons; for they will engage him into their own quarrels. When a traveller returneth home, let him not leave the countries where he hath travelled altogether behind him; but maintain a correspondence by letters with those of his acquaintance which are of most worth. And let his travel appear rather in his discourse than in his apparel or gesture;[14] and in his discourse let him be rather advised[15] in his answers, than forward[16] to tell stories; and let it appear that he doth not change his country manners* for those of foreign parts; but only prick in[17] some flowers[18] of that he hath learned abroad into the customs of his own country.

19. OF EMPIRE*

It is a miserable state of mind to have few things to desire, and many things to fear; and yet that commonly is the case of kings; who, being at

1 answer	2 magnet	3 dine	4 changing places	5 letter of introduction
6 of high rank	7 shorten, ease	8 household staff	9 absorb	10 find out
11 astuteness	12 questions of precedence	13 insults	14 behaviour	
15 deliberate, judicious	16 too eager	17 transplant	18 the choicest parts	

the highest, want[1] matter of desire, which makes their minds more languishing;[2] and have many representations* of perils and shadows, which makes their minds the less clear. And this is one reason also of that effect[3] which the Scripture speaketh of, that 'the king's heart is inscrutable'.* For multitude of jealousies,[4] and lack of some predominant desire that should marshal and put in order all the rest, maketh any man's heart hard to find or sound.[5] Hence it comes likewise, that princes many times make themselves desires, and set their hearts upon toys;[6] sometimes upon a building; sometimes upon erecting of an order;* sometimes upon the advancing[7] of a person; sometimes upon obtaining excellency in some art or feat of the hand; as Nero* for playing on the harp, Domitian* for certainty of the hand with the arrow, Commodus* for playing at fence, Caracalla* for driving chariots, and the like. This seemeth incredible unto those that know not the principle that 'the mind of man is more cheered and refreshed by profiting in small things, than by standing at a stay[8] in great'. We see also that kings that have been fortunate conquerors in their first years, it being not possible for them to go forward infinitely, but that they must have some check[9] or arrest in their fortunes, turn in their latter years to be superstitious and melancholy; as did Alexander* the Great; Diocletian;* and in our memory, Charles the Fifth;* and others. For he that is used to go forward, and findeth a stop,[10] falleth out of his own favour,[11] and is not the thing he was.

To speak now of the true temper* of empire; it is a thing rare and hard to keep; for both temper and distemper* consist of contraries. But it is one thing to mingle contraries, another to interchange them. The answer* of Apollonius to Vespasian is full of excellent instruction. Vespasian asked him, 'what was Nero's overthrow?' He answered, 'Nero could touch and tune the harp well; but in government sometimes he used to wind the pins too high, sometimes to let them down too low'. And certain it is that nothing destroyeth authority so much as the unequal[12] and untimely interchange of power pressed too far, and relaxed too much.

This is true, that the wisdom[13] of all these latter times in princes' affairs is rather fine[14] deliveries[15] and shiftings[16] of dangers and mischiefs

1 lack   2 inert, enervated   3 fact   4 suspicions
5 probe, discover the inclinations   6 trifles   7 promotion (as of a court favourite)
8 remaining passive, stagnant   9 rebuff   10 obstacle   11 self-respect
12 unbalanced   13 art (of government)   14 astute
15 means of escape from difficulties   16 subterfuges (to avoid danger)

when they are near, than solid and grounded courses to keep them aloof. But this is but to try masteries* with fortune. And let men beware how they neglect and suffer matter of trouble to be prepared; for no man can forbid¹ the spark, nor tell whence it may come. The difficulties in princes' business are many and great; but the greatest difficulty is often in their own mind. For it is common with princes (saith Tacitus) to will² contradictories: *Sunt plerumque regum voluntates vehementes, et inter se contrariae.** For it is the solecism* of power, to think to command the end, and yet not to endure the mean.³

Kings have to deal with their neighbours, their wives, their children, their prelates or clergy, their nobles, their second-nobles⁴ or gentlemen, their merchants, their commons, and their men of war; and from all these arise dangers, if care and circumspection be not used.

First for their neighbours: there can no general rule be given (the occasions are so variable), save one, which ever holdeth; which is, that princes do keep due sentinel, that none of their neighbours do overgrow so (by increase of territory, by embracing⁵ of trade, by approaches,* or the like), as they become more able to annoy them than they were. And this is generally the work of standing councils to foresee and to hinder it. During* that triumvirate of kings, King Henry the Eighth of England, Francis the First King of France, and Charles the Fifth Emperor, there was such a watch kept, that none of the three could win a palm of ground, but the other two would straightways⁶ balance it, either by confederation, or, if need were, by a war; and would not in any wise take up peace at interest.* And the like was done by that league* (which Guicciardine saith was the security of Italy) made between Ferdinando King of Naples, Lorenzius Medices, and Ludovicus Sforza, potentates, the one of Florence, the other of Milan. Neither is the opinion of some of the schoolmen* to be received,⁷ that 'a war cannot justly be made but upon a precedent injury or provocation'. For there is no question but a just fear of an imminent danger, though there be no blow given, is a lawful cause of a war.

For their wives: there are cruel examples of them. Livia is infamed* for the poisoning of her husband;* Roxalana, Solyman's wife, was the destruction* of that renowned prince Sultan Mustapha, and otherwise* troubled his house and succession; Edward the Second of England his queen* had the principal hand in the deposing and

---

1 prevent   2 desire   3 means   4 gentry   5 dominating
6 immediately   7 accepted

murther of her husband. This kind of danger is then to be feared chiefly, when the wives have plots for the raising[1] of their own children; or else that they be advoutresses.[2]

For their children: the tragedies likewise of dangers from them have been many. And generally, the entering of fathers into suspicion of their children hath been ever unfortunate. The destruction of Mustapha (that we named before) was so fatal to Solyman's line,[3] as the succession[4] of the Turks from Solyman until this day is suspected to be untrue, and of strange* blood; for that Selymus the Second was thought to be suppositious.[5] The destruction of Crispus,* a young prince of rare towardness,[6] by Constantinus the Great, his father, was in like manner fatal to his house;[7] for both Constantinus and Constance, his sons, died violent deaths; and Constantius, his other son, did little better; who died indeed of sickness, but after that Julianus had taken arms against him. The destruction of Demetrius,* son to Philip the Second* of Macedon, turned upon the father, who died of repentance. And many like examples there are; but few or none where the fathers had good by such distrust; except it were where the sons were up in open arms against them; as was Selymus* the First against Bajazet; and the three sons* of Henry the Second, King of England.

For their prelates: when they are proud and great, there is also danger from them; as it was in the times of Anselmus* and Thomas Becket,* Archbishops of Canterbury; who with their crosiers did almost try it[8] with the king's sword; and yet they had to deal with stout[9] and haughty kings; William Rufus, Henry the First, and Henry the Second. The danger is not from that state,* but[10] where it hath a dependance of foreign authority;* or where the churchmen come in and are elected, not by the collation* of the king, or particular patrons, but by the people.

For their nobles: to keep them at a distance, it is not amiss; but to depress[11] them, may make a king more absolute, but less safe; and less able to perform any thing that he desires. I have noted* it in my *History of King Henry the Seventh of England*, who depressed his nobility; whereupon it came to pass[12] that his times were full of difficulties and troubles; for the nobility, though they continued loyal unto him, yet

1 advancing   2 adulteresses   3 descent   4 dynasty   5 illegitimate
6 promise   7 lineage   8 measure their strength against   9 bold
10 except   11 lessen their power; humiliate   12 happened

did they not co-operate with him in his business. So that in effect he was fain[1] to do all things himself.

For their second[2] nobles: there is not much danger from them, being a body dispersed. They may sometimes discourse high,[3] but that doth little hurt; besides, they are a counterpoise to the higher nobility, that they grow not too potent; and, lastly, being the most immediate in authority with the common people, they do best temper popular commotions.

For their merchants: they are *vena porta*;* and if they flourish not, a kingdom may have good limbs, but will have empty veins, and nourish little. Taxes and imposts upon them do seldom good to the king's revenue; for that that he wins in the hundred* he leeseth in the shire;* the particular rates[4] being increased, but the total bulk of trading rather decreased.

For their commons:[5] there is little danger from them, except it be where they have great and potent heads;[6] or where you meddle with the point of religion, or their customs,[7] or means of life.

For their men of war: it is a dangerous state[8] where they live and remain in a body, and are used to donatives;[9] whereof we see examples in the janizaries,* and pretorian bands* of Rome; but trainings of men, and arming them in several[10] places, and under several commanders, and without donatives, are things of defence, and no danger.

Princes are like to heavenly bodies, which cause good or evil times; and which have much veneration, but no rest.* All precepts concerning kings are in effect comprehended in those two remembrances; *memento quod es homo*; and *memento quod es Deus*, or *vice Dei*;* the one bridleth their power, and the other their will.[11]

20. Of Counsel

The greatest trust between man and man is the trust of giving counsel. For in other* confidences men commit the parts of life; their lands, their goods, their children, their credit, some particular affair; but to such as they make their counsellors, they commit the whole: by how much the more they* are obliged to all faith and integrity. The wisest princes need not think it any diminution to their greatness, or deroga-

1 obliged   2 inferior   3 talk recklessly   4 revenues from tax
5 working classes   6 leaders   7 taxes, imposts   8 situation
9 special additional payments; generous presents   10 separate   11 desire

tion[1] to their sufficiency,[2] to rely upon counsel. God himself is not without, but hath made it one of the great names[3] of his blessed Son, 'The Counsellor'.* Salomon* hath pronounced that 'in counsel is stability'. Things will have their first or second agitation:[4] if they be not tossed upon the arguments of counsel, they will be tossed upon the waves of fortune; and be full of inconstancy, doing and undoing, like the reeling[5] of a drunken man. Salomon's son* found the force of counsel, as his father saw the necessity of it. For the beloved kingdom of God was first rent and broken by ill counsel;[6] upon which counsel there are set for our instruction the two marks whereby bad counsel is for ever best discerned; that it was young counsel, for the persons; and violent counsel, for the matter.[7]

The ancient times do set forth in figure[8] both the incorporation and inseparable conjunction of counsel with kings, and the wise and politic use of counsel by kings: the one, in that they say Jupiter did marry Metis, which signifieth counsel; whereby they intend[9] that Sovereignty is married to Counsel: the other in that which followeth, which was thus: They say, after Jupiter was married to Metis, she conceived by him and was with child, but Jupiter suffered her not[10] to stay till she brought forth, but ate her up; whereby he became himself with child, and was delivered of Pallas* armed, out of his head.* Which monstrous[11] fable containeth a secret of empire; how kings are to make use of their council of state.* That first they ought to refer matters unto them, which is the first begetting or impregnation; but when they are elaborate,[12] moulded, and shaped in the womb of their counsel, and grow ripe and ready to be brought forth, that then they suffer not their council to go through with the resolution and direction,[13] as if it depended on them; but take the matter back into their own hands, and make it appear to the world that the decrees and final directions (which, because they come forth with prudence and power, are resembled to Pallas armed) proceeded from themselves; and not only from their authority, but (the more to add reputation to themselves) from their head and device.[14]

Let us now speak of the inconveniences of counsel, and of the remedies. The inconveniences that have been noted in calling[15] and using

---

1 discredit   2 competence   3 major titles   4 motion; also debate
5 swaying unsteadily from side to side   6 bad advice   7 contents, substance
8 emblematically   9 mean, imply   10 did not allow   11 unnatural
12 developed   13 course of action   14 brain and ingenuity   15 inviting

counsel, are three. First, the revealing of affairs, whereby they become less secret. Secondly, the weakening of the authority of princes, as if they were less of themselves.[1] Thirdly, the danger of being unfaithfully counselled, and more for the good of them that counsel than of him that is counselled. For which inconveniences, the doctrine of Italy, and practice of France, in some kings' times, hath introduced cabinet councils;* a remedy worse than the disease.

As to secrecy; princes are not bound to communicate all matters with all counsellors; but may extract and select. Neither is it necessary that he that consulteth what he should do, should declare what he will do. But let princes beware that the unsecreting[2] of their affairs comes not from themselves. And as for cabinet councils, it may be their motto, *plenus rimarum sum*:* one futile[3] person that maketh it his glory to tell, will do more hurt than many that know it their duty to conceal. It is true there be some affairs which require extreme secrecy, which will hardly go beyond one or two persons* besides the king: neither are those counsels unprosperous; for, besides the secrecy, they commonly go on constantly in one spirit of direction,[4] without distraction. But then it must be a prudent king, such as is able to grind with a hand-mill;* and those inward[5] counsellors had need also be wise men, and especially true and trusty to the king's ends; as it was with King Henry the Seventh* of England, who in his greatest business imparted[6] himself to none, except it were to Morton and Fox.

For weakening of authority; the fable* showeth the remedy. Nay, the majesty of kings is rather exalted than diminished when they are in the chair of council; neither was there ever prince bereaved of his dependances* by his council; except where there hath been either an over-greatness in one counsellor or an over-strict combination* in divers; which are things soon found and holpen.[7]

For the last inconvenience, that men will counsel with an eye to themselves; certainly, *non inveniet fidem super terram** is meant of the nature of times,[8] and not of all particular persons. There be[9] that are in nature faithful, and sincere, and plain, and direct; not crafty and involved;[10] let princes, above all, draw to themselves such natures. Besides, counsellors are not commonly so united, but that one counsellor keepeth sentinel over another; so that if any do counsel out of

---

1 less capable   2 divulging   3 talkative, indiscreet
4 one consistent path or policy   5 intimate   6 revealed   7 remedied
8 epochs   9 There are some people   10 complicated, devious

faction or private ends, it commonly comes to the king's ear. But the best remedy is, if princes know their counsellors, as well as their counsellors know them:

*Principis est virtus maxima nosse suos.**

And on the other side, counsellors should not be too speculative[1] into their sovereign's person. The true composition of a counsellor is rather to be skilful in their master's business, than in his nature; for then he is like to advise him, and not feed his humour.[2] It is of singular[3] use to princes if they take the opinions of their council both separately and together. For private opinion is more free; but opinion before others is more reverent.[4] In private, men are more bold in their own humours; and in consort, men are more obnoxious[5] to others' humours; therefore it is good to take both; and of the inferior sort* rather in private, to preserve freedom; of the greater rather in consort, to preserve respect. It is in vain for princes to take counsel concerning matters,[6] if they take no counsel likewise concerning persons; for all matters are as dead images; and the life[7] of the execution of affairs resteth in the good choice of persons. Neither is it enough to consult concerning persons *secundum genera*,* as in an idea,[8] or mathematical description, what the kind and character of the person should be; for the greatest errors are committed, and the most[9] judgment is shown, in the choice of individuals. It was truly said, *optimi consiliarii mortui*;* books will speak plain when counsellors blanch.[10] Therefore it is good to be conversant[11] in them, specially the books of such as themselves have been actors upon the stage.

The councils at this day in most places are but familiar meetings, where matters are rather talked on[12] than debated. And they run too swift to the order or act of council.* It were better that in causes of weight, the matter were propounded one day and not spoken to till the next day; *in nocte consilium.** So was it done in the Commission of Union* between England and Scotland; which was a grave[13] and orderly assembly. I commend set[14] days for petitions; for both it gives the suitors more certainty for their attendance, and it frees the meetings for matters of estate,[15] that they may *hoc agere.** In choice of committees

---

1 inquisitive, prying   2 indulge his whims   3 unique   4 respectful
5 exposed to, under the influence of; deferential   6 affairs of state
7 vigour, success   8 abstract notion   9 greatest   10 whiten: either 'blench',
or 'blandish, flatter'   11 familiar with   12 gossiped about   13 important
14 fixed, agreed upon beforehand   15 state

for ripening business for the council, it is better to choose indifferent[1]
persons, than to make an indifferency[2] by putting in those that are
strong on both sides. I commend also standing commissions;[3] as for
trade, for treasure, for war, for suits,[4] for some provinces; for where
there be divers particular councils and but one council of estate (as it is
in Spain), they are, in effect, no more than standing commissions:
save[5] that they have greater authority. Let such as are to inform councils out of their particular professions, (as lawyers, seamen, mintmen,[6]
and the like), be first heard before committees; and then, as occasion
serves, before the council. And let them not come in multitudes, or in
a tribunitious* manner; for that is to clamour[7] councils, not to inform
them. A long table and a square table, or seats about the walls, seem
things of form, but are things of substance; for at a long table a few at
the upper end,* in effect, sway all the business; but in the other form
there is more use of the counsellors' opinions that sit lower. A king,
when he presides in council, let him beware how he opens his own inclination too much in that which he propoundeth; for else counsellors
will but take the wind of him,* and instead of giving free counsel, sing
him a song of *placebo*.*

21. OF DELAYS

Fortune is like the market; where many times, if you can stay[8] a little,
the price will fall. And again, it is sometimes like Sibylla's offer;*
which at first offereth the commodity at full, then consumeth part and
part, and still holdeth up the price. For 'occasion' (as it is in the common verse)* 'turneth a bald noddle,[9] after she hath presented her locks
in front, and no hold taken'; or at least turneth the handle of the bottle
first to be received, and after[10] the belly, which is hard to clasp. There
is surely no greater wisdom than well to time the beginnings and on-
sets of things. Dangers are no more light, if they once seem light; and
more dangers have deceived men than forced[11] them. Nay, it were better to meet some dangers half way, though they come nothing near,
than to keep too long a watch upon their approaches; for if a man watch
too long, it is odds he will fall asleep. On the other side, to be deceived
with too long shadows (as some have been when the moon was low and

1 impartial   2 balance (and possibly stalemate)   3 permanent committees
4 petitions   5 except   6 makers of coins   7 disturb   8 wait
9 back of the head   10 afterwards   11 harmed

shone on their enemies' back),* and so to shoot off before the time; or to teach dangers to come on, by over early buckling* towards them; is another extreme.

The ripeness or unripeness of the occasion (as we said) must ever be well weighed; and generally it is good to commit the beginnings of all great actions to Argos* with his hundred eyes, and the ends to Briareus* with his hundred hands; first to watch, and then to speed. For the helmet of Pluto,* which maketh the politique* man go invisible, is secrecy in the counsel and celerity in the execution. For when things are once come to the execution, there is no secrecy comparable to celerity; like the motion of a bullet in the air, which flieth so swift as it outruns the eye.

22. OF CUNNING

We take Cunning for a sinister or crooked wisdom. And certainly there is a great difference between a cunning man and a wise man; not only in point of honesty, but in point of ability. There be that can pack the cards,* and yet cannot play well; so there are some that are good in canvasses[1] and factions, that are otherwise weak men. Again, it is one thing to understand persons, and another thing to understand matters; for many are perfect[2] in men's humours, that are not greatly capable of the real part of business; which is the constitution[3] of one that hath studied men more than books. Such men are fitter for practice[4] than for counsel; and they are good but in their own alley:* turn them to new men, and they have lost their aim; so as the old rule to know a fool from a wise man, *Mitte ambos nudos ad ignotos, et videbis*,* doth scarce hold for them. And because these cunning men are like haberdashers[5] of small wares, it is not amiss to set forth their shop.*

It is a point of cunning, to wait upon[6] him with whom you speak, with your eye; as the Jesuits* give it in precept: for there be many wise men that have secret hearts and transparent countenances. Yet this would[7] be done with a demure[8] abasing of your eye sometimes, as the Jesuits also do use.

Another is, that when you have anything to obtain of present despatch,[9] you entertain and amuse the party with whom you deal with

---

1 intrigues   2 well versed   3 disposition   4 trickery, scheming
5 dealers in small goods   6 observe closely   7 ought to   8 modest
9 immediate urgency

some other discourse; that he be not too much awake to make objections. I knew a counsellor* and secretary, that never came to Queen Elizabeth of England with bills[1] to sign, but he would always first put her into some discourse of estate, that she might the less mind the bills.

The like surprise may be made by moving[2] things when the party is in haste, and cannot stay to consider advisedly of that is moved.

If a man would cross[3] a business that he doubts[4] some other would handsomely and effectually move, let him pretend to wish it well, and move it himself in such sort as may foil[5] it.

The breaking off in the midst of that one was about to say, as if he took himself up,* breeds a greater appetite in him with whom you confer to know more.

And because it works better when anything seemeth to be gotten from you by question, than if you offer it of yourself, you may lay a bait for a question, by showing another visage and countenance than you are wont; to the end to give occasion for the party to ask what the matter is of the change? As Nehemias did; 'And I had not before that time been sad before the king'.*

In things that are tender[6] and unpleasing, it is good to break the ice by some whose words are of less weight, and to reserve the more weighty voice to come in as by chance, so that he may be asked the question upon[7] the other's speech; as Narcissus* did, in relating to Claudius the marriage of Messalina and Silius.

In things that a man would not be seen in himself, it is a point of cunning to borrow the name of the world; as to say, 'The world says', or 'There is a speech abroad'.

I knew one that, when he wrote a letter, he would put that which was most material[8] in the postscript, as if it had been a bye matter.

I knew another that, when he came to have speech, he would pass over that that he intended most; and go forth, and come back again, and speak of it as of a thing that he had almost forgot.

Some procure themselves to be surprised at such times as it is like[9] the party that they work upon[10] will suddenly come upon[11] them; and to be found with a letter in their hand, or doing somewhat which they are not accustomed; to the end they may be apposed of[12] those things which of themselves they are desirous to utter.

---

1 petitions   2 proposing, supporting   3 thwart   4 fears, suspects
5 bring to naught   6 delicate, needing tact   7 following on   8 important
9 likely that   10 manipulate   11 encounter   12 questioned about

It is a point of cunning, to let fall those words in a man's own name, which he would have another man learn and use, and thereupon take advantage. I knew two that were competitors for the secretary's place* in Queen Elizabeth's time, and yet kept good quarter between themselves; and would confer one with another upon the business; and the one of them said, that to be a secretary 'in the declination[1] of a monarchy' was a ticklish[2] thing, and that he did not affect[3] it: the other straight[4] caught up those words, and discoursed with divers of his friends, that he had no reason to desire to be secretary in the declination of a monarchy. The first man took hold of it, and found means it was told the Queen; who hearing of 'a declination of a monarchy', took it so ill, as she would never after hear of the other's suit.

There is a cunning, which we in England call 'The turning of the cat in the pan';* which is, when that which a man says to another, he lays it as if another had said it to him. And to say truth, it is not easy, when such a matter passed between two, to make it appear from which of them it first moved and began.

It is a way that some men have, to glance and dart* at others by justifying themselves by negatives; as to say 'This I do not'; as Tigellinus did towards Burrhus, *Se non diversas spes, sed incolumitatem imperatoris simpliciter spectare*.*

Some have in readiness so many tales and stories, as there is nothing they would insinuate, but they can wrap it into a tale; which serveth both to keep themselves more in guard,[5] and to make others carry it[6] with more pleasure.

It is a good point of cunning, for a man to shape the answer he would have[7] in his own words and propositions; for it makes the other party stick[8] the less.

It is strange how long some men will lie in wait to speak somewhat they desire to say; and how far about they will fetch; and how many other matters they will beat over,[9] to come near it. It is a thing of great patience, but yet of much use.

A sudden, bold, and unexpected question doth many times surprise a man, and lay him open. Like to him that, having changed his name and walking in Paul's,* another suddenly came behind him and called him by his true name, whereat straightways[10] he looked back.

---

1 decline   2 tricky   3 like   4 immediately   5 to better protect themselves
6 accept the suggestion   7 would like to hear   8 hesitate   9 refer to
10 immediately

But these small wares and petty points[1] of cunning are infinite; and it were a good deed to make a list of them; for that[2] nothing doth more hurt in a state than that cunning men pass for wise.

But certainly some there are that know the resorts and falls* of business, that cannot sink into the main* of it; like a house that hath convenient stairs and entries, but never a fair[3] room. Therefore you shall see them find out pretty looses* in the conclusion, but are no ways able to examine or debate matters. And yet commonly they take advantage of their inability, and would be thought wits of direction.* Some build rather upon the abusing of others, and (as we now say) 'putting tricks upon them', than upon soundness of their own proceedings. But Salomon saith, *Prudens advertit ad gressus suos: stultus divertit ad dolos.**

23. OF WISDOM FOR A MAN'S SELF*

An ant is a wise* creature for itself, but it is a shrewd thing in an orchard or garden. And certainly men that are great lovers of themselves waste[4] the public. Divide[5] with reason between self-love[6] and society;* and be so true to thyself, as thou be not false to others; specially to thy king and country. It is a poor centre of a man's actions, *himself*. It is right earth.* For that only stands fast[7] upon his[8] own centre; whereas all things that have affinity with the heavens, move upon the centre of another, which they benefit. The referring of all to a man's self is more tolerable in a sovereign prince; because themselves are not only themselves, but their good and evil is at the peril of[9] the public fortune. But it is a desperate evil in a servant to a prince, or a citizen in a republic. For whatsoever affairs* pass such a man's hands, he crooketh them to his own ends; which must needs be often eccentric[10] to the ends of his master or state. Therefore let princes, or states, choose such servants as have not this mark; except they mean[11] their service should be made but the accessary. That which maketh the effect more pernicious is that all proportion* is lost. It were disproportion enough for the servant's good to be preferred before the master's; but yet it is a greater extreme, when a little good of the servant shall carry things[12] against a great good of the master's. And yet that is the case of bad officers,

1 trivial items   2 because   3 large, spacious   4 lay waste, destroy
5 distinguish   6 selfishness   7 depends on, has reference to   8 its
9 subject to risks from   10 removed, distant   11 intend, wish   12 prevail

treasurers, ambassadors, generals, and other false and corrupt servants; which set a bias upon their bowl,* of their own petty ends and envies,[1] to the overthrow of their master's great and important affairs. And for the most part, the good such servants receive is after the model* of their own fortune; but the hurt they sell* for that good is after the model of their master's fortune. And certainly it is the nature of extreme self-lovers, as they will set an house on fire, and it were but to roast their eggs; and yet these men many times hold credit with their masters, because their study is but to please them and profit themselves; and for either respect[2] they will abandon the good of their affairs.

Wisdom for a man's self is, in many branches thereof, a depraved thing. It is the wisdom of rats,* that will be sure to leave a house somewhat before it fall. It is the wisdom of the fox, that thrusts out the badger, who digged[3] and made room for him. It is the wisdom of crocodiles, that shed tears when they would devour.* But that which is specially to be noted is, that those which (as Cicero says of Pompey) are *sui amantes, sine rivali*,* are many times unfortunate. And whereas they have all their times sacrificed to themselves, they become in the end themselves sacrifices to the inconstancy of fortune; whose wings they thought by their self-wisdom to have pinioned.[4]

24. OF INNOVATIONS*

As the births[5] of living creatures at first are ill-shapen, so are all Innovations, which are the births of time. Yet notwithstanding, as those that first bring honour into their family are commonly more worthy[6] than most that succeed, so the first precedent (if it be good) is seldom attained[7] by imitation. For Ill,[8] to man's nature as it stands perverted,* hath a natural motion,* strongest in continuance; but Good, as a forced motion,* strongest at first. Surely every medicine is an innovation; and he that will not apply new remedies must expect new evils; for time is the greatest innovator; and if time of course[9] alter things to the worse, and wisdom and counsel shall not alter them to the better, what shall be the end? It is true, that what is settled by custom,

1 desires   2 consideration   3 dug   4 clipped   5 offspring
6 courageous, enterprising   7 reached, equalled in excellence   8 Evil
9 in its course, progress

though it be not good, yet at least it is fit;[1] and those things which have long gone together, are as it were confederate[2] within themselves; whereas new things piece* not so well; but though they help by their utility,[3] yet they trouble by their inconformity.[4] Besides, they are like strangers; more admired[5] and less favoured.

All this is true, if time stood still; which contrariwise moveth so round,[6] that a froward[7] retention of custom is as turbulent[8] a thing as an innovation; and they that reverence too much old times, are but a scorn to the new. It were good therefore that men in their innovations would follow the example of time itself; which indeed innovateth greatly, but quietly, and by degrees scarce to be perceived. For otherwise,[9] whatsoever is new is unlooked for; and ever it mends[10] some, and pairs[11] other; and he that is holpen[12] takes it for a fortune, and thanks the time; and he that is hurt, for a wrong, and imputeth it to the author.[13] It is good also not to try experiments in states, except the necessity be urgent, or the utility evident; and well to beware[14] that it be the reformation that draweth on[15] the change, and not the desire of change that pretendeth[16] the reformation. And lastly, that the novelty, though it be not rejected, yet be held for a suspect;* and, as the Scripture* saith, that 'we make a stand upon the ancient way, and then look about us, and discover what is the straight and right way, and so to walk in it'.

25. OF DISPATCH*

Affected dispatch[17] is one of the most dangerous things to business that can be. It is like that which the physicians call predigestion,[18] or hasty digestion; which is sure to fill the body full of crudities[19] and secret seeds of diseases. Therefore measure not dispatch by the times of sitting,[20] but by the advancement of the business. And as in races it is not the large stride or high lift[21] that makes the speed; so in business, the keeping close to the matter, and not taking of it[22] too much at once, procureth dispatch. It is the care of some only to come off speedily for

1 suitable, opportune   2 unified   3 usefulness   4 want of agreement
5 wondered at   6 swiftly, uninterruptedly   7 self-willed, stubborn   8 unruly
9 anyway   10 improves the conditions of   11 impairs, hurts
12 helped, benefited   13 initiator   14 take note   15 brings about
16 puts forward as a pretext   17 ostentatious haste   18 premature digestion
19 undigested matter in the stomach   20 length or frequency of meetings
21 the step of a horse   22 dealing with

the time;* or to contrive some false periods* of business, because[1] they may seem men of dispatch. But it is one thing to abbreviate by contracting,[2] another by cutting off. And business so handled at several sittings or meetings goeth commonly backward and forward in an unsteady manner. I knew a wise man* that had it for a by-word,[3] when he saw men hasten to a conclusion, 'Stay[4] a little, that we may make an end the sooner'.

On the other side, true dispatch is a rich[5] thing. For time is the measure of business, as money is of wares; and business is bought at a dear hand[6] where there is small dispatch. The Spartans and Spaniards* have been noted to be of small dispatch; *Mi venga la muerte de Spagna*; 'Let my death come from Spain'; for then it will be sure to be long in coming.

Give good hearing to those that give the first information in business; and rather direct them in the beginning, than interrupt them in the continuance of their speeches; for he that is put out of his own order will go forward and backward, and be more tedious while he waits upon his memory, than he could have been if he had gone on in his own course. But sometimes it is seen that the moderator[7] is more troublesome than the actor.[8]

Iterations[9] are commonly loss of time. But there is no such gain of time as to iterate often the state of the question; for it chaseth away many a frivolous speech as it is coming forth. Long and curious[10] speeches are as fit for dispatch, as a robe or mantle with a long train[11] is for race. Prefaces and passages,[12] and excusations,[13] and other speeches of reference to the person,[14] are great wastes of time; and though they seem to proceed of modesty, they are bravery.[15] Yet beware of being too material[16] when there is any impediment or obstruction in men's wills; for pre-occupation of mind[17] ever requireth preface of speech; like a fomentation[18] to make the unguent enter.

Above all things, order, and distribution,[19] and singling out of parts, is the life of dispatch; so as the distribution be not too subtle:[20] for he that doth not divide* will never enter well into business; and he that divideth too much will never come out of it clearly. To choose time is

1 in order that   2 reducing to essentials   3 proverbial saying   4 wait
5 precious   6 high price   7 chairman   8 orator   9 repetitions
10 elaborate   11 the part of a cloak or dress that trails on the ground
12 digressions   13 rhetorical apologies   14 speaker   15 ostentation
16 coming to the point too abruptly   17 being absorbed with problems
18 warm moist cloth used to open skin pores   19 classification   20 minute

to save time; and an unseasonable motion is but beating the air. There be three parts of business; the preparation, the debate or examination, and the perfection.[1] Whereof, if you look for dispatch, let the middle* only be the work of many, and the first and last the work of few. The proceeding[2] upon somewhat conceived in writing doth for the most part facilitate dispatch: for though it should be wholly rejected, yet that negative is more pregnant of direction[3] than an indefinite; as ashes are more generative than dust.*

26. Of Seeming Wise

It hath been an opinion, that the French are wiser than they seem, and the Spaniards seem wiser than they are. But howsoever it be between nations, certainly it is so between man and man. For as the Apostle saith of godliness, 'Having a shew of godliness, but denying the power[4] thereof';* so certainly there are in point of wisdom and sufficiency,[5] that do nothing or little very solemnly:[6] *magno conatu nugas.**

It is a ridiculous thing and fit for a satire to persons of judgment, to see what shifts[7] these formalists[8] have, and what prospectives* to make *superficies*[9] to seem body that hath depth and bulk. Some are so close and reserved, as they will not shew their wares but by a dark light;[10] and seem always to keep back somewhat; and when they know within themselves they speak of that they do not well know, would nevertheless seem to others to know of that which they may not well speak. Some help themselves with countenance and gesture, and are wise by signs;[11] as Cicero saith of Piso, that when he answered him, he fetched one of his brows up to his forehead, and bent the other down to his chin; *Respondes, altero ad frontem sublato, altero ad mentum depresso supercilio, crudelitatem tibi non placere.** Some think to bear it[12] by speaking a great word, and being peremptory; and go on, and take by admittance that which they cannot make good.* Some, whatsoever is beyond their reach, will seem to despise or make light of it as impertinent[13] or curious;[14] and so would have their ignorance seem judgment. Some are never without a difference,[15] and commonly by amusing men

1 completion   2 basing a discussion   3 suggestive, productive   4 essence
5 ability   6 superciliously   7 evasive tricks   8 impostors, 'solemn pretenders to wisdom' (*SOED*)   9 surface   10 furtively   11 grimaces
12 succeed, carry it off   13 irrelevant   14 insignificant   15 distinction

with a subtilty,[1] blanch[2] the matter; of whom A. Gellius saith, *Hominem delirum, qui verborum minutiis rerum frangit pondera.** Of which kind also, Plato* in his *Protagoras* bringeth in Prodicus in scorn, and maketh him make a speech that consisteth of distinctions from the beginning to the end. Generally, such men in all deliberations find ease to be of the negative side, and affect a credit to object* and foretell difficulties; for when propositions[3] are denied, there is an end of them; but if they be allowed, it requireth a new work; which false point of wisdom is the bane of business.

To conclude, there is no decaying merchant, or inward* beggar, hath so many tricks to uphold the credit of their wealth, as these empty persons have to maintain the credit of their sufficiency. Seeming wise men may make shift[4] to get opinion;[5] but let no man choose them for employment; for certainly you were better take for business a man somewhat absurd[6] than over-formal.

27. OF FRIENDSHIP

It had been hard for him that spake it to have put more truth and untruth together in few words, than in that speech, 'Whosoever is delighted in solitude is either a wild beast or a god'.* For it is most true that a natural[7] and secret hatred and aversation[8] towards society in any man, hath somewhat of the savage beast; but it is most untrue that it should have any character[9] at all of the divine nature; except it proceed, not out of a pleasure in solitude, but out of a love and desire to sequester[10] a man's self for a higher conversation:[11] such as is found to have been falsely and feignedly* in some of the heathen; as Epimenides* the Candian, Numa* the Roman, Empedocles* the Sicilian, and Apollonius of Tyana;* and truly and really in divers of the ancient hermits and holy fathers of the church. But little do men perceive what solitude is, and how far it extendeth. For a crowd is not company; and faces are but a gallery of pictures; and talk but a tinkling cymbal,* where there is no love. The Latin adage meeteth with it a little: *Magna civitas, magna solitudo;** because in a great town friends are scattered; so that there is not that fellowship, for the most part, which is in less[12]

1 trivial point   2 gloss over, evade   3 proposals   4 manage
5 gain reputation   6 deaf to reason, difficult   7 innate   8 aversion
9 distinctive trait   10 withdraw   11 company, way of life   12 smaller

neighbourhoods. But we may go further, and affirm most truly that it is a mere[1] and miserable solitude to want[2] true friends; without which the world is but a wilderness; and even in this sense also of solitude, whosoever in the frame[3] of his nature and affections is unfit for friendship, he taketh it of the beast, and not from humanity.

A principal fruit of friendship is the ease and discharge of the fullness and swellings of the heart,* which passions of all kinds do cause and induce. We know diseases of stoppings[4] and suffocations are the most dangerous in the body; and it is not much otherwise in the mind; you may take sarza* to open[5] the liver, steel* to open the spleen, flower of sulphur* for the lungs, castoreum[6] for the brain; but no receipt[7] openeth the heart, but a true friend; to whom you may impart griefs, joys, fears, hopes, suspicions, counsels, and whatsoever lieth upon the heart to oppress it, in a kind of civil shrift* or confession.

It is a strange thing to observe how high a rate great kings and monarchs do set upon this fruit of friendship whereof we speak: so great, as they purchase it many times at the hazard of their own safety and greatness. For princes, in regard of the distance of their fortune from that of their subjects and servants, cannot gather this fruit, except (to make themselves capable thereof) they raise some persons to be as it were companions and almost equals to themselves, which many times sorteth to[8] inconvenience. The modern languages give unto such persons the name of favourites, or privadoes;[9] as if it were matter of grace,[10] or conversation.[11] But the Roman name attaineth[12] the true use and cause thereof, naming them *participes curarum;** for it is that which tieth the knot.[13] And we see plainly that this hath been done, not by weak and passionate[14] princes only, but by the wisest and most politique that ever reigned; who have oftentimes joined to themselves some of their servants; whom both themselves have called friends, and allowed others likewise to call them in the same manner; using the word which is received[15] between private men.

L. Sulla, when he commanded Rome, raised Pompey (after surnamed the Great) to that height, that Pompey vaunted himself for Sulla's over-match. For when he had carried[16] the consulship for a friend of his, against the pursuit[17] of Sulla, and that Sulla did a little

---

1 absolute   2 lack   3 constitution   4 physical obstructions   5 purge, relieve
6 castor oil   7 medical prescription   8 results in   9 Spanish word for intimates or favourites   10 favour   11 familiarity   12 arrives at   13 unites people
14 emotional   15 common, current   16 gained   17 competition

resent thereat, and began to speak great, Pompey turned upon him again, and in effect bade him be quiet; 'for that more men adored the sun rising than the sun setting'.* With Julius Caesar,* Decimus Brutus had obtained that interest,[1] as he set him down in his testament for heir in remainder after his nephew.* And this was the man that had power with him to draw him forth to his death. For when Caesar would have discharged[2] the senate, in regard of some ill presages, and specially a dream of Calpurnia; this man lifted him gently by the arm out of his chair, telling him he hoped he would not dismiss the senate till his wife had dreamt a better dream. And it seemeth his favour[3] was so great, as Antonius, in a letter which is recited *verbatim* in one of Cicero's *Philippics*,* calleth him *venefica*, 'witch'; as if he had enchanted Caesar.

Augustus raised Agrippa (though of mean birth) to that height, as when he consulted with Maecenas* about the marriage of his daughter Julia, Maecenas took the liberty to tell him, that 'he must either marry his daughter to Agrippa, or take away his life: there was no third way, he had made him so great'. With Tiberius Caesar, Sejanus had ascended to that height, as they two were termed and reckoned as a pair of friends.* Tiberius in a letter to him saith, *haec pro amicitia nostra non occultavi*;* and the whole senate dedicated an altar to Friendship, as to a goddess, in respect of the great dearness of friendship between them two. The like or more was between Septimius Severus* and Plautianus. For he forced his eldest son to marry the daughter of Plautianus; and would often maintain[4] Plautianus in doing affronts to his son; and did write also in a letter to the senate, by these words:* 'I love the man so well, as I wish he may over-live me'. Now if these princes had been as a Trajan* or a Marcus Aurelius,* a man might have thought that this had proceeded of an abundant goodness of nature; but being men so wise,[5] of such strength and severity of mind, and so extreme lovers of themselves, as all these were, it proveth most plainly that they found their own felicity (though as great as ever happened to mortal men) but as an half piece,* except they might have a friend to make it entire; and yet, which is more, they were princes that had wives, sons, nephews;* and yet all these could not supply the comfort of friendship.

It is not to be forgotten what Comineus* observeth of his first master, Duke Charles the Hardy; namely, that he would communicate his

[1] ascendancy   [2] dismissed   [3] standing, popularity   [4] support, uphold
[5] shrewd

secrets with none; and least of all, those secrets which troubled him most. Whereupon he goeth on and saith that towards his latter time that 'closeness[1] did impair and a little perish[2] his understanding'. Surely Comineus might have made the same judgment also, if it had pleased him, of his second master Lewis the Eleventh, whose closeness was indeed his tormentor. The parable of Pythagoras* is dark, but true; *Cor ne edito*; 'Eat not the heart'. Certainly, if a man would give it a hard phrase,[3] those that want friends to open themselves unto are cannibals of their own hearts. But one thing is most admirable (wherewith I will conclude this first fruit of friendship), which is, that this communicating of a man's self to his friend works two contrary effects; for it redoubleth joys, and cutteth griefs in halfs. For there is no man that imparteth[4] his joys to his friend, but he joyeth the more: and no man that imparteth his griefs to his friend, but he grieveth the less. So that it is in truth of operation* upon a man's mind, of like virtue[5] as the alchymists use to attribute to their stone* for man's body; that it worketh all contrary effects, but still to the good and benefit of nature. But yet without praying in aid of[6] alchymists, there is a manifest image[7] of this in the ordinary course of nature. For in bodies,* union[8] strengtheneth and cherisheth any natural action; and on the other side weakeneth and dulleth any violent impression:[9] and even so it is of minds.

The second fruit of friendship is healthful and sovereign[10] for the understanding, as the first is for the affections.[11] For friendship maketh indeed a fair day in the affections, from[12] storm and tempests; but it maketh daylight in the understanding,[13] out of darkness and confusion of thoughts. Neither is this to be understood only of faithful counsel, which a man receiveth from his friend; but before you come to that, certain it is that whosoever hath his mind fraught[14] with many thoughts, his wits and understanding do clarify and break up, in the communicating and discoursing with another; he tosseth[15] his thoughts more easily; he marshalleth[16] them more orderly; he seeth how they look when they are turned into words: finally, he waxeth wiser than himself; and that more by an hour's discourse than by a day's meditation.* It was well said by Themistocles to the king of

1 secrecy   2 corrupt, destroy   3 put it bluntly   4 communicates
5 effectiveness   6 calling in, as an advocate   7 figure
8 composition (as in an alloy)   9 impact, force   10 remedial   11 passions
12 out of   13 intellect   14 occupied, worried   15 moves   16 sorts

Persia, that 'speech was like cloth of Arras,* opened and put abroad;* whereby the imagery[1] doth appear in figure; whereas in thoughts they lie but as in packs'.* Neither is this second fruit of friendship, in opening the understanding, restrained[2] only to such friends as are able to give a man counsel (they indeed are best); but even without that, a man learneth of himself, and bringeth his own thoughts to light, and whetteth* his wits as against a stone, which itself cuts not. In a word, a man were better relate himself to a statua or picture, than to suffer his thoughts to pass in smother.[3]

Add now, to make this second fruit of friendship complete, that other point which lieth more open and falleth within vulgar[4] observation; which is faithful counsel from a friend. Heraclitus* saith well in one of his enigmas, 'Dry light is ever the best'. And certain it is, that the light that a man receiveth by counsel from another, is drier and purer than that which cometh from his own understanding and judgment; which is ever infused and drenched* in his affections and customs. So as there is as much difference between the counsel that a friend giveth, and that a man giveth himself, as there is between the counsel of a friend and of a flatterer.* For there is no such flatterer as is a man's self; and there is no such remedy against flattery of a man's self, as the liberty of a friend. Counsel is of two sorts; the one concerning manners,[5] the other concerning business.[6] For the first, the best preservative[7] to keep the mind in health is the faithful admonition of a friend. The calling of a man's self to a strict account* is a medicine, sometime, too piercing and corrosive. Reading good books of morality is a little flat[8] and dead. Observing our faults in others is sometimes improper for our case. But the best receipt (best, I say, to work, and best to take)[9] is the admonition of a friend. It is a strange thing to behold what gross errors and extreme absurdities many (especially of the greater sort) do commit, for want of a friend to tell them of them;* to the great damage both of their fame and fortune: for, as St James saith,* they are as men that 'look sometimes into a glass, and presently[10] forget their own shape and favour'.[11]

As for business, a man may think, if he will, that two eyes see no more than one; or that a gamester[12] seeth always more than a looker-on; or that a man in anger is as wise as he that hath said over the four and

1 pattern, picture   2 limited   3 concealed, undisclosed   4 common, widespread   5 morals   6 public, active life   7 medicament   8 insipid   9 have a lasting effect   10 immediately   11 feature   12 player at any game

twenty letters;* or that a musket may be shot off as well upon the arm as upon a rest;[1] and such other fond and high[2] imaginations, to think himself all in all.* But when all is done, the help of good counsel is that which setteth business straight. And if any man think that he will take counsel, but it shall be by pieces;[3] asking counsel in one business of one man, and in another business of another man; it is well (that is to say, better perhaps than if he asked none at all); but he runneth two dangers; one, that he shall not be faithfully counselled; for it is a rare thing, except it be from a perfect and entire friend, to have counsel given, but such as shall be bowed and crooked[4] to some ends which he hath that giveth it. The other, that he shall have counsel given, hurtful and unsafe (though with good meaning),[5] and mixed partly of mischief and partly of remedy; even as if you would call a physician that is thought good for the cure of the disease you complain of, but is unacquainted with your body; and therefore may put you in way for* a present[6] cure, but overthroweth your health in some other kind;[7] and so cure the disease and kill the patient. But a friend that is wholly acquainted with a man's estate[8] will beware, by furthering any present business, how he dasheth upon[9] other inconvenience. And therefore rest not upon scattered counsels; they will rather distract and mislead, than settle and direct.

After these two noble fruits of friendship (peace in the affections, and support of the judgment), followeth the last fruit; which is like the pomegranate, full of many kernels; I mean aid and bearing a part in all actions and occasions. Here the best way to represent to life the manifold use of friendship, is to cast[10] and see how many things there are which a man cannot do himself; and then it will appear that it was a sparing speech[11] of the ancients, to say,* that 'a friend is another himself'; for that a friend is far more than himself. Men have their time,* and die many times in desire of some things which they principally take to heart; the bestowing[12] of a child, the finishing of a work, or the like. If a man have a true friend, he may rest almost secure that the care of those things will continue after him. So that a man hath, as it were, two lives in his desires.* A man hath a body, and that body is confined to a place; but where friendship is, all offices[13] of life are as it were

---

1 support for a firearm   2 foolish, exaggerated   3 from different people
4 bent, perverted   5 intention   6 immediate   7 respect   8 condition
9 meets with   10 reckon, count up   11 understatement
12 settling a patrimony on, placing in life   13 duties

granted to him and his deputy. For he may exercise them by his friend. How many things are there which a man cannot, with any face or comeliness,* say or do himself?* A man can scarce allege his own merits with modesty, much less extol them; a man cannot sometimes brook[1] to supplicate or beg; and a number of the like. But all these things are graceful in a friend's mouth, which are blushing in a man's own. So again, a man's person[2] hath many proper relations which he cannot put off. A man cannot speak to his son but as a father; to his wife but as a husband; to his enemy but upon terms:[3] whereas a friend may speak as the case requires, and not as it sorteth with[4] the person. But to enumerate these things were endless; I have given the rule, where a man cannot fitly play his own part: if he have not a friend, he may quit the stage.

28. OF EXPENSE

Riches are for spending, and spending for honour* and good actions. Therefore extraordinary expense must be limited[5] by the worth of the occasion; for voluntary undoing* may be as well for a man's country as for the kingdom of heaven.* But ordinary expense ought to be limited by a man's estate; and governed with such regard, as it be within his compass;[6] and not subject to deceit and abuse[7] of servants; and ordered to the best shew,[8] that the bills may be less than the estimation abroad.* Certainly, if a man will keep but of even hand,[9] his ordinary expenses ought to be but to the half of his receipts;[10] and if he think to wax rich, but to the third part. It is no baseness for the greatest to descend and look into their own estate. Some forbear it, not upon negligence alone, but doubting[11] to bring themselves into melancholy, in respect they shall find it broken.* But wounds cannot be cured without searching.[12] He that cannot look into his own estate at all, had need both choose well those whom he employeth, and change them often; for new are more timorous and less subtle.[13] He that can look into his estate but seldom, it behoveth him to turn all to certainties.* A man had need, if he be plentiful in some kind of expense, to be as saving again in some

1 bear   2 role (persona) that he has to play in society   3 formally, on agreed conditions   4 suits   5 measured, appropriate   6 limits, control   7 larceny   8 make the best impression   9 equally balanced   10 income   11 fearing   12 examination   13 deceitful, cunning

other. As if he be plentiful in diet,[1] to be saving in apparel; if he be plentiful in the hall,[2] to be saving in the stable; and the like. For he that is plentiful in expenses of all kinds will hardly be preserved from decay.[3] In clearing[4] of a man's estate, he may as well hurt himself in being too sudden,[5] as in letting it run on too long. For hasty selling is commonly as disadvantageable as interest.[6] Besides, he that clears at once will relapse; for finding himself out of straits,[7] he will revert to his customs:[8] but he that cleareth by degrees induceth a habit of frugality, and gaineth as well upon his mind as upon his estate. Certainly, who hath a state[9] to repair, may not despise small things; and commonly it is less dishonourable to abridge[10] petty[11] charges,[12] than to stoop to petty gettings. A man ought warily to begin charges which once begun will continue: but in matters that return not* he may be more magnificent.

29. OF THE TRUE GREATNESS OF KINGDOMS AND ESTATES

The speech* of Themistocles the Athenian, which was haughty and arrogant in taking so much to himself, had[13] been a grave and wise observation and censure,[14] applied at large to others. Desired at a feast to touch a lute, he said, 'He could not fiddle,* but yet he could make a small town a great city'. These words (holpen[15] a little with a metaphor)* may express two differing abilities in those that deal in business of estate.[16] For if a true survey be taken of counsellors and statesmen, there may be found (though rarely) those which can make a small state great, and yet cannot fiddle: as on the other side, there will be found a great many that can fiddle very cunningly, but yet are so far from being able to make a small state great, as their gift lieth the other way; to bring a great and flourishing estate to ruin and decay. And, certainly those degenerate arts and shifts,[17] whereby many counsellors and governors gain both favour with their masters and estimation with the vulgar, deserve no better name than fiddling; being things rather pleasing for the time, and graceful to themselves only, than tending to the weal[18] and

---

1 food and drink   2 hospitality   3 undoing   4 settling the accounts, outstanding debts   5 precipitous   6 paying interest on a loan   7 difficulties 8 habits   9 estate   10 reduce   11 trivial   12 expenses   13 would have 14 judgement, opinion   15 helped   16 affairs of state   17 skills and tricks 18 welfare

advancement of the state which they serve. There are also (no doubt) counsellors and governors which may be held sufficient[1] (*negotiis pares*),* able to manage affairs, and to keep them from precipices and manifest inconveniences; which nevertheless are far from the ability to raise and amplify an estate in power, means,[2] and fortune. But be the workmen what they may be, let us speak of the work; that is, the true Greatness[3] of Kingdoms and Estates, and the means[4] thereof. An argument[5] fit for great and mighty princes to have in their hand; to the end that neither by over-measuring[6] their forces, they leese themselves in vain enterprises; nor on the other side, by undervaluing them, they descend to fearful[7] and pusillanimous counsels.[8]

The greatness of an estate in bulk and territory, doth fall under measure;[9] and the greatness of finances and revenue doth fall under computation. The population may appear[10] by musters;[11] and the number and greatness of cities and towns by cards[12] and maps. But yet there is not anything amongst civil affairs more subject to error, than the right valuation and true judgment concerning the power and forces of an estate. The kingdom of heaven is compared,* not to any great kernel or nut, but to a grain of mustard-seed; which is one of the least grains, but hath in it a property and spirit hastily to get up and spread. So are there states great in territory, and yet not apt[13] to enlarge or command; and some that have but a small dimension of stem,* and yet apt to be the foundations of great monarchies.

Walled towns, stored[14] arsenals and armories, goodly races[15] of horse, chariots of war, elephants, ordnance,[16] artillery,* and the like; all this is but a sheep in a lion's skin,* except the breed and disposition of the people be stout[17] and warlike. Nay, number (itself) in armies importeth[18] not much, where the people is of weak courage; for (as Virgil* saith) 'It never troubles a wolf how many the sheep be'. The army of the Persians in the plains of Arbela was such a vast sea of people, as it did somewhat astonish the commanders in Alexander's army; who came to him therefore, and wished him to set upon them by night; but he answered,* 'He would not pilfer the victory'. And the defeat was easy. When Tigranes the Armenian, being encamped upon a hill with four hundred thousand men, discovered the army of the Romans,

---

1 competent   2 resources   3 magnitude; grandeur   4 ways of achieving
5 topic, subject for consideration   6 overestimating   7 timid   8 resolutions
9 can be measured   10 be displayed, computed   11 registers   12 plans, maps
13 adapted, suitable   14 fully stocked   15 breeds; stables
16 military stores or supplies   17 bold, courageous   18 signifies

being not above fourteen thousand, marching towards him, he made himself merry with it, and said,* 'Yonder men are too many for an ambassage,[1] and too few for a fight'. But, before the sun set, he found them enough to give him the chase with infinite slaughter. Many are the examples of the great odds[2] between number and courage: so that a man may truly make a judgment, that the principal point of greatness in any state is to have a race of military men.* Neither is money the sinews of war (as it is trivially said),* where the sinews of men's arms, in base and effeminate people, are failing. For Solon* said well to Croesus (when in ostentation he shewed him his gold), 'Sir, if any other come that hath better iron than you, he will be master of all this gold'. Therefore let any prince or state think soberly[3] of his forces, except his militia* of natives be of good and valiant soldiers. And let princes, on the other side, that have subjects of martial disposition, know their own strength; unless they be otherwise wanting unto themselves.* As for mercenary forces (which is the help[4] in this case), all examples show that whatsoever estate or prince doth rest* upon them, he may spread[5] his feathers for a time, but he will mew[6] them soon after.

The blessing* of Judah and Issachar will never meet; that 'the same people or nation should be both the lion's whelp and the ass between burthens';* neither will it be, that a people overlaid[7] with taxes should ever become valiant and martial. It is true that taxes levied by consent of the estate[8] do abate[9] men's courage less: as it hath been seen notably in the excises* of the Low Countries; and, in some degree, in the subsidies* of England. For you must note that we speak now of the heart and not of the purse. So that although the same tribute[10] and tax, laid by consent or by imposing, be all one to the purse, yet it works diversely upon the courage. So that you may conclude, that no people over-charged with tribute is fit for empire.

Let states that aim at greatness, take heed how their nobility and gentlemen do multiply too fast. For that maketh the common subject grow to be a peasant[11] and base swain,[12] driven out of heart, and in effect but the gentleman's labourer. Even as you may see in coppice woods; if you leave your staddles* too thick, you shall never have clean underwood, but shrubs and bushes. So in countries, if the gentlemen be too many, the commons will be base;[13] and you will bring it to that,

---

1 embassy   2 difference, disproportion   3 cautiously   4 remedy
5 display   6 moult, shed   7 burdened   8 state   9 beat down, depress
10 levy   11 serf   12 peasant   13 degraded (morally)

that not the hundred poll will be fit for an helmet;* especially as to the infantry, which is the nerve of an army;* and so there will be great population and little strength. This which I speak of hath been no where better seen than by comparing of England and France; whereof England, though far less in territory and population, hath been (nevertheless) an over-match; in regard[1] the middle people* of England make good soldiers, which the peasants of France do not. And herein the device[2] of king Henry the Seventh (whereof I have spoken* largely in the history of his life) was profound and admirable; in making farms and houses of husbandry[3] of a standard;* that is, maintained with such a proportion of land unto them, as may breed a subject to live in convenient[4] plenty and no servile condition; and to keep the plough in the hands of the owners, and not mere hirelings.* And thus indeed you shall attain to Virgil's character which he gives to ancient Italy:

*Terra potens armis atque ubere glebae.**

Neither is that state[5] (which, for anything I know, is almost peculiar to England, and hardly to be found anywhere else, except it be perhaps in Poland) to be passed over; I mean the state of free servants* and attendants upon noblemen and gentlemen; which are no ways inferior unto the yeomanry* for arms. And therefore out of all question, the splendour and magnificence and great retinues and hospitality of noblemen and gentlemen, received into custom,[6] doth much conduce[7] unto martial greatness. Whereas, contrariwise, the close and reserved living of noblemen and gentlemen causeth a penury of military forces.

By all means it is to be procured, that the trunk of Nebuchadnezzar's tree* of monarchy be great enough to bear the branches and the boughs;* that is, that the natural[8] subjects of the crown or state bear a sufficient proportion to the stranger[9] subjects that they govern. Therefore all states that are liberal of naturalisation towards strangers are fit for empire.[10] For to think that an handful of people can, with the greatest courage and policy in the world, embrace too large extent of dominion, it may hold for a time, but it will fail suddenly. The Spartans were a nice* people in point of naturalisation; whereby, while they kept their compass,[11] they stood firm; but when they did spread, and their boughs were becomen too great for their stem, they became a windfall*

---

1 because   2 plan   3 agriculture   4 suitable   5 social class
6 an accepted practice   7 contribute   8 indigenous, native
9 foreign, naturalized   10 able to expand   11 limits, bounds

upon the sudden. Never any state was in this point so open to receive strangers into their body as were the Romans. Therefore it sorted with[1] them accordingly; for they grew to the greatest monarchy.* Their manner was to grant naturalisation (which they called *jus civitatis*),* and to grant it in the highest degree; that is, not only *jus commercii, jus connubii, jus haereditatis*; but also *jus suffragii*, and *jus honorum*.* And this not to singular[2] persons alone, but likewise to whole families; yea to cities, and sometimes to nations. Add to this their custom of plantation of colonies;* whereby the Roman plant was removed into the soil of other nations. And putting both constitutions* together, you will say that it was not the Romans that spread upon the world, but it was the world that spread upon the Romans; and that was the sure way of greatness. I have marvelled sometimes at Spain, how they clasp and contain[3] so large dominions with so few natural[4] Spaniards; but sure the whole compass of Spain is a very great body of a tree; far above Rome and Sparta at the first.[5] And besides, though they have not had that usage to naturalise liberally, yet they have that which is next to it; that is, to employ almost indifferently all nations in their militia of ordinary soldiers; yea and sometimes in their highest* commands. Nay it seemeth at this instant they are sensible[6] of this want of natives; as by the Pragmatical Sanction,* now published, appeareth.

It is certain, that sedentary and within-door arts,* and delicate manufactures* (that require rather the finger than the arm), have in their nature a contrariety to a military disposition. And generally, all warlike people are a little idle, and love danger better than travail. Neither must they be too much broken of[7] it, if they shall be preserved in vigour. Therefore it was great advantage in the ancient states of Sparta, Athens, Rome, and others, that they had the use of slaves, which commonly did rid those manufactures.* But that is abolished,* in greatest part, by the Christian law. That which cometh nearest to it, is to leave those arts chiefly to strangers (which for that purpose are the more easily to be received),[8] and to contain[9] the principal bulk of the vulgar natives[10] within those three kinds,—tillers of the ground; free servants; and handicraftsmen[11] of strong and manly arts, as smiths, masons, carpenters, &c: not reckoning professed[12] soldiers.

1 resulted   2 single   3 hold in, control   4 native   5 at their beginnings
6 aware   7 worn out by   8 accepted   9 restrain, direct
10 common citizens   11 artisans   12 having as a profession

But above all, for empire and greatness, it importeth[1] most that a nation do profess arms as their principal honour, study, and occupation. For the things which we formerly have spoken of are but habilitations* towards arms; and what is habilitation without intention and act?* Romulus,* after his death (as they report or feign), sent a present* to the Romans, that above all they should intend[2] arms; and then they should prove the greatest empire of the world. The fabric of the state of Sparta was wholly (though not wisely) framed[3] and composed to that scope and end. The Persians and Macedonians had it for a flash.[4] The Gauls, Germans, Goths, Saxons, Normans, and others, had it for a time. The Turks have it at this day, though in great declination.[5] Of Christian Europe, they that have it are, in effect, only the Spaniards. But it is so plain that every man profiteth in that he most intendeth, that it needeth not to be stood upon. It is enough to point at it; that no nation which doth not directly[6] profess arms, may look to have greatness fall into their mouths. And on the other side, it is a most certain oracle of time,* that those states that continue long in that profession (as the Romans and Turks principally have done) do wonders. And those that have professed arms but for an age, have notwithstanding commonly attained that greatness in that age which maintained them long after, when their profession and exercise of arms hath grown to decay.

Incident to this point is, for a state to have those laws or customs which may reach forth unto them just occasions (as may be pretended) of war. For there is that justice imprinted in the nature of men, that they enter not upon wars (whereof so many calamities do ensue) but upon some, at the least specious,[7] grounds and quarrels. The Turk hath at hand, for cause of war, the propagation of his law or sect;* a quarrel that he may always command. The Romans, though they esteemed the extending the limits of their empire to be great honour to their generals when it was done, yet they never rested upon that alone to begin a war. First therefore, let nations that pretend to[8] greatness have this; that they be sensible of wrongs, either upon borderers,* merchants, or politique ministers;* and that they sit not too long upon a provocation. Secondly, let them be prest[9] and ready to give aids and succours to their confederates; as it ever was with the Romans;

---

1 is important   2 aim at, dedicate themselves to   3 contrived
4 brief moment   5 decline   6 straightforwardly, absolutely
7 attractive, plausible   8 aspire to   9 prepared

insomuch as, if the confederates had leagues defensive with divers other states, and, upon invasion offered, did implore their aids severally,[1] yet the Romans would ever be the foremost, and leave it to none other to have the honour. As for the wars which were anciently made on the behalf of a kind of party,[2] or tacit conformity* of estate, I do not see how they may be well justified: as when the Romans* made a war for the liberty of Graecia; or when the Lacedaemonians and Athenians* made wars to set up or pull down democracies and oligarchies; or when wars were made by foreigners, under the pretence of justice or protection, to deliver the subjects of others from tyranny and oppression; and the like. Let it suffice, that no estate expect to be great, that is not awake upon any just occasion of arming.

No body can be healthful without exercise, neither natural body nor politic; and certainly to a kingdom or estate, a just and honourable war is the true exercise. A civil war indeed is like the heat of a fever; but a foreign war is like the heat of exercise, and serveth to keep the body in health; for in a slothful peace,* both courages[3] will effeminate[4] and manners corrupt. But howsoever it be for happiness, without all question, for greatness it maketh, to be still for the most part in arms; and the strength of a veteran[5] army (though it be a chargeable[6] business) always on foot,* is that which commonly giveth the law,* or at least the reputation, amongst all neighbour states; as may well be seen in Spain, which hath had, in one part or other, a veteran army almost continually, now by the space of six score years.

To be master of the sea is an abridgment* of a monarchy. Cicero, writing to Atticus of Pompey his preparation against Caesar, saith, *Consilium Pompeii plane Themistocleum est; putat enim, qui mari potitur, eum rerum potiri.** And, without doubt, Pompey had[7] tired out Caesar, if upon vain confidence[8] he had not left that way.* We see the great effects of battles by sea. The battle of Actium* decided the empire of the world. The battle of Lepanto* arrested the greatness of the Turk. There be many examples where sea-fights have been final[9] to the war; but this is when princes or states have set up their rest* upon the battles. But thus much is certain, that he that commands the sea is at great liberty, and may take as much and as little* of the war as he will. Whereas those that be strongest by land are many times nevertheless in

1 separately   2 faction   3 spirits, resolve   4 grow soft
5 skilled, professional   6 expensive   7 would have   8 presumption
9 decisive

great straits.[1] Surely, at this day, with us of Europe, the vantage[2] of strength at sea (which is one of the principal dowries of this kingdom of Great Britain) is great; both because most of the kingdoms of Europe are not merely[3] inland, but girt with the sea most part of their compass;[4] and because the wealth of both Indies seems in great part but an accessary* to the command of the seas.

The wars of latter ages seem to be made in the dark, in respect of the glory and honour which reflected upon men from the wars in ancient time. There be now, for martial encouragement, some degrees[5] and orders of chivalry; which nevertheless are conferred promiscuously[6] upon soldiers and no soldiers;* and some remembrance perhaps upon the scutcheon;* and some hospitals* for maimed soldiers; and such like things. But in ancient times, the trophies erected upon the place of the victory; the funeral laudatives and monuments for those that died in the wars; the crowns and garlands personal;* the style of Emperor,* which the great kings of the world after[7] borrowed; the triumphs of the generals upon their return; the great donatives[8] and largesses[9] upon the disbanding of the armies; were things able to inflame all men's courages. But above all, that of the Triumph,* amongst the Romans, was not pageants or gaudery,[10] but one of the wisest and noblest institutions that ever was. For it contained three things; honour to the general; riches to the treasury out of the spoils; and donatives to the army. But that honour perhaps were not fit for monarchies; except it be in the person of the monarch himself, or his sons, as it came to pass in the times of the Roman emperors, who did impropriate[11] the actual triumphs to themselves and their sons, for such wars as they did achieve[12] in person; and left only, for wars achieved by subjects, some triumphal garments and ensigns[13] to the general.

To conclude: no man can 'by care taking' (as the Scripture* saith) 'add a cubit to his stature', in this little model of a man's body; but in the great frame of kingdoms and commonwealths, it is in the power of princes or estates to add amplitude and greatness[14] to their kingdoms; for by introducing such ordinances, constitutions, and customs, as we have now touched,[15] they may sow greatness to[16] their posterity and

---

1 difficulties   2 advantage   3 entirely   4 boundaries   5 honorary titles
6 indifferently   7 afterwards   8 rewards made by the emperors to victorious soldiers   9 generous presents   10 finery, cheap display   11 appropriate
12 carry to successful completion   13 badges or flags, insignia
14 greater extent, area   15 briefly discussed   16 for the advantage of

succession. But these things are commonly not observed,* but left to take their chance.

30. OF REGIMENT[1] OF HEALTH

There is a wisdom in this* beyond the rules of physic:[2] a man's own observation, what he finds good of, and what he finds hurt of,* is the best physic to preserve health. But it is a safer conclusion to say, 'This agreeth not well with me, therefore I will not continue it'; than this, 'I find no offence of this, therefore I may use it'. For strength of nature in youth passeth over many excesses, which are owing a man till his age. Discern of the coming on of years, and think not to do the same things still;[3] for age will not be defied. Beware of sudden change in any great point of diet, and if necessity inforce it, fit the rest to it. For it is a secret both in nature and state, that it is safer to change many things than one.* Examine thy customs of diet, sleep, exercise, apparel, and the like; and try, in any thing thou shalt judge hurtful, to discontinue it by little and little; but so, as if thou dost find any inconvenience by the change, thou come back to it again: for it is hard to distinguish that which is generally held good and wholesome, from that which is good particularly,[4] and fit for thine own body. To be free-minded and cheerfully disposed at hours of meat and of sleep and of exercise, is one of the best precepts of long lasting. As for the passions and studies* of the mind: avoid envy; anxious fears; anger fretting inwards;* subtle and knotty inquisitions;[5] joys and exhilarations in excess; sadness not communicated. Entertain[6] hopes; mirth rather than joy; variety of delights, rather than surfeit of them; wonder and admiration, and therefore novelties; studies that fill the mind with splendid and illustrious objects, as histories, fables, and contemplations of nature.

If you fly physic in health altogether,* it will be too strange[7] for your body when you shall need it. If you make it too familiar, it will work no extraordinary effect when sickness cometh. I commend[8] rather some diet for certain seasons, than frequent use of physic, except it be grown into a custom.[9] For those diets alter the body more, and trouble it less. Despise no new accident[10] in your body, but ask opinion of it. In sickness, respect* health principally; and in health, action.[11] For those

1 control, regimen   2 medicine   3 always   4 individually
5 investigations   6 cultivate   7 unaccustomed   8 recommend
9 become a habit   10 sudden change, symptom   11 activity, physical exercise

that put their bodies to endure[1] in health, may in most sicknesses, which are not very sharp, be cured only with diet and tendering.[2] Celsus* could never have spoken* it as a physician, had he not been a wise man withal, when he giveth it for one of the great precepts of health and lasting,[3] that a man do vary and interchange contraries,[4] but with an inclination to the more benign extreme: use fasting and full eating, but rather full eating; watching[5] and sleep, but rather sleep; sitting[6] and exercise, but rather exercise; and the like. So shall nature be cherished, and yet taught masteries.*

Physicians are some of them so pleasing[7] and conformable to the humour* of the patient, as they press[8] not the true cure of the disease; and some other are so regular in proceeding according to art[9] for the disease, as they respect not sufficiently the condition of the patient. Take one of a middle temper; or if it may not be found in one man, combine two of either[10] sort; and forget not to call as well the best acquainted with your body, as the best reputed of for his faculty.[11]

31. OF SUSPICION

Suspicions amongst thoughts are like bats amongst birds, they ever fly by twilight. Certainly they are to be repressed, or at the least well guarded: for they cloud the mind; they leese[12] friends; and they check with[13] business, whereby business cannot go on currently[14] and constantly. They dispose kings to tyranny, husbands to jealousy, wise men to irresolution and melancholy. They are defects, not in the heart,* but in the brain; for they take place[15] in the stoutest[16] natures; as in the example of Henry the Seventh of England. There was not a more suspicious* man, nor a more stout.[17] And in such a composition* they do small hurt. For commonly they are not admitted, but with examination, whether they be likely or no? But in fearful[18] natures they gain ground too fast. There is nothing makes a man suspect much, more than to know little; and therefore men should remedy suspicion by procuring to know more, and not to keep their suspicions in smother.[19]

1 bear exertions   2 careful nursing   3 long life   4 opposed states
5 staying awake   6 repose   7 obliging   8 penetrate to, discover
9 medical precepts   10 each   11 professional ability   12 cause the loss of
13 hinder, interfere with   14 in a smooth current   15 have effect
16 most vigorous   17 firm, resolute   18 timid   19 covered up, stifled

What would men have? Do they think those they employ and deal with are saints? Do they not think they will have their own ends, and be truer to themselves than to them? Therefore there is no better way to moderate suspicions, than to account upon[1] such suspicions as true and yet to bridle[2] them as false. For so far a man ought to make use of suspicions, as to provide,[3] as if that should be true that he suspects, yet it may do him no hurt.

Suspicions that the mind of itself gathers are but buzzes;[4] but suspicions that are artificially[5] nourished, and put into men's heads by the tales and whisperings of others, have stings. Certainly, the best mean to clear the way in this same wood of suspicions, is frankly to communicate them with the party[6] that he suspects; for thereby he shall be sure to know more of the truth of them than he did before; and withal[7] shall make that party more circumspect not to give further cause of suspicion. But this would[8] not be done to men of base[9] natures; for they, if they find themselves once suspected, will never be true. The Italian says, *Sospetto licentia fede*;* as if suspicion did give a passport[10] to faith; but it ought rather to kindle it to discharge itself.*

32. Of Discourse*

Some in their discourse desire rather commendation of wit,* in being able to hold[11] all arguments, than of judgment, in discerning what is true; as if it were a praise to know what might be said, and not what should be thought.* Some have certain common places and themes* wherein they are good, and want variety;* which kind of poverty is for the most part tedious, and when it is once perceived, ridiculous. The honourablest part[12] of talk is to give the occasion;[13] and again to moderate[14] and pass to somewhat else; for then a man leads the dance. It is good, in discourse and speech of conversation, to vary and intermingle speech of the present occasion with arguments,* tales with reasons,[15] asking of questions with telling of opinions, and jest with earnest: for it is a dull thing to tire, and, as we say now, to jade,[16] any thing too far.

---

1 regard 2 restrain 3 arrange 4 empty noise 5 maliciously
6 person 7 at the same time 8 should 9 despicable
10 permission to depart 11 maintain 12 action 13 suggest a topic
14 sum up, pronounce judgement 15 statements 16 to tire, weary

As for jest,[1] there be certain things which ought to be privileged[2] from it; namely, religion, matters of state, great persons, any man's present business of importance, and any case that deserveth pity. Yet there be some that think their wits have been asleep, except they dart out[3] somewhat that is piquant, and to the quick.[4] That is a vein* which would[5] be bridled;

*Parce, puer, stimulis, et fortius utere loris.**

And generally, men ought to find the difference between saltness[6] and bitterness. Certainly, he that hath a satirical vein, as he maketh others afraid of his wit, so he had need be afraid of others' memory.

He that questioneth much, shall learn much, and content[7] much; but especially if he apply[8] his questions to the skill of the persons whom he asketh; for he shall give them occasion to please themselves in speaking, and himself shall continually gather knowledge. But let his questions not be troublesome; for that is fit for a poser.[9] And let him be sure to leave other men their turns to speak. Nay, if there be any that would reign and take up all the time, let him find means to take them off,* and to bring others on; as musicians use to do with those that dance too long galliards.*

If you dissemble sometimes your knowledge of that you are thought to know, you shall be thought another time to know that you know not. Speech of a man's self* ought to be seldom, and well chosen. I knew one was wont to say in scorn, 'He must needs be a wise man, he speaks so much of himself': and there is but one case wherein a man may commend himself with good grace, and that is in commending virtue in another; especially if it be such a virtue whereunto himself pretendeth.[10]

Speech of touch towards others should be sparingly used; for discourse ought to be as a field, without coming home* to any man. I knew two noblemen, of the west part of England, whereof the one was given to scoff,[11] but kept ever royal cheer[12] in his house; the other would ask of those that had been at the other's table, 'Tell truly, was there never a flout[13] or dry blow[14] given?' To which the guest would answer, 'Such and such a thing passed'. The lord would say, 'I thought he would mar[15] a good dinner'.

---

1 joking   2 exempt   3 utter sharply   4 penetrating, hurting   5 ought to
6 satiric wit   7 please others   8 adapt   9 an examiner, who 'poses' or puts
questions   10 aspires   11 mockery   12 entertainment, feasting
13 mocking speech   14 scornful jest   15 spoil

Discretion of speech is more than eloquence; and to speak agree-ably[1] to him with whom we deal, is more than to speak in good words or in good order. A good continued* speech, without a good speech of interlocution,* shews slowness; and a good reply or second speech, without a good settled speech, sheweth shallowness and weakness. As we see in beasts, that those that are weakest in the course, are yet nim-blest in the turn;* as it is betwixt the greyhound and the hare. To use too many circumstances[2] ere[3] one come to the matter, is wearisome; to use none at all, is blunt.

33. Of Plantations*

Plantations are amongst ancient, primitive, and heroical[4] works. When the world was young* it begat more children; but now it is old it begets fewer: for I may justly account new plantations to be the children of former kingdoms. I like a plantation in a pure soil;* that is, where people are not displanted* to the end to plant in others. For else it is rather an extirpation[5] than a plantation. Planting of countries is like planting of woods; for you must make account[6] to leese[7] almost twenty years profit, and expect your recompense[8] in the end. For the principal thing[9] that hath been the destruction of most plantations, hath been the base and hasty drawing* of profit in the first years. It is true, speedy profit is not to be neglected, as far as may stand with[10] the good of the plantation, but no further.

It is a shameful and unblessed thing to take the scum of people,* and wicked condemned men, to be the people with whom you plant; and not only so, but it spoileth the plantation; for they will ever live like rogues, and not fall to work, but be lazy, and do mischief, and spend[11] victuals,[12] and be quickly weary, and then certify* over to their country to the discredit of the plantation. The people wherewith you plant ought to be gardeners, ploughmen, labourers, smiths, carpenters, joiners, fishermen, fowlers,[13] with some few apothecaries, surgeons, cooks, and bakers.

In a country of plantation, first look about what kind of victual the country yields of itself to hand; as chestnuts, wallnuts, pine-apples,

---

1 fitly, suitably   2 introductory comments   3 before   4 performed by heroes
5 weeding out, killing   6 reckon   7 lose   8 reward   9 cause
10 be compatible with   11 consume   12 food supplies   13 bird catchers

olives, dates, plums, cherries, wild honey, and the like; and make use of them. Then consider what victual or esculent[1] things there are, which grow speedily, and within the year; as parsnips, carrots, turnips, onions, radish, artichokes of Hierusalem,* maize, and the like. For wheat, barley, and oats, they ask too much labour; but with pease and beans you may begin, both because they ask less labour, and because they serve for meat* as well as for bread. And of rice likewise cometh a great increase, and it is a kind of meat. Above all, there ought to be brought store[2] of biscuit,[3] oat-meal, flour, meal,* and the like, in the beginning, till bread may be had. For beasts, or birds, take chiefly such as are least subject to diseases, and multiply fastest; as swine, goats, cocks, hens, turkeys, geese, house-doves, and the like. The victual in plantations ought to be expended[4] almost as in a besieged town; that is, with certain allowance.[5] And let the main part of the ground employed to gardens or corn, be to a common stock;[6] and to be laid in,[7] and stored up, and then delivered out in proportion;* besides some spots of ground that any particular person will manure[8] for his own private.[9]

Consider likewise what commodities the soil where the plantation is doth naturally yield, that they may some way help to defray the charge[10] of the plantation, (so it be not, as was said, to the untimely prejudice[11] of the main business), as it hath fared with tobacco* in Virginia. Wood commonly aboundeth but too much; and therefore timber is fit to be one.* If there be iron ore, and streams whereupon to set the mills, iron is a brave* commodity where wood aboundeth. Making of bay-salt,* if the climate be proper for it, would be put in experience. Growing silk* likewise, if any be, is a likely[12] commodity. Pitch and tar, where store of firs and pines are, will not fail. So drugs and sweet woods,* where they are, cannot but yield great profit. Soap-ashes* likewise, and other things that may be thought of. But moil[13] not too much under ground; for the hope of mines* is very uncertain, and useth to make the planters lazy in other things.

For government, let it be in the hands of one, assisted with some council; and let them have commission[14] to exercise martial laws,[15] with some limitation. And above all, let men make that profit of being in the wilderness, as they have God always, and his service, before their

---

1 edible 2 large supply 3 ship's biscuit, hard tack 4 consumed
5 fixed ration 6 public granary 7 gathered, harvested 8 cultivate
9 personal use 10 initial costs 11 damage 12 sought-after
13 toil, labour 14 authority 15 military laws, with severe penalties

eyes. Let not the government of the plantation depend upon too many counsellors and undertakers[1] in the country that planteth, but upon a temperate number; and let those be rather noblemen and gentlemen, than merchants; for they look ever to the present[2] gain. Let there be freedoms from custom,[3] till the plantation be of strength; and not only freedom from custom, but freedom to carry their commodities where they may make their best of them, except there be some special cause of caution.

Cram not in people, by sending too fast company[4] after company; but rather hearken[5] how they waste,[6] and send supplies[7] proportionably; but so as the number may live well in the plantation, and not by surcharge[8] be in penury. It hath been a great endangering to the health of some plantations, that they have built along the sea and rivers, in marish[9] and unwholesome grounds. Therefore, though you begin there, to avoid carriage* and other like discommodities, yet build still[10] rather upwards[11] from the streams, than along. It concerneth likewise the health of the plantation that they have good store of salt with them, that they may use it in their victuals when it shall be necessary.

If you plant where savages are, do not only entertain[12] them with trifles and gingles;[13] but use them justly and graciously, with sufficient guard nevertheless; and do not win their favour by helping them to invade their enemies, but for their defence it is not amiss;* and send oft of them over to the country that plants, that they may see a better condition[14] than their own, and commend it when they return. When the plantation grows to strength, then it is time to plant with women as well as with men; that the plantation may spread into generations,* and not be ever pieced[15] from without. It is the sinfullest thing in the world to forsake or destitute* a plantation once in forwardness;[16] for besides the dishonour, it is the guiltiness of blood* of many commiserable[17] persons.

34. Of Riches

I cannot call Riches better than the baggage* of virtue. The Roman word is better, *impedimenta*. For as the baggage is to an army, so is

1 shareholders   2 immediate   3 customs duties   4 shipments of people
5 ascertain   6 dwindle   7 reinforcements   8 overpopulation   9 marshy
10 always   11 away   12 deal with; amuse   13 cheap jewellery
14 level of existence   15 patched up   16 prosperity   17 pitiable

riches to virtue. It cannot be spared nor left behind, but it hindereth the march; yea and the care of it sometimes loseth or disturbeth the victory. Of great riches there is no real use, except it be in the distribution;[1] the rest is but conceit.[2] So saith Salomon, 'Where much is, there are many to consume it; and what hath the owner but the sight of it with his eyes?'* The personal fruition[3] in any man cannot reach to feel[4] great riches: there is a custody of them; or a power of dole and donative[5] of them; or a fame of them; but no solid use to the owner. Do you not see what feigned[6] prices are set upon little stones and rarities? and what works of ostentation are undertaken, because[7] there might seem to be some use of great riches? But then you will say, they may be of use to buy men[8] out of dangers or troubles. As Salomon saith, 'Riches are as a stronghold, in the imagination of the rich man'.* But this is excellently expressed that it is in imagination, and not always in fact. For certainly great riches have sold* more men than they have bought out.[9] Seek not proud riches, but such as thou mayest get justly, use soberly, distribute cheerfully, and leave contentedly. Yet have no abstract nor friarly* contempt of them. But distinguish, as Cicero saith well of Rabirius Posthumus, *In studio rei amplificandae apparebat, non avaritiae praedam, sed instrumentum bonitati quaeri.** Hearken also to Salomon, and beware of hasty gathering of riches; *Qui festinat ad divitias, non erit insons.** The poets feign,* that when Plutus* (which is Riches) is sent from Jupiter, he limps and goes slowly; but when he is sent from Pluto,* he runs and is swift of foot. Meaning that riches gotten by good means and just labour pace[10] slowly; but when they come by the death of others (as by the course of inheritance, testaments, and the like), they come tumbling upon a man. But it might be applied likewise to Pluto, taking him for the devil. For when riches come from the devil (as by fraud and oppression and unjust means), they come upon speed.[11]

The ways to enrich are many, and most of them foul. Parsimony is one of the best, and yet is not innocent; for it withholdeth men from works of liberality and charity. The improvement of the ground is the most natural obtaining of riches; for it is our great mother's blessing, the earth's; but it is slow. And yet where men of great wealth do stoop* to husbandry,[12] it multiplieth riches exceedingly. I knew a nobleman*

1 spending   2 fantasy, imagination   3 pleasure arising from possession
4 experience   5 charitable distribution and gift   6 fanciful   7 in order that
8 ransom   9 redeemed   10 proceed   11 all of a sudden
12 managing their own estates (agriculture)

in England, that had the greatest audits[1] of any man in my time; a great grazier,[2] a great sheep-master,[3] a great timber man,[4] a great collier,[5] a great corn-master,[6] a great lead-man,[7] and so of iron, and a number of the like points of husbandry.* So as the earth seemed a sea to him, in respect of the perpetual importation. It was truly observed by one,* that himself came very hardly[8] to a little riches, and very easily to great riches. For when a man's stock is come to that, that he can expect the prime[9] of markets, and overcome those bargains* which for their greatness[10] are few men's money,[11] and be partner in the industries[12] of younger men, he cannot but increase mainly.

The gains of ordinary trades[13] and vocations[14] are honest; and furthered by two things chiefly; by diligence, and by a good name for good and fair dealing. But the gains of bargains[15] are of a more doubtful nature; when men shall wait upon[16] others' necessity, broke[17] by servants and instruments[18] to draw them on, put off others cunningly that would be better chapmen,[19] and the like practices,[20] which are crafty and naught.[21] As for the chopping[22] of bargains, when a man buys not to hold but to sell over again, that commonly grindeth double,[23] both upon the seller and upon the buyer. Sharings[24] do greatly enrich, if the hands be well chosen that are trusted. Usury is the certainest[25] means of gain, though one of the worst; as that whereby a man doth eat his bread *in sudore vultus alieni;** and besides, doth plough upon Sundays.* But yet certain though it be, it hath flaws;[26] for that the scriveners and brokers* do value* unsound[27] men to serve their own turn.

The fortune in being the first in an invention or in a privilege,* doth cause sometimes a wonderful overgrowth in riches; as it was with the first sugar man in the Canaries.* Therefore if a man can play the true logician,* to have as well judgment as invention, he may do great matters; especially if the times be fit. He that resteth upon gains certain,* shall hardly grow to great riches; and he that puts all upon adventures,[28] doth oftentimes break and come to poverty: it is good therefore to guard adventures with certainties, that may uphold[29] losses.

---

1 revenues, receipts　　2 cattle-farmer　　3 owner of sheep　　4 proprietor of timber　　5 owner of coal-mines　　6 owner of corn　　7 owner of lead-mines 8 with difficulty　　9 wait for the most favourable conditions　　10 size 11 resources　　12 commercial activities　　13 handicrafts　　14 professions 15 speculations　　16 watch　　17 negotiate, do business　　18 intermediaries 19 buyers　　20 frauds　　21 false, despicable　　22 bartering, speculating 23 cuts in both directions　　24 joint enterprises　　25 most certain 26 weak points　　27 unreliable　　28 risky enterprises　　29 make up for

Monopolies, and coemption of wares* for re-sale, where they are not restrained,[1] are great means to enrich; especially if the party have intelligence* what things are like to come into request, and so store[2] himself beforehand. Riches gotten by service, though it be of the best rise,[3] yet when they are gotten by flattery, feeding humours,* and other servile conditions, they may be placed amongst the worst. As for fishing for testaments and executorships* (as Tacitus saith of Seneca, *testamenta et orbos tamquam indagine capi*),* it is yet worse; by how much men submit themselves to meaner persons than in service.

Believe not much them that[4] seem to despise riches; for they despise them that despair of them; and none worse when they come to them. Be not penny-wise;* riches have wings, and sometimes they fly away of themselves,* sometimes they must be set flying to bring in more. Men leave their riches either to their kindred, or to the public; and moderate portions prosper best in both. A great state[5] left to an heir, is as a lure to all the birds of prey round about to seize on him, if he be not the better stablished[6] in years and judgment. Likewise glorious[7] gifts and foundations are like 'sacrifices without salt';* and but the painted sepulchres* of alms, which soon will putrefy* and corrupt inwardly. Therefore measure not thine advancements[8] by quantity, but frame them by measure: and defer not charities till death; for, certainly, if a man weigh it rightly, he that doth so is rather liberal of another man's than of his own.*

35. OF PROPHECIES

I mean not to speak of divine prophecies;* nor of heathen oracles; nor of natural* predictions; but only of prophecies that have been of certain memory, and from hidden causes. Saith the Pythonissa* to Saul,* 'To-morrow thou and thy son shall be with me'. Homer hath these verses:

At domus Aeneae cunctis dominabitur oris,
*Et nati natorum, et qui nascentur ab illis.**

A prophecy, as it seems, of the Roman empire. Seneca the tragedian hath these verses:

1 restricted, forbidden   2 make large provisions   3 origin, source   4 who
5 estate, fortune   6 thoroughly settled   7 ostentatious   8 gifts

> *Venient annis*
> *Saecula seris, quibus Oceanus*
> *Vincula rerum laxet, et ingens*
> *Pateat Tellus, Tiphysque novos*
> *Detegat orbes; nec sit terris*
> *Ultima Thule.**

—a prophecy of the discovery of America. The daughter of Poly-crates* dreamed that Jupiter bathed her father, and Apollo anointed him; and it came to pass that he was crucified in an open place, where the sun made his body run with sweat, and the rain washed it. Philip of Macedon* dreamed he sealed up his wife's belly; whereby he did ex-pound it, that his wife should be barren; but Aristander the sooth-sayer[1] told him his wife was with child, because men do not use to seal vessels that are empty. A phantasm[2] that appeared to M. Brutus in his tent, said to him, *Philippis iterum me videbis.** Tiberius said to Galba, *Tu quoque, Galba, degustabis imperium.** In Vespasian's time,* there went a prophecy in the East, that those that should come forth of Judea should reign over the world: which though it may be was meant of our Saviour, yet Tacitus expounds it of Vespasian. Domitian* dreamed, the night before he was slain, that a golden head was growing out of the nape of his neck: and indeed the succession[3] that followed him, for many years, made golden times. Henry the Sixth* of England said of Henry the Seventh, when he was a lad, and gave him water, 'This is the lad that shall enjoy the crown for which we strive'.

When I was in France,* I heard from one Dr. Pena, that the Queen Mother,* who was given to curious[4] arts, caused the King her hus-band's nativity[5] to be calculated, under a false name; and the astrologer gave a judgment, that he should be killed in a duel; at which the Queen laughed, thinking her husband to be above challenges and duels: but he was slain upon a course at tilt,* the splinters of the staff of Montgomery going in at his beaver.* The trivial prophecy, which I heard when I was a child, and queen Elizabeth was in the flower of her years, was,

> When hempe* is sponne
> England's done:

whereby it was generally conceived, that after the princes had reigned which had the principal* letters of that word 'hempe' (which were

---

1 truth-teller, of future events   2 ghost, spirit   3 successors   4 occult
5 horoscope

Henry, Edward, Mary, Philip, and Elizabeth), England should come to utter confusion;[1] which, thanks be to God, is verified only in the change of the name; for that the King's style is now no more of England, but of Britain.* There was also another prophecy, before the year of eighty-eight,* which I do not well understand.

> There shall be seen upon a day,
> Between the Baugh and the May,*
> The black fleet of Norway.
> When that that is come and gone,
> England build houses of lime and stone,
> For after wars shall you have none.

It was generally conceived to be meant of the Spanish fleet that came in eighty-eight: for that the king of Spain's surname, as they say, is Norway. The prediction of Regiomontanus,*

Octogesimus octavus mirabilis annus, *

was thought likewise accomplished in the sending of that great fleet, being the greatest in strength, though not in number, of all that ever swam upon the sea. As for Cleon's dream,* I think it was a jest. It was, that he was devoured of a long dragon; and it was expounded of a maker of sausages, that troubled him exceedingly. There are numbers of the like kind; especially if you include dreams, and predictions of astrology. But I have set down these few only of certain credit,[2] for example.

My judgment is, that they ought all to be despised;[3] and ought to serve but for winter talk[4] by the fireside. Though when I say 'despised', I mean it as for belief; for otherwise, the spreading or publishing of them is in no sort to be despised. For they have done much mischief; and I see many severe laws* made to suppress them. That that hath given them grace,[5] and some credit, consisteth in three things. First, that men mark[6] when they hit, and never mark when they miss; as they do generally also of dreams. The second is, that probable conjectures, or obscure traditions, many times turn themselves into prophecies; while the nature of man, which coveteth divination,[7] thinks it no peril to foretell that which indeed they do but collect.[8] As that of Seneca's verse.* For so much was then* subject to demonstration, that the globe

---

1 complete chaos   2 definite authenticity   3 ignored   4 idle chatter
5 favour   6 notice   7 earnestly desires predictions   8 deduce, infer

of the earth had great parts[1] beyond the Atlantic, which might be probably conceived not to be all sea: and adding thereto the tradition in Plato's *Timaeus*, and his *Atlanticus*,* it might encourage one to turn it to a prediction. The third and last (which is the great* one) is, that almost all of them, being infinite in number, have been impostures, and by idle and crafty[2] brains merely[3] contrived and feigned after the event past.

36. OF AMBITION

Ambition* is like choler;* which is an humour that maketh men active, earnest, full of alacrity, and stirring,[4] if it be not stopped. But if it be stopped, and cannot have his way, it becometh adust,[5] and thereby malign and venomous. So ambitious men, if they find the way open for their rising, and still[6] get forward, they are rather busy[7] than dangerous; but if they be checked in their desires, they become secretly discontent, and look upon men and matters with an evil eye, and are best pleased when things go backward; which is the worst property[8] in a servant of a prince or state. Therefore it is good for princes, if they use ambitious men, to handle it so as they be still progressive[9] and not retrograde;* which because it cannot be without inconvenience, it is good not to use such natures at all. For if they rise not with their service,[10] they will take order[11] to make their service fall with them.

But since we have said it were good not to use men of ambitious natures, except it be upon necessity, it is fit we speak in what cases they are of necessity. Good commanders in the wars must be taken, be they never so ambitious; for the use of their service dispenseth with the rest; and to take a soldier without ambition is to pull off his spurs. There is also great use of ambitious men in being screens[12] to princes in matters of danger and envy;[13] for no man will take that part, except he be like a seeled* dove, that mounts and mounts because he cannot see about him. There is use also of ambitious men in pulling down the greatness of any subject that overtops;[14] as Tiberius used Macro in the pulling down of Sejanus.*

1 regions   2 thoughtless and malicious   3 wholly   4 energetic
5 scorched, parched, causing irritation   6 always
7 intriguing, prying into people's affairs   8 characteristic   9 going forward
10 duties   11 take measures   12 protecting walls   13 discontent
14 rises beyond their station

Since therefore they must be used in such cases, there resteth to speak how they are to be bridled,[1] that they may be less dangerous. There is less danger of them if they be of mean birth, than if they be noble; and if they be rather harsh of nature, than gracious[2] and popular:* and if they be rather new[3] raised, than grown cunning and fortified in their greatness. It is counted by some a weakness in princes to have favourites; but it is of all others the best remedy against ambitious great-ones. For when the way of pleasuring and displeasuring lieth by the favourite, it is impossible any other should be over-great. Another means to curb them, is to balance them by others as proud as they. But then there must be some middle counsellors, to keep things steady; for without that ballast the ship will roll too much. At the least, a prince may animate and inure[4] some meaner[5] persons, to be as it were scourges[6] to ambitious men. As for the having of them obnoxious[7] to ruin; if they be of fearful[8] natures, it may do well; but if they be stout[9] and daring, it may precipitate their designs, and prove dangerous. As for the pulling of them down, if the affairs require it, and that it may not be done with safety suddenly, the only way is, the interchange continually of favours and disgraces; whereby they may not know what to expect, and be as it were in a wood.[10]

Of ambitions, it is less harmful,[11] the ambition to prevail in great things, than that other to appear in every thing; for that breeds confusion,[12] and mars[13] business. But yet it is less danger to have an ambitious man stirring in business, than great in dependances.[14] He that seeketh to be eminent amongst able men hath a great task; but that is ever good for the public. But he that plots to be the only figure amongst ciphers* is the decay of a whole age.

Honour[15] hath three things in it; the vantage[16] ground to do good; the approach to kings and principal persons; and the raising of a man's own fortunes. He that hath the best of these intentions, when he aspireth, is an honest man; and that prince that can discern of these intentions in another that aspireth, is a wise prince. Generally, let princes and states choose such ministers as are more sensible[17] of duty than of rising; and such as love business rather upon conscience[18] than upon bravery;[19] and let them discern a busy nature from a willing mind.

1 controlled   2 endowed with charm   3 recently   4 habituate, train
5 less ambitious   6 punishing restraints   7 exposed to, in danger of   8 timid
9 bold, courageous   10 lost, bewildered   11 pernicious   12 chaos
13 spoils or damages   14 having many followers   15 social eminence
16 superior position   17 responsive to   18 moral sense   19 display

37. Of Masques and Triumphs*

These things are but toys,[1] to come amongst such serious observations.* But yet, since princes will have such things, it is better they should be graced with elegancy than daubed with cost.*

Dancing to song,* is a thing of great state[2] and pleasure. I understand it, that the song be in quire,[3] placed aloft,[4] and accompanied with some broken music;* and the ditty fitted to the device.* Acting in song,* especially in dialogues, hath an extreme good grace; I say acting, not dancing* (for that is a mean and vulgar thing); and the voices of the dialogue would[5] be strong and manly, (a bass and a tenor; no treble);[6] and the ditty high and tragical;* not nice or dainty.[7] Several[8] quires, placed one over against another,* and taking the voice by catches, anthem-wise, give great pleasure. Turning dances into figure* is a childish curiosity.[9] And generally let it be noted, that those things which I here set down are such as do naturally take the sense,[10] and not respect[11] petty wonderments.[12] It is true, the alterations* of scenes, so it be quietly and without noise, are things of great beauty and pleasure; for they feed and relieve the eye, before it be full of the same object.

Let the scenes abound with light, specially coloured and varied; and let the masquers,* or any other, that are to come down from the scene,* have some motions* upon the scene itself before their coming down; for it draws the eye strangely, and makes it with great pleasure to desire to see that it cannot perfectly discern. Let the songs be loud and cheerful, and not chirpings or pulings.* Let the music likewise be sharp* and loud, and well placed. The colours that shew[13] best by candle-light, are white, carnation, and a kind of sea-water-green; and oes,* or spangs, as they are of no great cost, so they are of most glory. As for rich embroidery, it is lost* and not discerned. Let the suits[14] of the masquers be graceful, and such as become the person when the vizards* are off; not after examples of known attires; Turks, soldiers, mariners, and the like.

Let anti-masques* not be long; they have been commonly of fools, satyrs, baboons, wild-men, antics,[15] beasts, sprites,[16] witches, Ethiops,* pigmies, turquets,* nymphs, rustics, Cupids, statua's moving, and the like. As for angels, it is not comical enough to put them in

1 trivialities   2 stateliness, splendour   3 choir   4 above, in the gallery
5 ought to   6 boy sopranos   7 fastidious, elaborate   8 Separate
9 elaborate trick   10 appeal to the senses   11 are concerned with   12 surprises
13 stand out   14 costumes   15 grotesque figures, buffoons   16 spirits

anti-masques; and any thing that is hideous, as devils, giants, is on the other side as unfit. But chiefly, let the music of them be recreative, and with some strange changes.* Some sweet odours[1] suddenly coming forth, without any drops falling, are, in such a company as there is steam[2] and heat, things of great pleasure and refreshment. Double masques, one of men, another of ladies, addeth state[3] and variety. But all is nothing except the room be kept clear and neat.

For jousts, and tourneys,* and barriers;* the glories of them are chiefly in the chariots, wherein the challengers make their entry; especially if they be drawn with strange beasts: as lions, bears, camels, and the like; or in the devices[4] of their entrance; or in the bravery[5] of their liveries; or in the goodly furniture[6] of their horses and armour. But enough of these toys.

38. OF NATURE IN MEN

Nature* is often hidden; sometimes overcome; seldom extinguished. Force maketh nature more violent in the return;* doctrine[7] and discourse[8] maketh nature less importune;[9] but custom[10] only doth alter and subdue nature. He that seeketh victory over his nature, let him not set himself too great nor too small tasks; for the first will make him dejected by often failings; and the second will make him a small proceeder, though by often prevailings. And at the first let him practise with helps, as swimmers do with bladders[11] or rushes;[12] but after a time let him practise with disadvantages, as dancers do with thick shoes. For it breeds great perfection, if the practice be harder than the use. Where nature is mighty, and therefore the victory hard, the degrees[13] had need be, first to stay and arrest nature in time;* like to him that would say over the four and twenty letters* when he was angry; then to go less in quantity; as if one should, in forbearing[14] wine, come from drinking healths[15] to a draught[16] at a meal; and lastly, to discontinue altogether. But if a man have the fortitude and resolution to enfranchise[17] himself at once,[18] that is the best:

1 fine sprays of perfume   2 humidity, or body-odours   3 splendour
4 invented plots   5 rich display   6 trappings, harness   7 teaching, education
8 precepts   9 importunate, pressing   10 habit, practice
11 bladder of an animal used as a float   12 plants with hollow stems   13 stages
14 giving up   15 toasts   16 a glass of wine or beer   17 set free, liberate
18 at one go

*Optimus ille animi vindex laedentia pectus
Vincula qui rupit, dedoluitque semel.**

Neither is the ancient rule* amiss,[1] to bend nature as a wand[2] to a contrary extreme, whereby to set it right; understanding it,* where the
contrary extreme is no vice. Let not a man force a habit upon himself
with a perpetual continuance, but with some intermission. For both
the pause reinforceth the new onset; and if a man that is not perfect be
ever in practice, he shall as well practise his errors as his abilities, and
induce one habit of both;* and there is no means to help this but by seasonable intermissions. But let not a man trust his victory over his nature too far; for nature will lay[3] buried a great time, and yet revive upon
the occasion or temptation. Like as it was with Aesop's damsel,*
turned from a cat to a woman, who sat very demurely at the board's
end, till a mouse ran before her. Therefore let a man either avoid the
occasion altogether; or put himself often to it, that he may be little
moved with it.

A man's nature is best perceived in privateness, for there is no affectation; in passion, for that putteth a man out of his precepts; and in
a new case or experiment,[4] for there custom leaveth him. They are
happy men whose natures sort with[5] their vocations; otherwise they
may say, *multum incola fuit anima mea,** when they converse[6] in those
things they do not affect.[7] In studies, whatsoever a man commandeth
upon himself, let him set hours[8] for it; but whatsoever is agreeable to
his nature, let him take no care for any set times; for his thoughts will
fly to it of themselves; so as the spaces[9] of other business or studies will
suffice. A man's nature runs either to herbs or weeds; therefore let him
seasonably water the one, and destroy the other.

39. OF CUSTOM AND EDUCATION

Men's thoughts are much according to their inclination;[10] their discourse and speeches according to their learning and infused[11] opinions; but their deeds are after as they have been accustomed. And
therefore as Machiavel* well noteth (though in an evil-favoured instance), there is no trusting to the force of nature nor to the bravery[12]

1 inapplicable   2 stick   3 lie   4 experience   5 agree with
6 are engaged   7 like, enjoy   8 assign fixed times   9 intervals
10 natural tendencies   11 inculcated, received   12 courage; also boastfulness

of words, except it be corroborate[1] by custom. His instance is, that for the achieving[2] of a desperate conspiracy, a man should not rest[3] upon the fierceness of any man's nature, or his resolute undertakings;[4] but take such an one as hath had his hands formerly in blood. But Machiavel knew not of a friar Clement, nor a Ravillac, nor a Jaureguy, nor a Baltazar Gerard;* yet his rule holdeth still, that nature, nor the engagement[5] of words, are not so forcible[6] as custom. Only superstition is now so well advanced,[7] that men of the first blood* are as firm as butchers by occupation;[8] and votary resolution* is made equipollent[9] to custom even in matter of blood. In other things the predominancy of custom is everywhere visible; insomuch as a man would wonder to hear men profess, protest, engage, give great words, and then do just as they have done before; as if they were dead images,* and engines moved only by the wheels of custom.

We see also the reign or tyranny of custom, what it is. The Indians* (I mean the sect of their wise men) lay themselves quietly upon a stack of wood, and so sacrifice themselves by fire. Nay the wives strive to be burned with the corpses of their husbands. The lads of Sparta,* of ancient time, were wont to be scourged upon the altar of Diana, without so much as queching.* I remember, in the beginning of Queen Elizabeth's time of England, an Irish rebel* condemned, put up a petition to the Deputy* that he might be hanged in a with,* and not in an halter; because it had been so used with former rebels. There be monks in Russia, for penance,[10] that will sit a whole night in a vessel of water, till they be engaged* with hard ice. Many examples may be put of the force of custom, both upon mind and body.

Therefore, since custom is the principal magistrate[11] of man's life, let men by all means endeavour to obtain good customs. Certainly custom is most perfect when it beginneth in young years: this we call education; which is, in effect, but an early custom. So we see, in languages the tongue is more pliant* to all expressions and sounds, the joints are more supple to all feats of activity and motions,[12] in youth than afterwards. For it is true that late learners cannot so well take the ply;[13] except it be in some minds that have not suffered themselves to fix,[14] but

---

1 strengthened, confirmed 2 success 3 rely, depend 4 brave promises
5 obligation 6 effective 7 disseminated 8 profession
9 of equal importance 10 penitence 11 schoolmaster, guide
12 movements 13 receive a new shape 14 grow rigid

have kept themselves open and prepared to receive continual amendment, which is exceeding rare.

But if the force of custom simple and separate be great, the force of custom copulate[1] and conjoined and collegiate* is far greater. For there example teacheth, company comforteth,[2] emulation quickeneth,[3] glory raiseth: so as in such places the force of custom is in his exaltation.[4] Certainly the great multiplication of virtues upon human nature resteth upon[5] societies[6] well ordained and disciplined. For commonwealths and good governments do nourish virtue grown, but do not much mend[7] the seeds. But the misery is, that the most effectual means are now applied to the ends least to be desired.*

40. OF FORTUNE

It cannot be denied, but[8] outward accidents[9] conduce[10] much to fortune; favour,[11] opportunity, death of others, occasion fitting virtue.* But chiefly, the mould[12] of a man's fortune is in his own hands. *Faber quisque fortunae suae,** saith the poet. And the most frequent of external causes is, that the folly of one man is the fortune of another. For no man prospers so suddenly as by others' errors. *Serpens nisi serpentem comederit non fit draco.** Overt and apparent[13] virtues bring forth praise; but there be secret and hidden virtues that bring forth fortune; certain deliveries* of a man's self, which have no name. The Spanish name, *desemboltura*,[14] partly expresseth them; when there be not stonds[15] nor restiveness[16] in a man's nature; but that the wheels of his mind keep way[17] with the wheels of his fortune. For so Livy (after he had described Cato Major* in these words, *In illo viro tantum robur corporis et animi fuit, ut quocunque loco natus esset, fortunam sibi facturus videretur*),* falleth upon* that, that he had *versatile ingenium.** Therefore if a man look sharply and attentively, he shall see Fortune: for though she be blind,* yet she is not invisible. The way of fortune is like the milken way in the sky; which is a meeting or knot of a number of small stars; not seen asunder, but giving light together. So are there a number of little and scarce discerned virtues, or rather faculties and customs,[18]

1 coupled with   2 strengthens   3 stimulates   4 highest point, of greatest influence   5 depends on   6 social institutions   7 improve   8 that
9 external events   10 contribute   11 kindness, patronage   12 formation
13 manifest   14 boldness, cheek   15 obstructions, hindrances   16 obstinacy
17 keep pace   18 abilities and habits

that make men fortunate. The Italians note some of them, such as a man would little think. When they speak of one that cannot do amiss, they will throw in into his other conditions, that he hath *Poco di matto*.* And certainly there be not two more fortunate properties,[1] than to have a little of the fool, and not too much of the honest. Therefore extreme lovers of their country or masters were never fortunate, neither can they be. For when a man placeth his thoughts without[2] himself, he goeth not his own way. An hasty fortune[3] maketh an enterpriser and remover* (the French hath it better, *entreprenant*, or *remuant*); but the exercised[4] fortune maketh the able man.

Fortune is to be honoured and respected, and it be but for her daughters, Confidence[5] and Reputation. For those two felicity[6] breedeth; the first within a man's self, the latter in others towards him. All wise men, to decline[7] the envy of their own virtues,* use to ascribe them to Providence and Fortune; for so they may the better assume[8] them: and, besides, it is greatness in a man to be the care[9] of the higher powers. So Caesar said to the pilot in the tempest, *Caesarem portas, et fortunam ejus*.* So Sulla chose the name of *Felix*, and not of *Magnus*.* And it hath been noted, that those who ascribe openly too much to their own wisdom and policy, end infortunate. It is written that Timotheus* the Athenian, after he had, in the account he gave to the state of his government, often interlaced[10] this speech, 'and in this Fortune had no part', never prospered in anything he undertook afterwards. Certainly there be, whose fortunes are like Homer's verses, that have a slide* and easiness more than the verses of other poets; as Plutarch saith of Timoleon's fortune, in respect of that of Agesilaus or Epaminondas. And that this should be, no doubt it is much* in a man's self.

41. OF USURY

Many have made witty invectives against Usury. They say that it is a pity the devil should have God's part, which is the tithe.* That the usurer is the greatest sabbath-breaker,* because his plough goeth every Sunday. That the usurer is the drone that Virgil speaketh of;

1 qualities   2 outside   3 sudden riches   4 acquired with difficulty
5 credit   6 prosperity   7 turn aside   8 take possession of, put on
9 object of attention   10 inserted

*Ignavum fucos pecus a praesepibus arcent.**

That the usurer breaketh the first law* that was made for mankind after the fall, which was, *in sudore vultus tui comedes panem tuum*; not, *in sudore vultus alieni.** That usurers should have orange-tawny bonnets,* because they do judaize.* That it is against nature* for money to beget money; and the like. I say this only, that usury is a *concessum propter duritiem cordis*:* for since there must be borrowing and lending, and men are so hard of heart as they will not lend freely, usury must be permitted. Some others have made suspicious[1] and cunning propositions of banks, discovery of men's estates, and other inventions. But few have spoken of usury usefully. It is good to set before us the incommodities and commodities of usury, that the good may be either weighed out[2] or culled[3] out; and warily to provide, that while we make forth[4] to that which is better, we meet not with that which is worse.

The discommodities of usury are, First, that it makes fewer merchants. For were it not for this lazy trade of usury, money would not lie still, but would in great part be employed upon merchandizing; which is the *vena porta** of wealth in a state. The second, that it makes poor merchants. For as a farmer cannot husband[5] his ground so well if he sit at a great rent;* so the merchant cannot drive his trade so well, if he sit at great usury. The third is incident[6] to the other two; and that is the decay of customs[7] of kings or states, which ebb or flow with merchandizing. The fourth, that it bringeth the treasure of a realm or state[8] into a few hands. For the usurer being at certainties,[9] and others at uncertainties, at the end of the game most of the money will be in the box;* and ever a state flourisheth when wealth is more equally spread.[10] The fifth, that it beats down the price of land; for the employment of money is chiefly either merchandizing or purchasing;[11] and usury waylays[12] both. The sixth, that it doth dull and damp[13] all industries, improvements, and new inventions, wherein money would be stirring, if it were not for this slug.[14] The last, that it is the canker[15] and ruin of many men's estates; which in process of time breeds a public poverty.

On the other side, the commodities of usury are, first, that howsoever usury in some respect hindereth merchandizing, yet in some

1 exciting suspicion   2 weighed and dispensed in portions accordingly
3 picked out for rejection   4 proceed   5 farm, cultivate   6 naturally connected
7 decline in excise duties   8 monarchy or republic   9 having guaranteed returns
10 like manure   11 permanently acquiring (as of land)
12 ambushes, obstructs (like a highwayman)   13 suffocates   14 obstacle
15 anything that corrupts and destroys

other it advanceth[1] it; for it is certain that the greatest part of trade is driven by young merchants, upon borrowing at interest; so as if the usurer either call in or keep back his money, there will ensue presently[2] a great stand[3] of trade. The second is, that were it not for this easy borrowing upon interest, men's necessities[4] would draw upon them a most sudden undoing;[5] in that they would be forced to sell their means[6] (be it lands or goods) far under foot;[7] and so, whereas usury doth but gnaw upon them, bad markets would swallow them quite up. As for mortgaging or pawning,* it will little mend the matter: for either men will not take pawns without use;* or if they do, they will look precisely for the forfeiture.* I remember a cruel monied man in the country, that would say, 'The devil take this usury, it keeps us from forfeitures of mortgages and bonds'. The third and last is, that it is a vanity[8] to conceive that there would be ordinary borrowing without profit; and it is impossible to conceive the number of inconveniences that will ensue, if borrowing be cramped.[9] Therefore to speak of the abolishing of usury is idle.* All states have ever had it, in one kind or rate,[10] or other. So as that opinion must be sent to Utopia.*

To speak now of the reformation and reiglement[11] of usury; how the discommodities of it may be best avoided, and the commodities retained. It appears by the balance of commodities and discommodities of usury, two things are to be reconciled. The one, that the tooth of usury be grinded,* that it bite not too much; the other, that there be left open a means to invite monied men to lend to the merchants, for the continuing and quickening of trade. This cannot be done, except you introduce two several[12] sorts of usury, a less and a greater.[13] For if you reduce usury to one low rate, it will ease the common borrower, but the merchant will be to seek for* money. And it is to be noted, that the trade of merchandize, being the most lucrative, may bear usury at a good rate: other contracts[14] not so.

To serve both intentions,[15] the way would be briefly thus. That there be two rates of usury; the one free, and general for all; the other under licence only, to certain persons and in certain places of merchandizing. First therefore, let usury in general be reduced to five in the hundred;[16] and let that rate be proclaimed to be free and current;[17] and let the state

1 promotes   2 immediately   3 standstill   4 things necessary for daily life
5 ruin   6 assets   7 below their real value   8 silly idea   9 suppressed
10 interest rate   11 regulation   12 distinct   13 a lower, and a higher rate
14 forms of business   15 purposes   16 5 per cent   17 negotiable and official

shut itself out to take any penalty* for the same. This will preserve borrowing from any general stop or dryness.[1] This will ease infinite borrowers in the country. This will, in good part, raise the price of land, because land purchased at sixteen years' purchase* will yield six in the hundred, and somewhat more; whereas this rate of interest yields but five. This by like reason will encourage and edge[2] industrious and profitable improvements; because many will rather venture in that kind than take five in the hundred, especially having been used to greater profit. Secondly, let there be certain persons licensed to lend to known merchants upon usury at a higher rate; and let it be with the cautions following. Let the rate be, even with the merchant himself, somewhat more easy than that he used formerly to pay; for by that means all borrowers shall have some ease by this reformation, be he merchant, or whosoever. Let it be no bank or common[3] stock, but every man be master of his own money. Not that I altogether mislike* banks, but they will hardly be brooked,[4] in regard of certain suspicions. Let the state be answered some small matter* for the licence,[5] and the rest left to the lender; for if the abatement[6] be but small, it will no whit discourage the lender. For he, for example, that took before ten or nine in the hundred, will sooner descend to eight in the hundred, than give over his trade of usury, and go from certain gains to gains of hazard.[7] Let these licensed lenders be in number indefinite, but restrained to certain principal cities and towns of merchandizing; for then they will be hardly able to colour* other men's monies in the country: so as the licence of nine will not suck away the current rate of five; for no man will send his monies far off, nor put them into unknown hands.

If it be objected that this doth in a sort authorize usury, which before was in some places but permissive; the answer is, that it is better to mitigate usury by declaration,[8] than to suffer it to rage by connivance.

42. Of Youth and Age

A man that is young in years may be old in hours, if he have lost no time.* But that happeneth rarely. Generally, youth is like the first cogitations,[9] not so wise as the second. For there is a youth in thoughts, as

1 lack of circulation   2 urge, stimulate   3 joint   4 put up with
5 official permission   6 deduction   7 risky profits   8 official recognition
9 reflections

well as in ages. And yet the invention[1] of young men is more lively than that of old; and imaginations[2] stream into their minds better, and as it were more divinely. Natures that have much heat* and great and violent desires and perturbations, are not ripe for action till they have passed the meridian* of their years; as it was with Julius Caesar, and Septimius Severus.* Of the latter of whom it is said, *Juventutem egit erroribus, imo furoribus, plenam.** And yet he was the ablest emperor, almost, of all the list. But reposed natures may do well in youth. As it is seen in Augustus Caesar, Cosmus Duke of Florence, Gaston de Fois,* and others. On the other side, heat and vivacity in age is an excellent composition[3] for business.[4]

Young men are fitter to invent than to judge;* fitter for execution than for counsel;* and fitter for new projects than for settled[5] business. For the experience of age, in things that fall within the compass[6] of it, directeth[7] them; but in new things, abuseth[8] them. The errors of young men are the ruin of business; but the errors of aged men amount but to this, that more might have been done, or sooner. Young men, in the conduct and manage of actions, embrace more than they can hold; stir more than they can quiet;[9] fly to the end, without consideration of the means and degrees;* pursue some few principles which they have chanced upon absurdly;[10] care not to innovate, which draws unknown inconveniences; use extreme remedies at first; and that which doubleth[11] all errors, will not acknowledge or retract them; like an unready horse, that will neither stop nor turn. Men of age object too much, consult too long, adventure too little,* repent too soon, and seldom drive business home to the full period,[12] but content themselves with a mediocrity of success.

Certainly it is good to compound[13] employments of both; for that will be good for the present, because the virtues of either age may correct the defects of both; and good for succession,[14] that young men may be learners, while men in age are actors;* and, lastly, good for extern accidents,* because authority followeth old men, and favour and popularity youth. But for the moral* part, perhaps youth will have the preeminence, as age hath for the politic.* A certain rabbin,* upon the text, 'Your young men shall see visions, and your old men shall dream

1 inventiveness   2 ideas, projects   3 temperament   4 public life
5 routine   6 range   7 keeps on a straight path   8 deceives
9 resolve, settle   10 without good grounds   11 intensifies
12 completion, conclusion   13 combine   14 continuity, future

dreams', inferreth that young men are admitted nearer to God than old, because vision is a clearer revelation than a dream. And certainly, the more a man drinketh of the world, the more it intoxicateth: and age doth profit rather in the powers of understanding, than in the virtues of the will and affections.[1] There be some have an over-early ripeness in their years, which fadeth betimes.[2] These are, first, such as have brittle[3] wits, the edge[4] whereof is soon turned; such as was Hermogenes* the rhetorician, whose books are exceeding subtle; who afterwards waxed stupid. A second sort is of those that have some natural dispositions which have better grace in youth than in age; such as is a fluent and luxuriant* speech; which becomes youth well, but not age: so Tully saith of Hortensius, *Idem manebat, neque idem decebat.** The third is of such as take too high a strain[5] at the first, and are magnanimous more than tract[6] of years can uphold. As was Scipio Africanus, of whom Livy saith in effect, *Ultima primis cedebant.**

43. OF BEAUTY

Virtue is like a rich stone, best plain set;[7] and surely virtue is best in a body that is comely, though not of delicate[8] features; and that hath rather dignity of presence,[9] than beauty of aspect.[10] Neither is it almost[11] seen, that very beautiful persons are otherwise of great virtue; as if nature were rather busy not to err, than in labour to produce excellency. And therefore they prove accomplished, but not of great spirit; and study rather behaviour than virtue.* But this holds not always: for Augustus Caesar, Titus Vespasianus, Philip le Bel of France, Edward the Fourth of England, Alcibiades of Athens, Ismael the Sophy* of Persia, were all high and great spirits;* and yet the most beautiful men of their times. In beauty, that of favour[12] is more than that of colour;* and that of decent and gracious motion* more than that of favour. That is the best part of beauty, which a picture cannot express; no nor the first sight of the life.*

There is no excellent beauty that hath not some strangeness in the proportion.* A man cannot tell whether Apelles* or Albert Durer* were the more trifler;[13] whereof the one would make a personage[14] by

---

1 passions   2 soon   3 weak, thin   4 acumen, sharpness of mind
5 make too great an effort   6 length   7 mounted simply   8 sensual
9 bearing, deportment   10 appearance   11 generally   12 feature, countenance
13 greater time-waster   14 representation of the human face

geometrical proportions; the other, by taking the best parts out of divers faces, to make one excellent. Such personages, I think, would please nobody but the painter that made them. Not but I think a painter may make a better face than ever was; but he must do it by a kind of felicity[1] (as a musician that maketh an excellent air in music), and not by rule. A man shall see faces, that if you examine them part by part, you shall find never a good; and yet altogether do well. If it be true that the principal part of beauty is in decent motion,[2] certainly it is no marvel though[3] persons in years seem many times more amiable; *pulchrorum autumnus pulcher*;* for no youth can be comely but by pardon,* and considering the youth as to make up[4] the comeliness. Beauty is as summer fruits, which are easy to corrupt, and cannot last; and for the most part it makes a dissolute youth,* and an age a little out of countenance;[5] but yet certainly again, if it light well,[6] it maketh virtue shine, and vices blush.*

44. OF DEFORMITY

Deformed persons* are commonly even[7] with nature; for as nature hath done ill by them, so do they by nature; being for the most part (as the Scripture* saith), 'void of natural affection'; and so they have their revenge of nature. Certainly there is a consent[8] between the body and the mind; and where nature erreth in the one, she ventureth[9] in the other: *Ubi peccat in uno, periclitatur in altero.* But because there is in man an election[10] touching the frame[11] of his mind, and a necessity in the frame of his body, the stars of natural inclination are sometimes obscured by the sun of discipline[12] and virtue. Therefore it is good to consider of deformity, not as a sign, which is more deceivable;[13] but as a cause, which seldom faileth of[14] the effect.

Whosoever hath any thing fixed[15] in his person[16] that doth induce[17] contempt, hath also a perpetual spur in himself to rescue and deliver himself from scorn. Therefore all deformed persons are extreme bold. First, as in their own defence, as being exposed to scorn; but in process of time by a general habit. Also it stirreth in them industry, and

1 happy skill   2 dignified bearing   3 if   4 contribute
5 upset, discomforted   6 alight on a worthy owner   7 got even with, revenged on
8 sympathy   9 risks failure   10 liberty of choice   11 framework, make-up
12 education, training   13 apt to be deceptive   14 misses
15 permanent deformity   16 body   17 generate

especially of this kind, to watch and observe the weakness of others, that they may have somewhat to repay.[1] Again, in their superiors, it quencheth jealousy towards them, as persons that they think they may at pleasure despise: and it layeth their competitors and emulators asleep;[2] as never believing they should be in possibility of advancement, till they see them in possession.[3] So that upon the matter,[4] in a great wit,[5] deformity is an advantage to rising.[6]

Kings in ancient times (and at this present in some countries) were wont to put great trust in eunuchs; because they that are envious towards all are more obnoxious[7] and officious[8] towards one. But yet their trust towards them hath rather been as to good spials[9] and good whisperers,[10] than good magistrates and officers. And much like is the reason[11] of deformed persons. Still[12] the ground is, they will, if they be of spirit,[13] seek to free themselves from scorn; which must be either by virtue or malice; and therefore let it not be marvelled if sometimes they prove excellent persons; as was Agesilaus, Zanger the son of Solyman, Aesop, Gasca President of Peru; and Socrates* may go likewise amongst them; with others.

45 . OF BUILDING

Houses are built to live in, and not to look on; therefore let use be preferred before uniformity,[14] except where both may be had. Leave the goodly fabrics of houses, for beauty only, to the enchanted palaces* of the poets; who build them with small cost. He that builds a fair house upon an ill seat,[15] committeth himself to prison. Neither do I reckon it an ill seat only where the air[16] is unwholesome; but likewise where the air is unequal;[17] as you shall see many fine seats[18] set upon a knap[19] of ground, environed with higher hills round about it; whereby the heat of the sun is pent in,[20] and the wind gathereth as in troughs;[21] so as you shall have, and that suddenly, as great diversity of heat and cold as if you dwelt in several[22] places. Neither is it ill air only that maketh an ill seat, but ill ways, ill markets: and, if you will consult with Momus,* ill

---

1 revenge   2 off guard   3 in office   4 in fact; on the whole
5 intellect, gifted person   6 making a career   7 submissive, obsequious
8 dutiful   9 spies   10 malicious informers, detractors   11 motive force, rationale
12 always   13 enterprising, talented   14 symmetry   15 a bad site
16 climate   17 variable   18 houses   19 small hill, knoll
20 captured, concentrated   21 collects, as if canalized   22 different

neighbours. I speak not of many more: want of water; want of wood, shade, and shelter; want of fruitfulness, and mixture[1] of grounds of several natures; want of prospect;[2] want of level grounds; want of places at some near distance for sports of hunting, hawking, and races; too near the sea, too remote; having [not] the commodity of navigable rivers, or the discommodity of their overflowing; too far off from great cities, which may hinder business, or too near them, which lurcheth* all provisions,[3] and maketh every thing dear; where a man hath a great living[4] laid together, and where he is scanted:[5] all which, as it is impossible perhaps to find together, so it is good to know them, and think of them, that a man may take[6] as many as he can; and if he have several dwellings, that he sort[7] them so, that what he wanteth in the one he may find in the other. Lucullus* answered Pompey well; who, when he saw his stately galleries,[8] and rooms so large and lightsome,[9] in one of his houses, said, 'Surely an excellent place for summer, but how do you in winter?' Lucullus answered, 'Why, do you not think me as wise as some fowl[10] are, that ever change their abode towards the winter?'

To pass from the seat to the house itself; we will do as Cicero doth in the orator's art; who writes books *De Oratore*, and a book he entitles *Orator*; whereof the former delivers[11] the precepts of the art, and the latter the perfection.[12] We will therefore describe a princely palace, making a brief model thereof. For it is strange to see, now in Europe, such huge buildings as the Vatican* and Escurial* and some others be, and yet scarce a very fair[13] room in them.

First therefore, I say you cannot have a perfect palace, except you have two several sides;[14] a side for the banquet,[15] as is spoken of in the book of Hester,* and a side for the household;[16] the one for feasts and triumphs,[17] and the other for dwelling. I understand both these sides to be not only returns,* but parts of the front; and to be uniform without, though severally partitioned within; and to be on both sides of a great and stately tower in the midst of the front, that, as it were, joineth them together on either hand. I would have on the side of the banquet, in front, one only goodly room above stairs, of some forty foot high; and under it a room for a dressing or preparing place* at times of triumphs.

1 lacking the proper variety of terrain   2 view   3 supplies of food and drink
4 large property   5 lacking   6 take into account   7 arrange, dispose of
8 arcades   9 full of light   10 bird (of any kind)   11 describes
12 completion, perfect realization   13 habitable, comfortable
14 separate buildings   15 dining hall   16 domestic offices, residential quarters
17 magnificent shows

On the other side, which is the household side, I wish it divided at the first* into a hall and a chapel (with a partition between); both of good state[1] and bigness; and those not to go all the length, but to have at the further end a winter and a summer parlour,[2] both fair.[3] And under these rooms, a fair and large cellar sunk under ground; and likewise some privy[4] kitchens, with butteries[5] and pantries,[6] and the like. As for the tower, I would have it two stories, of eighteen foot high a piece,[7] above the two wings; and a goodly leads[8] upon the top, railed[9] with statua's interposed; and the same tower to be divided into rooms, as shall be thought fit. The stairs likewise to the upper rooms, let them be upon a fair open newel,* and finely railed in with images of wood,* cast into a brass colour; and a very fair landing-place[10] at the top. But this to be, if you do not point[11] any of the lower rooms for a dining place of servants. For otherwise you shall have the servants' dinner after your own: for the steam of it will come up as in a tunnel.[12] And so much for the front. Only I understand the height of the first stairs to be sixteen foot, which is the height of the lower room.*

Beyond this front is there to be a fair court, but three sides of it, of a far lower building than the front. And in all the four corners of that court fair stair-cases, cast into turrets, on the outside,* and not within the row of buildings themselves. But those towers are not to be of the height of the front, but rather proportionable to the lower building. Let the court not be paved, for that striketh up[13] a great heat in summer, and much cold in winter. But* only some side alleys, with a cross, and the quarters to graze,* being kept shorn, but not too near shorn. The row of return* on the banquet side, let it be all stately galleries: in which galleries let there be three, or five fine cupolas in the length of it, placed at equal distance; and fine coloured windows of several[14] works.* On the household side, chambers of presence* and ordinary entertainments,* with some bed-chambers; and let all three sides be a double house,* without thorough lights* on the sides, that you may have rooms from[15] the sun, both for forenoon and afternoon. Cast it also, that you may have rooms both for summer and winter; shady for summer, and warm for winter. You shall have sometimes fair houses so full of glass, that one cannot tell where to become[16] to be out of the sun

1 proportion   2 smaller room, for conversation and less formal meals
3 handsome   4 private   5 storerooms for provisions
6 rooms for storing and cleaning kitchenware   7 each   8 well covered with lead
9 adorned   10 landing   11 appoint   12 chimney-flue   13 reflects
14 different   15 away from   16 betake oneself

or cold. For inbowed[1] windows, I hold them of good use (in cities, indeed, upright[2] do better, in respect of the uniformity[3] towards the street); for they be pretty[4] retiring places for conference;[5] and besides, they keep both the wind and sun off; for that which would strike[6] almost thorough the room doth scarce pass the window. But let them be but few, four in the court, on the sides* only.

Beyond this court, let there be an inward[7] court, of the same square[8] and height; which is to be environed with the garden on all sides; and in the inside, cloistered[9] on all sides,[10] upon decent[11] and beautiful arches, as high as the first story.[12] On the under story, towards the garden, let it be turned to a grotta,[13] or place of shade, or estivation.* And only have opening and windows towards the garden; and be level upon the floor, no whit sunken under ground, to avoid all dampishness. And let there be a fountain, or some fair work of statua's in the midst of this court; and to be paved as the other court was. These buildings to be for privy lodgings on both sides; and the end for privy galleries. Whereof you must foresee[14] that one of them be for an infirmary,* if the prince or any special person should be sick, with chambers, bed-chamber, antecamera, and recamera,* joining to it. This upon the second story. Upon the ground story, a fair gallery,* open, upon pillars; and upon the third story likewise, an open gallery,[15] upon pillars, to take[16] the prospect and freshness of the garden. At both corners of the further side, by way of return, let there be two delicate or rich cabinets,[17] daintily[18] paved, richly hanged,[19] glazed with crystalline* glass, and a rich cupola in the midst; and all other elegancy that may be thought upon. In the upper gallery too, I wish that there may be, if the place will yield[20] it, some fountains running in divers places from the wall, with some fine avoidances.*

And thus much for the model of the palace; save[21] that you must have, before you come to the front, three courts. A green court plain,* with a wall about it; a second court of the same, but more garnished, with little turrets, or rather embellishments, upon the wall; and a third court, to make a square with the front, but not to be built,[22] nor yet enclosed with a naked wall, but enclosed with tarrasses,* leaded aloft,

1 bay windows, like balconies   2 not projecting   3 symmetrical appearance
4 useful   5 conversation   6 penetrate (the sun's rays)   7 interior   8 area
9 surrounded with cloisters   10 both (lateral) sides   11 appropriately sized
12 storey   13 grotto, artificial cave   14 provide   15 loggia, covered terrace
16 partake of, enjoy   17 small rooms for displaying art objects   18 elegantly
19 with ornate wall-hangings   20 permit   21 except   22 built up, enclosed

and fairly garnished, on the three sides; and cloistered on the inside,
with pillars, and not with arches below. As for offices,* let them stand
at distance, with some low galleries,[1] to pass from them to the palace
itself.

46. Of Gardens

God Almighty first planted a Garden.* And indeed it is the purest of
human pleasures. It is the greatest refreshment to the spirits of man;
without which, buildings and palaces are but gross handy-works:* and
a man shall ever see that when ages grow to civility[2] and elegancy, men
come to build stately sooner than to garden finely;[3] as if gardening
were the greater perfection. I do hold[4] it, in the royal ordering[5] of gardens, there ought to be gardens for all the months in the year; in which
severally[6] things of beauty may be then in season. For December, and
January, and the latter part of November, you must take such things as
are green all winter: holly; ivy; bays; juniper; cypress-trees; yew; pine-
apple trees;[7] fir-trees; rosemary; lavender; periwinkle, the white, the
purple, and the blue; germander;* flags;* orange-trees; lemon-trees;
and myrtles, if they be stooved;* and sweet marjoram, warm set.[8]
There followeth, for the latter part of January and February, the me-
zereon-tree,[9] which then blossoms; crocus vernus,* both the yellow
and the grey; primroses; anemones; the early tulippa; hyacinthus ori-
entalis; chamaïris;[10] fritellaria. For March, there come[11] violets, specially the single blue, which are the earliest; the yellow daffodil; the
daisy; the almond-tree in blossom; the peach-tree in blossom; the cor-
nelian-tree[12] in blossom; sweet-briar. In April follow the double white
violet; the wall-flower; the stock-gilliflower; the cowslip; flower-de-
lices, and lilies of all natures;[13] rosemary-flowers; the tulippa; the double
piony; the pale daffodil; the French honeysuckle; the cherry-tree in
blossom; the dammasin[14] and plum-trees in blossom; the white thorn[15]
in leaf; the lilac-tree. In May and June come pinks[16] of all sorts, specially the blush-pink; roses of all kinds, except the musk, which comes
later; honeysuckles; strawberries; bugloss;* columbine; the French

1 arcades   2 civilization   3 skilfully   4 maintain, believe   5 arrangement
6 separately   7 pine-trees, bearing cones   8 planted in a sunny spot
9 the dwarf bay tree, or German olive   10 the dwarf iris   11 flower
12 the male cornel-tree   13 kinds   14 damson-tree   15 hawthorn
16 carnations

marigold; flos Africanus;[1] cherry-tree in fruit; ribes;[2] figs in fruit; rasps;[3] vine-flowers; lavender in flowers; the sweet satyrian,[4] with the white flower; herba muscaria;[5] lilium convallium;[6] the apple-tree in blossom. In July come gilliflowers of all varieties; musk-roses; the lime-tree in blossom; early pears and plums in fruit; genitings, quadlins.* In August come[7] plums of all sorts in fruit; pears; apricocks; barberries;* filberds;[8] musk-melons;[9] monks-hoods, of all colours. In September come grapes; apples; poppies of all colours; peaches; melo-cotones;[10] nectarines; cornelians;* wardens;[11] quinces. In October and the beginning of November come services;* medlars;* bullaces;[12] roses cut or removed to come late; holly-oaks; and such like. These particu-lars are for the climate of London; but my meaning is perceived, that you may have *ver perpetuum*,* as the place* affords.

And because the breath[13] of flowers is far sweeter in the air (where it comes and goes like the warbling of music) than in the hand, therefore nothing is more fit for that delight, than to know what be the flowers and plants that do best perfume the air. Roses, damask and red,* are fast[14] flowers of their smells; so that you may walk by a whole row of them, and find nothing of their sweetness; yea though it be in a morn-ing's dew. Bays likewise yield no smell as they grow. Rosemary little; nor sweet marjoram. That which above all others yields the sweetest smell in the air, is the violet, specially the white double violet, which comes twice a year; about the middle of April, and about Bartholomew-tide.* Next to that is the musk-rose. Then the straw-berry-leaves dying, which [yield]* a most excellent cordial[15] smell. Then the flower of the vines; it is a little dust,* like the dust of a bent,* which grows upon the cluster in the first coming forth. Then sweet-briar. Then wall-flowers, which are very delightful to be set under a parlour or lower chamber window. Then pinks and gilliflowers, spe-cially the matted pink and clove gilliflower. Then the flowers of the lime-tree. Then the honeysuckles, so[16] they be somewhat afar off. Of bean-flowers I speak not, because they are field flowers. But those which perfume the air most delightfully, not passed by[17] as the rest, but being trodden upon and crushed, are three; that is, burnet,* wild-thyme,

---

1 type of marigold   2 redcurrants   3 raspberries   4 variety of orchis
5 type of hyacinth   6 lily of the valley   7 ripen   8 hazelnuts
9 water-melons   10 melon peaches   11 winter pears   12 wild plums (black)
13 scent, odour   14 retentive   15 stimulating   16 provided that
17 when one walks past

and watermints. Therefore you are to set whole alleys of them, to have the pleasure when you walk or tread.

For gardens (speaking of those which are indeed prince-like, as we have done of buildings), the contents ought not well to be under thirty acres* of ground; and to be divided into three parts; a green in the entrance; a heath or desert* in the going forth;[1] and the main garden in the midst; besides alleys on both sides.* And I like well that four acres of ground be assigned to the green; six to the heath; four and four to either side; and twelve to the main garden. The green hath two pleasures: the one, because nothing is more pleasant to the eye than green grass kept finely shorn; the other, because it will give you a fair alley in the midst, by which you may go in front upon* a stately hedge, which is to enclose the garden. But because the alley will be long, and, in great heat of the year or day, you ought not to buy[2] the shade in the garden by going in the sun thorough[3] the green, therefore you are, of either side the green, to plant a covert alley,* upon carpenter's work,* about twelve foot in height, by which you may go in shade into the garden. As for the making of knots or figures with divers coloured earths,* that they may lie under the windows of the house on that side which the garden stands, they be but toys: you may see as good sights many times in tarts.

The garden is best to be square, encompassed on all the four sides with a stately arched hedge. The arches to be upon pillars of carpenter's work, of some ten foot high, and six foot broad; and the spaces between of the same dimension with the breadth of the arch. Over the arches let there be an entire[4] hedge of some four foot high, framed also upon carpenter's work; and upon the upper hedge, over every arch, a little turret, with a belly,[5] enough to receive a cage of birds; and over every space between the arches some other little figure, with broad plates of round coloured glass gilt, for the sun to play upon. But this hedge I intend to be raised upon a bank, not steep, but gently slope, of some six foot, set all with flowers. Also I understand, that this square of the garden should not be the whole breadth of the ground, but to leave on either side ground enough for diversity of side alleys; unto which the two covert alleys of the green may deliver[6] you. But there must be no alleys with hedges at either end of this great enclosure; not at the hither end, for letting your prospect[7] upon this fair hedge from

1 outlet, exit   2 pay a high price for   3 through   4 complete
5 a protruding part   6 let in, admit   7 which will obstruct the view

the green; nor at the further end, for letting your prospect from the hedge through the arches upon the heath.

For the ordering[1] of the ground within the great hedge, I leave it to variety of device;[2] advising nevertheless that whatsoever form you cast it into, first, it be not too busy,[3] or full of work. Wherein I, for my part, do not like images cut out* in juniper or other garden stuff; they be for children. Little low hedges, round, like welts,[4] with some pretty pyramides,* I like well; and in some places, fair columns upon frames of carpenter's work. I would also have the alleys spacious and fair. You may have closer[5] alleys upon the side grounds, but none in the main garden. I wish also, in the very middle, a fair mount,* with three ascents,* and alleys, enough for four to walk abreast; which I would have to be perfect circles, without any bulwarks[6] or embossments;[7] and the whole mount to be thirty foot high; and some fine banqueting-house,* with some chimneys neatly cast,* and without too much glass.

For fountains, they are a great beauty and refreshment; but pools* mar[8] all, and make the garden unwholesome, and full of flies and frogs. Fountains I intend to be of two natures: the one that sprinkleth or spouteth water; the other a fair receipt[9] of water, of some thirty or forty foot square, but without fish, or slime, or mud. For the first, the ornaments of images gilt, or of marble, which are in use, do well: but the main matter is so to convey the water, as it never stay,[10] either in the bowls or in the cistern;[11] that the water be never by rest discoloured, green or red or the like; or gather any mossiness or putrefaction. Besides that, it is to be cleansed every day by the hand. Also some steps up to it, and some fine pavement about it, doth well. As for the other kind of fountain, which we may call a bathing pool, it may admit much curiosity* and beauty; wherewith we will not trouble ourselves: as, that the bottom be finely paved, and with images;[12] the sides likewise; and withal embellished with coloured glass, and such things of lustre;[13] encompassed also with fine rails of low statua's. But the main point is the same which we mentioned in the former kind of fountain; which is, that the water be in perpetual motion, fed by a water higher than the pool, and delivered[14] into it by fair spouts,* and then discharged away under ground, by some equality of bores,* that it stay little.

---

1 disposition   2 design, contrivance   3 over-elaborate   4 ornamental edgings or borders (of a dress)   5 narrower   6 ramparts, projections
7 ornaments with raised work   8 spoil   9 receptacle, basin   10 stand still
11 tank   12 figures, designs   13 shining   14 admitted

And for fine devices, of arching water without spilling, and making it rise in several forms (of feathers, drinking glasses, canopies,* and the like), they be pretty things to look on, but nothing to health and sweetness.

For the heath, which was the third part of our plot,[1] I wish it to be framed,[2] as much as may be, to a natural wildness. Trees I would have none in it, but some thickets made only of sweet-briar and honeysuckle, and some wild vine amongst;[3] and the ground set with violets, strawberries, and primroses. For these are sweet, and prosper in the shade. And these to be in the heath, here and there, not in any order. I like also little heaps, in the nature of mole-hills (such as are in wild heaths), to be set, some with wild thyme; some with pinks; some with germander, that gives a good flower to the eye; some with periwinkle; some with violets; some with strawberries; some with cowslips; some with daisies; some with red roses; some with lilium convallium; some with sweet-williams red; some with bear's-foot:[4] and the like low flowers, being withal sweet[5] and sightly.[6] Part of which heaps are to be with standards[7] of little bushes pricked[8] upon their top, and part without. The standards to be roses; juniper; holly; barberries (but[9] here and there, because of the smell of their blossom); red currants; gooseberries; rosemary; bays; sweet-briar; and such like. But these standards to be kept with cutting, that they grow not out of course.*

For the side grounds, you are to fill them with variety of alleys, private,* to give a full shade, some of them, wheresoever the sun be. You are to frame[10] some of them likewise for shelter, that when the wind blows sharp, you may walk as in a gallery. And those alleys must be likewise hedged at both ends, to keep out the wind; and these closer alleys must be ever finely gravelled, and no grass, because of going wet.* In many of these alleys likewise, you are to set fruit-trees of all sorts; as well upon the walls as in ranges.[11] And this would[12] be generally observed, that the borders wherein you plant your fruit-trees be fair and large, and low, and not steep; and set with fine flowers, but thin and sparingly, lest they deceive[13] the trees. At the end of both the side grounds, I would have a mount of some pretty height, leaving the wall of the enclosure breast high, to look abroad into the fields.

---

1 project (also 'plot of ground')   2 arranged, ordered   3 intermixed
4 stinking hellebore   5 sweet-smelling   6 pleasant to look at
7 shrubs, trees standing upright   8 set, planted   9 only   10 ordain
11 ranks, rows   12 should   13 deprive of nutriment

For the main garden, I do not deny but there should be some fair alleys ranged on both sides, with fruit trees; and some pretty tufts of fruit trees, and arbours with seats, set in some decent order; but these to be by no means set too thick; but to leave the main garden so as it be not close, but the air open and free. For as for shade, I would have you rest upon[1] the alleys of the side grounds, there to walk, if you be disposed, in the heat of the year or day; but to make account[2] that the main garden is for the more temperate parts of the year; and in the heat of summer, for the morning and the evening, or overcast days.

For aviaries, I like them not, except they be of that largeness as they may be turfed,[3] and have living plants and bushes set in them; that the birds may have more scope,[4] and natural nestling, and that no foulness[5] appear in the floor of the aviary.

So I have made a platform[6] of a princely garden, partly by precept, partly by drawing, not a model,[7] but some general lines of it; and in this I have spared for no cost. But it is nothing for great princes, that for the most part taking advice with workmen,[8] with no less cost set their things together; and sometimes add statua's, and such things, for state and magnificence,[9] but nothing[10] to the true pleasure of a garden.

47. OF NEGOTIATING*

It is generally better to deal by speech than by letter; and by the mediation of a third than by a man's self.* Letters are good, when a man would draw[11] an answer by letter back again; or when it may serve for a man's justification afterwards to produce his own letter; or where it may be danger[12] to be interrupted, or heard by pieces.[13] To deal in person is good, when a man's face breedeth regard,[14] as commonly with inferiors; or in tender[15] cases, where a man's eye upon the countenance[16] of him with whom he speaketh may give him a direction how far to go; and generally, where a man will reserve to himself liberty either to disavow* or to expound.* In choice of instruments,[17] it is better to choose men of a plainer sort, that are like[18] to do that that is committed to them, and to report back again faithfully the success,[19] than those

---

1 keep to   2 consider   3 covered with grass-roots   4 can fly about more freely
5 dirt, ordure   6 plan, outline   7 strict pattern (graphic design to be followed in construction)   8 skilled craftsmen   9 ostentatious display
10 adding nothing   11 obtain, elicit   12 dangerous   13 incompletely
14 inspires respect   15 tricky, delicate   16 behaviour, reactions
17 go-betweens   18 likely   19 outcome (good or bad)

that are cunning to contrive out of other men's business somewhat to grace[1] themselves, and will help the matter in report for satisfaction sake.* Use also such persons as affect[2] the business wherein they are employed; for that quickeneth much;[3] and such as are fit for the matter; as bold men for expostulation,[4] fair-spoken men for persuasion, crafty[5] men for inquiry and observation, froward[6] and absurd[7] men for business that doth not well bear out[8] itself. Use also such as have been lucky, and prevailed[9] before in things wherein you have employed them; for that breeds confidence, and they will strive to maintain their prescription.[10] It is better to sound[11] a person with whom one deals afar off,[12] than to fall upon[13] the point at first; except you mean to surprise him by some short[14] question. It is better dealing with men in appetite,[15] than with those that are where they would be. If a man deal with another upon conditions,* the start or first performance[16] is all; which a man cannot reasonably demand, except either the nature of the thing be such, which must go before;* or else a man can persuade the other party[17] that he shall still need him in some other thing; or else that he* be counted the honester man. All practice[18] is to discover,[19] or to work.[20] Men discover themselves in trust, in passion, at unawares,* and of necessity, when they would have somewhat done and cannot find an apt pretext. If you would work any man, you must either know his nature and fashions,[21] and so lead him; or his ends, and so persuade him; or his weakness and disadvantages,[22] and so awe[23] him; or those that have interest in[24] him, and so govern him. In dealing with cunning persons, we must ever consider their ends, to interpret their speeches; and it is good to say little to them, and that which they least look for. In all negotiations of difficulty, a man may not look to sow and reap at once; but must prepare business, and so ripen it by degrees.

48. OF FOLLOWERS AND FRIENDS

Costly followers are not to be liked; lest while a man maketh his train* longer, he make his wings shorter. I reckon to be costly, not them alone

1 ingratiate 2 have a liking for 3 is efficacious 4 protest, complaint
5 astute 6 perverse, contrary 7 unreasonable 8 back up, confirm
9 succeeded 10 title, reputation 11 probe 12 indirectly 13 come to
14 brusque, unexpected 15 desirous of rising, ambitious 16 action performed
17 person 18 plotting 19 reveal the true nature of someone
20 influence, manipulate 21 habits 22 infirmities 23 influence by awe
24 are involved with

which charge[1] the purse, but which are wearisome and importune[2] in suits.[3] Ordinary followers ought to challenge[4] no higher conditions[5] than countenance,[6] recommendation, and protection from wrongs. Factious[7] followers are worse to be liked, which follow not upon affection to him with whom they range[8] themselves, but upon discontentment conceived against some other; whereupon commonly ensueth[9] that ill intelligence[10] that we many times see between great personages. Likewise glorious[11] followers, who make themselves as trumpets of the commendation of those they follow, are full of inconvenience; for they taint[12] business through want of secrecy; and they export honour from a man, and make him a return* in envy. There is a kind of followers likewise which are dangerous, being indeed espials;[13] which inquire the secrets of the house,* and bear tales of them to others. Yet such men, many times, are in great favour; for they are officious,[14] and commonly exchange tales.* The following by certain estates[15] of men, answerable[16] to that which a great person himself professeth (as of soldiers to him that hath been employed in the wars, and the like), hath ever been a thing civil,[17] and well taken even in monarchies; so[18] it be without too much pomp or popularity.[19] But the most honourable kind of following is to be followed as one that apprehendeth[20] to advance[21] virtue and desert[22] in all sorts of persons. And yet, where there is no eminent odds in sufficiency,* it is better to take with* the more passable,[23] than with the more able. And besides, to speak truth, in base[24] times active men are of more use than virtuous.[25] It is true that in government[26] it is good to use men of one rank equally: for to countenance some extraordinarily, is to make them insolent, and the rest discontent; because they may claim a due.[27] But contrariwise,[28] in favour,[29] to use men with much difference and election[30] is good; for it maketh the persons preferred more thankful, and the rest more officious: because all is of favour.* It is good discretion not to make too much[31] of any man at the first; because one cannot hold out[32] that proportion.[33] To be

---

1 burden   2 importunate   3 petitions, requests for favour   4 claim
5 treatment, favours   6 approval, moral support   7 partisan   8 ally
9 results   10 misunderstandings   11 boastful, ostentatious   12 spoil
13 spies   14 forward to do office   15 classes   16 corresponding
17 decent, orderly   18 provided   19 courting popular favour   20 studies, strives
21 promote, reward   22 merit   23 generally acceptable, tolerable
24 corrupt   25 able   26 normal employment, business   27 demand favours
as if by right   28 on the contrary   29 when it comes to distributing favours
30 discrimination, choice   31 take too much notice of; or 'treat favourably'
32 sustain   33 level of treatment

governed (as we call it) by one,* is not safe; for it shews softness,[1] and
gives a freedom to scandal and disreputation;[2] for those that would not
censure or speak ill of a man immediately,[3] will talk more boldly of
those that are so great with[4] them, and thereby wound their* honour.
Yet to be distracted[5] with many is worse; for it makes men to be of the
last impression,* and full of change. To take advice of some few friends
is ever honourable; for 'lookers-on many times see more than
gamesters';[6] and 'the vale best discovereth the hill'.* There is little
friendship in the world, and least of all between equals, which was
wont to be magnified.* That that is, is between superior and inferior,
whose fortunes may comprehend[7] the one the other.

49. Of Suitors

Many ill matters and projects* are undertaken;* and private suits do
putrefy* the public good. Many good matters are undertaken with bad
minds; I mean not only corrupt minds, but crafty minds, that intend
not performance.[8] Some embrace* suits, which never mean to deal[9] effectually in them; but if they see there may be life in the matter by some
other mean,* they will be content to win a thank, or take a second[10] reward, or at least to make use in the mean time of the suitor's hopes.
Some take hold of suits only for an occasion to cross[11] some other; or to
make[12] an information whereof they could not otherwise have apt pretext; without care what become of the suit when that turn is served; or,
generally, to make other men's business a kind of entertainment* to
bring in their own. Nay some undertake suits, with a full purpose to let
them fall; to the end[13] to gratify the adverse party or competitor. Surely
there is in some sort[14] a right in every suit; either a right in equity,[15] if it
be a suit of controversy;* or a right of desert,[16] if it be a suit of petition.*
If affection[17] lead a man to favour the wrong side in justice, let him
rather use his countenance[18] to compound[19] the matter than to carry[20]
it. If affection lead a man to favour the less worthy in desert, let him do
it without depraving or disabling* the better deserver. In suits which a

1 indulgence   2 discredit   3 directly   4 acquainted with, friendly
5 receive conflicting advice   6 gamblers   7 include, reciprocally depend on
8 doing what they promised   9 behave, act   10 secondary, less important
11 thwart, obstruct   12 gain, obtain   13 in order   14 measure
15 moral justice   16 merit   17 liking, partiality   18 influence
19 settle by agreement, compromise   20 pursue, prosecute

man doth not well understand, it is good to refer them to some friend of trust and judgment, that may report whether he may deal[1] in them with honour: but let him choose well his referendaries,[2] for else he may be led by the nose. Suitors are so distasted[3] with delays and abuses,[4] that plain dealing in denying to deal in suits at first,[5] and reporting the success barely,* and in challenging[6] no more thanks than one hath deserved, is grown not only honourable but also gracious.[7] In suits of favour,* the first coming[8] ought to take little place:[9] so far forth consideration may be had of his* trust, that if intelligence[10] of the matter could not otherwise have been had but by him, advantage be not taken of the note,[11] but the party* left to his other means; and in some sort recompensed for his discovery.[12] To be ignorant of the value[13] of a suit is simplicity;[14] as well as to be ignorant of the right[15] thereof is want of conscience. Secrecy in suits is a great mean[16] of obtaining; for voicing[17] them to be in forwardness[18] may discourage some kind of suitors, but doth quicken and awake others. But timing of the suit is the principal. Timing, I say, not only in respect of the person that should grant it, but in respect of those which are like[19] to cross it. Let a man, in the choice of his mean,[20] rather choose the fittest mean than the greatest mean; and rather them that deal in certain[21] things, than those that are general. The reparation of a denial[22] is sometimes equal to the first grant;[23] if a man shew himself neither dejected nor discontented. *Iniquum petas ut aequum feras*,* is a good rule, where a man hath strength of favour:* but otherwise a man were better rise in his suit;[24] for he that would have ventured at first to have lost the suitor, will not in the conclusion lose both the suitor and his own former favour. Nothing is thought so easy a request to a great person, as his letter; and yet, if it be not in a good cause, it is so much out of his reputation. There are no worse instruments than these general contrivers* of suits; for they are but a kind of poison and infection to public proceedings.

1 act, take part   2 referees, advisers   3 disgusted, offended   4 deceits
5 from the outset   6 claiming   7 agreeable, deserving thanks
8 priority in presenting one's petition   9 have little effect, not give precedence
10 knowledge   11 information   12 disclosure of information
13 relevance, import   14 naivety, stupidity   15 justice   16 means, condition
17 divulging   18 preparation   19 likely   20 go-between, instrument
21 definite, specific   22 reversal of a refusal   23 what was originally requested
24 gradually increase his requests

50. Of Studies

Studies serve for delight, for ornament, and for ability.* Their chief
use for delight, is in privateness and retiring;* for ornament, is in discourse;* and for ability, is in the judgment and disposition of business.* For expert men can execute, and perhaps judge of particulars,
one by one; but the general counsels,[1] and the plots and marshalling*
of affairs, come best from those that are learned. To spend too much
time in studies is sloth;* to use them too much for ornament, is affectation; to make judgment wholly by their rules, is the humour of a
scholar.* They perfect nature, and are perfected by experience: for
natural abilities are like natural plants, that need proyning[2] by study;
and studies themselves do give forth directions too much at large,* except they be bounded in by experience. Crafty[3] men contemn* studies,
simple* men admire[4] them, and wise[5] men use them; for they teach not
their own use;* but that is a wisdom without them, and above them,*
won by observation.

Read not to contradict and confute; nor to believe and take for
granted; nor to find talk and discourse; but to weigh and consider.
Some books are to be tasted, others to be swallowed, and some few to
be chewed and digested; that is, some books are to be read only in parts;
others to be read, but not curiously;[6] and some few to be read wholly,
and with diligence and attention. Some books also may be read by
deputy,* and extracts made of them by others; but that would[7] be only
in the less important arguments,[8] and the meaner sort of books; else
distilled books* are like common distilled waters,* flashy[9] things.

Reading maketh a full man; conference[10] a ready man; and writing
an exact man. And therefore, if a man write little, he had need have a
great memory; if he confer[11] little, he had need have a present wit;[12]
and if he read little, he had need have much cunning, to seem to know
that he doth not. Histories make men wise; poets witty;[13] the mathematics subtile; natural philosophy deep; moral grave; logic and
rhetoric able to contend. *Abeunt studia in mores.** Nay there is no
stond[14] or impediment in the wit,[15] but may be wrought out[16] by fit
studies: like as diseases of the body may have appropriate exercises.

1 arrangements   2 pruning, cultivating   3 cunning   4 wonder at
5 prudent, judicious   6 with minute attention   7 should   8 matters
9 insipid, tasteless   10 consultation   11 consult   12 quick, alert mind
13 ingenious, full of ideas   14 obstruction, obstacle   15 mind   16 eliminated

Bowling[1] is good for the stone and reins;* shooting[2] for the lungs and breast; gentle walking for the stomach; riding for the head; and the like. So if a man's wit be wandering, let him study the mathematics; for in demonstrations,[3] if his wit be called away never so little, he must begin again. If his wit be not apt to distinguish or find differences,* let him study the schoolmen;[4] for they are *cymini sectores.** If he be not apt to beat over[5] matters, and to call up one thing to prove[6] and illustrate[7] another, let him study the lawyers' cases.* So every defect of the mind may have a special receipt.[8]

51. OF FACTION*

Many have an opinion not wise,* that for a prince to govern his estate,[9] or for a great person to govern his proceedings,[10] according to the respect of[11] factions, is a principal part of policy;* whereas contrariwise,[12] the chiefest wisdom is either in ordering[13] those things which are general, and wherein men of several[14] factions do nevertheless agree; or in dealing with correspondence to* particular persons, one by one. But I say not that the consideration of factions is to be neglected. Mean men, in their rising, must adhere;* but great men, that have strength in themselves, were better to maintain themselves indifferent[15] and neutral. Yet even in beginners, to adhere so moderately, as he be a man of the one faction which is most passable[16] with the other, commonly giveth best way.[17] The lower and weaker faction is the firmer in conjunction;[18] and it is often seen that a few that are stiff[19] do tire out a greater number that are more moderate. When one of the factions is extinguished,[20] the remaining subdivideth; as the faction between Lucullus* and the rest of the nobles of the senate (which they called *Optimates*)* held out awhile against the faction of Pompey and Caesar; but when the senate's authority was pulled down, Caesar and Pompey soon after brake.* The faction or party of Antonius and Octavianus Caesar against Brutus and Cassius, held out likewise for a time; but when Brutus and Cassius were overthrown, then soon after

1 playing bowls   2 archery   3 mathematical proofs
4 medieval 'scholastic' philosophers   5 reflect upon, compare
6 test (by comparison)   7 clarify   8 recipe, treatment   9 state   10 actions
11 considering the wishes of   12 on the contrary   13 disposing, executing
14 distinct, different   15 impartial   16 acceptable
17 opens the best path (to office)   18 cohesion   19 determined   20 eliminated

Antonius and Octavianus brake and subdivided. These examples are of wars, but the same holdeth in private factions. And therefore those that are seconds[1] in factions do many times, when the faction subdivideth, prove principals; but many times also they prove ciphers[2] and cashiered:[3] for many a man's strength is in opposition; and when that faileth he groweth out of use.[4] It is commonly seen that men once placed[5] take in with the contrary faction to that by which they enter:[6] thinking belike[7] that they have the first sure, and now are ready for a new purchase. The traitor in faction lightly goeth away with it;* for when matters have stuck long in balancing,[8] the winning of some one man casteth* them, and he getteth all the thanks. The even carriage[9] between two factions proceedeth not always of moderation, but of a trueness to a man's self,[10] with end[11] to make use of both. Certainly in Italy they hold it a little suspect in popes, when they have often in their mouth *Padre commune*:* and take it to be a sign of one that meaneth to refer* all to the greatness of his own house. Kings had need beware how they side[12] themselves, and make themselves as of a faction or party; for leagues within the state are ever pernicious to monarchies: for they raise[13] an obligation paramount[14] to obligation of sovereignty, and make the king *tanquam unus ex nobis*;* as was to be seen in the League of France.* When factions are carried too high and too violently,* it is a sign of weakness in princes;* and much to the prejudice both of their authority and business. The motions of factions under kings ought to be like the motions (as the astronomers speak) of the inferior orbs, which may have their proper[15] motions, but yet still are quietly carried by the higher motion of *primum mobile*.*

52. Of Ceremonies and Respects*

He that is only real,* had need have exceeding great parts of virtue;[16] as the stone had need to be rich that is set without foil.* But if a man mark it well, it is in praise and commendation of men as it is in gettings and gains: for the proverb is true, that 'light gains make heavy purses'; for light gains come thick,[17] whereas great come but now and then. So

1 secondary figures   2 nonentities   3 dismissed in disgrace   4 practice
5 settled in place, position   6 begin   7 probably   8 equilibrium
9 impartial proceeding   10 loyalty to one's own interests   11 intention
12 take sides, align   13 give rise to   14 superior   15 own, individual
16 merits   17 frequently

it is true that small matters win great commendation, because they are continually in use and in note: whereas the occasion of any great virtue cometh but on festivals.[1] Therefore it doth much add to a man's reputation, and is (as queen Isabella* said) 'like perpetual letters commendatory',* to have good forms.[2] To attain[3] them it almost sufficeth not to despise them; for so[4] shall a man observe them in others; and let him trust himself with the rest.[5] For if he labour too much to express them, he shall lose their grace; which is to be natural and unaffected.* Some men's behaviour is like a verse, wherein every syllable is measured; how can a man comprehend[6] great matters, that breaketh[7] his mind too much to small observations?

Not to use ceremonies at all, is to teach others not to use them again; and so diminisheth respect to himself; especially they be not to be omitted to strangers and formal natures; but the dwelling upon them, and exalting them above the moon, is not only tedious, but doth diminish the faith and credit of him that speaks. And certainly there is a kind of conveying[8] of effectual and imprinting[9] passages[10] amongst compliments,[11] which is of singular use, if a man can hit upon it. Amongst a man's peers a man shall be sure of familiarity; and therefore it is good a little to keep state.[12] Amongst a man's inferiors one shall be sure of reverence; and therefore it is good a little to be familiar. He that is too much in anything, so that he giveth another occasion of satiety, maketh himself cheap. To apply[13] one's self to others is good; so it be with demonstration that a man doth it upon regard,[14] and not upon facility.[15] It is a good precept generally in seconding[16] another, yet to add somewhat of one's own: as if you will grant his opinion, let it be with some distinction; if you will follow his motion,[17] let it be with condition; if you allow his counsel,[18] let it be with alleging further reason.

Men had need beware how they be too perfect[19] in compliments; for be they never so sufficient[20] otherwise, their enviers will be sure to give them that attribute, to the disadvantage of their greater virtues. It is loss also in business[21] to be too full of respects,[22] or to be curious[23] in observing times and opportunities.* Salomon saith, 'He that considereth the wind shall not sow, and he that looketh to the clouds shall not

1 rarely   2 manners   3 acquire   4 provided that
5 practising them himself   6 deal with   7 trains, accustoms   8 insinuating
9 striking   10 phrases   11 courtly flattery   12 be a bit formal, dignified
13 adapt, accommodate   14 out of personal respect, affection   15 pliancy
16 agreeing with   17 proposal   18 approve of his advice   19 too meticulous
20 capable   21 affairs, practical life   22 ceremonious   23 precise

reap'.* A wise man will make more opportunities than he finds. Men's behaviour should be like their apparel, not too strait[1] or point device,[2] but free for exercise or motion.

53. OF PRAISE

Praise is the reflection of virtue.* But it is as[3] the glass or body which giveth the reflection. If it be from the common people, it is commonly false and naught;[4] and rather followeth vain[5] persons than virtuous. For the common people understand not many excellent virtues. The lowest virtues draw praise from them; the middle virtues work in them astonishment or admiration; but of the highest virtues they have no sense[6] or perceiving at all. But shews,[7] and *species virtutibus similes*,* serve best with them. Certainly fame is like a river, that beareth up things light and swoln,* and drowns things weighty and solid. But if persons of quality[8] and judgment[9] concur, then it is (as the Scripture saith), *Nomen bonum instar unguenti fragrantis*.* It filleth all round about, and will not easily away. For the odours of ointments[10] are more durable than those of flowers.

There be so many false points of praise, that a man may justly hold it a suspect. Some praises proceed merely of flattery; and if he be an ordinary flatterer, he will have certain common attributes, which may serve every man; if he be a cunning flatterer, he will follow the arch-flatterer,* which is a man's self; and wherein a man thinketh best of himself, therein the flatterer will uphold[11] him most: but if he be an impudent flatterer, look[12] wherein a man is conscious to himself that he is most defective, and is most out of countenance* in himself, that will the flatterer entitle[13] him to perforce,[14] *spreta conscientia*.* Some praises come of good wishes and respects,[15] which is a form[16] due in civility to kings and great persons, *laudando praecipere*;* when by telling men what they are, they represent to them what they should be.* Some men are praised maliciously to their hurt, thereby to stir envy and jealousy towards them; *pessimum genus inimicorum laudantium*;* insomuch as it was a proverb amongst the Grecians,* that 'he that was praised to

1 tight, constricting   2 very precisely fashioned   3 it varies with, depends on
4 worthless   5 conceited, superficial   6 capacity, mental apprehension
7 false appearances   8 rank, high status   9 wisdom, experience   10 perfumes
11 endorse, agree with   12 watch out   13 impute   14 of necessity
15 paying compliments   16 mode of behaviour

his hurt, should have a push rise upon his nose'; as we say, that 'a blister will rise upon one's tongue that tells a lie'. Certainly moderate praise, used with opportunity,[1] and not vulgar, is that which doth the good. Salomon saith, 'He that praiseth his friend aloud, rising early, it shall be to him no better than a curse'.* Too much magnifying of man or matter doth irritate[2] contradiction, and procure envy and scorn.

To praise a man's self cannot be decent,[3] except it be in rare cases; but to praise a man's office or profession, he* may do it with good grace, and with a kind of magnanimity.[4] The Cardinals of Rome, which are theologues, and friars, and schoolmen, have a phrase of notable[5] contempt and scorn towards civil business:* for they call all temporal business of wars, embassages,[6] judicature, and other employments, *sbirrerie*,[7] which is 'under-sheriffries';[8] as if they were but matters for under-sheriffs and catch-poles:[9] though many times those under-sheriffries do more good than their high speculations. St Paul, when he boasts of himself, he doth oft interlace,[10] 'I speak like a fool';* but speaking of his calling, he saith, *magnificabo apostolatum meum*.*

54. OF VAIN-GLORY*

It was prettily devised* of Aesop; 'the fly sat upon the axle-tree of the chariot wheel, and said, "What a dust do I raise!" ' So are there some vain[11] persons, that whatsoever goeth alone[12] or moveth upon greater means,[13] if they have never so little hand in it, they think it is they that carry[14] it. They that are glorious* must needs be factious;[15] for all bravery stands upon comparisons.* They must needs be violent, to make good their own vaunts.[16] Neither can they be secret, and therefore not effectual;* but according to the French proverb, *Beaucoup de bruit, peu de fruit*; 'Much bruit, little fruit'. Yet certainly there is use of this quality in civil affairs. Where there is an opinion and fame to be created either of virtue or greatness, these men are good trumpeters. Again, as Titus Livius noteth in the case of Antiochus and the Aetolians, 'There are sometimes great effects of cross[17] lies';* as if a man that negotiates between two princes, to draw them to join in a war against the third,

1 at the right time   2 provoke   3 proper   4 generosity, nobility
5 remarkable   6 diplomatic activities   7 trivial affairs
8 bailiffs and constables   9 petty officers of justice   10 insert
11 empty-headed, silly   12 by its own motion   13 superior power
14 perform   15 quarrelsome   16 boasts   17 reciprocal, interchanged

doth extol the forces of either[1] of them above measure, the one to the other: and sometimes he that deals between man and man, raiseth his own credit with both, by pretending greater interest[2] than he hath in either. And in these and the like kinds, it often falls out that somewhat is produced of nothing;* for lies are sufficient to breed opinion,[3] and opinion brings on substance.*

In military commanders and soldiers, vain-glory is an essential point;[4] for as iron sharpens iron,* so by glory one courage sharpeneth another. In cases of great enterprise upon charge and adventure,* a composition[5] of glorious natures doth put life into business; and those that are of solid and sober natures have more of the ballast than of the sail.* In fame of learning, the flight* will be slow without some feathers of ostentation. *Qui de contemnenda gloria libros scribunt, nomen suum inscribunt.** Socrates, Aristotle, Galen,* were men full of ostentation. Certainly vain-glory helpeth to perpetuate a man's memory; and virtue was never so beholding[6] to human nature, as it received his due at the second hand.* Neither had the fame of Cicero, Seneca, Plinius Secundus,* borne her age so well, if it had not been joined with some vanity in themselves; like unto varnish, that makes ceilings[7] not only shine but last.

But all this while, when I speak of vain-glory, I mean not of that property[8] that Tacitus doth attribute to Mucianus; *Omnium, quae dixerat feceratque, arte quadam ostentator:** for that proceeds not of vanity, but of natural magnanimity[9] and discretion;[10] and in some persons is not only comely, but gracious. For excusations,[11] cessions,[12] modesty itself well governed, are but arts of ostentation. And amongst those arts there is none better than that which Plinius Secundus speaketh of, which is to be liberal[13] of praise and commendation to others, in that wherein a man's self hath any perfection. For saith Pliny very wittily,[14] 'In commending another you do yourself right; for he that you commend is either superior to you in that you commend, or inferior. If he be inferior, if he be to be commended, you much more; if he be superior, if he be not to be commended, you much less'.*

Glorious men are the scorn of wise men, the admiration[15] of fools, the idols of parasites,* and the slaves of their own vaunts.

1 each   2 influence over   3 reputation   4 characteristic   5 combination
6 indebted   7 panelling, wainscotting   8 characteristic   9 great-heartedness
10 sagacity, judgement   11 excuses   12 making concessions, being compliant
13 generous   14 ingeniously   15 objects of scorn . . . admiration

55. OF HONOUR AND REPUTATION

The winning* of Honour is but the revealing[1] of a man's virtue and worth without disadvantage.[2] For some in their actions do woo and affect[3] honour and reputation; which sort of men are commonly much talked of, but inwardly[4] little admired. And some, contrariwise, darken their virtue in the shew of it; so as they be undervalued in opinion. If a man perform that which hath not been attempted before; or attempted and given over;[5] or hath been achieved, but not with so good circumstance;* he shall purchase[6] more honour, than by effecting a matter of greater difficulty or virtue,[7] wherein he is but a follower.[8] If a man so temper his actions, as in some one of them he doth content every faction or combination[9] of people, the music will be the fuller. A man is an ill husband[10] of his honour, that entereth into any action, the failing wherein may disgrace him more than the carrying of it through can honour him.* Honour that is gained and broken* upon another* hath the quickest reflexion, like diamonds cut with facets.* And therefore let a man contend[11] to excel any competitors of his in honour, in outshooting them, if he can, in their own bow.* Discreet followers and servants help much to reputation. *Omnis fama a domesticis emanat.** Envy, which is the canker[12] of honour, is best extinguished by declaring[13] a man's self in his ends rather to seek merit than fame; and by attributing a man's successes rather to divine Providence and felicity,[14] than to his own virtue or policy.[15] The true marshalling[16] of the degrees of sovereign honour are these. In the first place are *conditores imperiorum*,* founders of states and commonwealths;[17] such as were Romulus, Cyrus, Caesar, Ottoman, Ismael.* In the second place are *legislatores*, lawgivers; which are also called 'second founders', or *perpetui principes*,* because they govern by their ordinances after they are gone; such were Lycurgus, Solon, Justinian, Eadgar, Alphonsus of Castile, the wise, that made the *Siete partidas*.* In the third place are *liberatores*, or *salvatores*,* such as compound[18] the long miseries of civil wars, or deliver their countries from servitude of strangers or tyrants; as Augustus Caesar, Vespasianus, Aurelianus, Theodoricus, King Henry

1 recognition   2 injustices   3 pretend to, counterfeit   4 in private
5 abandoned   6 acquire   7 ability   8 imitator   9 group   10 manager
11 strive, exert himself   12 an eating sore, corruption   13 demonstrating
14 good fortune   15 astuteness   16 hierarchy, disposition   17 republics
18 settle, put an end to

the Seventh of England, King Henry the Fourth* of France. In the
fourth place are *propagatores* or *propugnatores imperii*;* such as in honourable wars enlarge their territories, or make noble defence against
invaders. And in the last place are *patres patriae*,* which reign justly,
and make the times good wherein they live. Both which last kinds need
no examples, they are in such number. Degrees of honour in subjects
are, first *participes curarum*,* those upon whom princes do discharge
the greatest weight of their affairs; their 'right hands', as we call them.
The next are *duces belli*,* great leaders; such as are princes' lieutenants,[1] and do them notable services in the wars. The third are *gratiosi*, favourites; such as exceed not this scantling,[2] to be solace to the
sovereign, and harmless to the people. And the fourth, *negotiis pares*;*
such as have great places under princes, and execute their places[3] with
sufficiency.[4] There is an honour, likewise, which may be ranked
amongst the greatest, which happeneth rarely; that is, of such as
sacrifice themselves to death or danger for the good of their country; as
was M. Regulus,* and the two Decii.*

56. OF JUDICATURE

Judges ought to remember that their office is *jus dicere*, and not *jus
dare*;* to interpret law, and not to make law, or give law. Else will it be
like the authority claimed by the church of Rome, which under pretext
of exposition of Scripture doth not stick[5] to add and alter; and to pronounce[6] that which they do not find; and by shew of antiquity to introduce novelty.* Judges ought to be more learned than witty,[7] more
reverend than plausible,* and more advised[8] than confident. Above all
things, integrity is their portion and proper virtue. 'Cursed' (saith the
law) 'is he that removeth the landmark'.* The mislayer[9] of a mere-
stone[10] is to blame. But it is the unjust judge that is the capital[11] remover of landmarks, when he defineth amiss[12] of lands and property.
One foul sentence* doth more hurt than many foul examples. For these
do but corrupt the stream, the other corrupteth the fountain. So saith
Salomon, *Fons turbatus, et vena corrupta, est justus cadens in causa sua*

---

1 second-in-command   2 measure, limit   3 duties   4 ability   5 scruple
6 give authoritative utterance   7 ingenious   8 deliberate, acting on reflection
9 one who misplaces   10 boundary mark (recording land-ownership)   11 chief
12 gives an erroneous judgement

coram adversario.* The office of judges may have reference* unto the parties that sue,* unto the advocates that plead, unto the clerks and ministers of justice underneath them, and to the sovereign or state[1] above them.

First, for the causes* or parties that sue. 'There be' (saith the Scripture) 'that turn judgment into wormwood';* and surely there be also that turn it into vinegar; for injustice maketh it bitter, and delays make it sour. The principal duty of a judge is to suppress force and fraud;* whereof force is the more pernicious when it is open, and fraud when it is close[2] and disguised. Add thereto contentious suits,* which ought to be spewed out, as the surfeit[3] of courts. A judge ought to prepare his way to a just sentence, as God useth to prepare his way, by raising valleys and taking down hills:* so when there appeareth on either side an high hand,[4] violent prosecution,* cunning advantages taken, combination,[5] power, great counsel,* then is the virtue of a judge seen, to make inequality equal; that he may plant his judgment as upon an even ground. *Qui fortiter emungit, elicit sanguinem*;* and where the wine-press is hard wrought,[6] it yields a harsh wine, that tastes of the grape-stone. Judges must beware of hard constructions[7] and strained inferences; for there is no worse torture* than the torture of laws. Specially in case of laws penal, they ought to have care that that which was meant for terror be not turned into rigour;* and that they bring not upon the people that shower whereof the Scripture speaketh, *Pluet super eos laqueos*;* for penal laws pressed are a 'shower of snares'[8] upon the people. Therefore let penal laws, if they have been sleepers of long,* or if they be grown unfit for the present time, be by wise judges confined[9] in the execution: *Judicis officium est, ut res, ita tempora rerum*,* &c. In causes of life and death, judges ought (as far as the law permitteth) in justice* to remember mercy; and to cast a severe eye upon the example,[10] but a merciful eye upon the person.

Secondly, for the advocates and counsel[11] that plead. Patience and gravity of hearing is an essential part of justice; and an overspeaking* judge is no well-tuned cymbal.* It is no grace to a judge first to find* that which he might have heard in due time from the bar;* or to show quickness of conceit[12] in cutting off evidence or counsel too short; or to

---

1 monarchy or republic   2 cunningly concealed   3 overeating, causing disgust
4 overbearing use of authority   5 conspiracy   6 worked too vigorously
7 extreme interpretations   8 traps   9 restricted   10 deed, act
11 advocate for the defence   12 understanding

prevent[1] information by questions, though pertinent. The parts[2] of a judge in hearing are four: to direct the evidence;* to moderate length, repetition, or impertinency[3] of speech; to recapitulate, select, and collate the material points of that which hath been said; and to give the rule* or sentence. Whatsoever is above these is too much; and proceedeth either of glory[4] and willingness[5] to speak, or of impatience to hear, or of shortness of memory, or of want of a staid and equal[6] attention. It is a strange thing to see that the boldness of advocates should prevail with judges; whereas they* should imitate God, in whose seat they sit; who 'represseth the presumptuous, and giveth grace to the modest'.* But it is more strange, that judges should have noted[7] favourites; which cannot but cause multiplication of fees,[8] and suspicion of bye-ways.[9] There is due from the judge to the advocate some commendation and gracing,[10] where causes are well handled and fair pleaded; especially towards the side which obtaineth[11] not; for that upholds in the client the reputation of his counsel, and beats down in him the conceit[12] of his cause. There is likewise due to the public a civil[13] reprehension of advocates, where there appeareth cunning counsel, gross neglect, slight[14] information, indiscreet pressing,* or an overbold defence. And let not the counsel at the bar chop[15] with the judge, nor wind himself into the handling of the cause anew after the judge hath declared his sentence; but on the other side, let not the judge meet the cause half way, nor give occasion for the party to say his counsel or proofs were not heard.

Thirdly, for that that concerns clerks and ministers.* The place of justice is an hallowed place; and therefore not only the bench, but the foot-pace* and precincts and purprise* thereof, ought to be preserved without scandal and corruption. For certainly 'Grapes' (as the Scripture saith) 'will not be gathered of thorns or thistles';* neither can justice yield her fruit with sweetness amongst the briars and brambles of catching and polling* clerks and ministers. The attendance[16] of courts is subject to four bad instruments. First, certain persons that are sowers of suits;* which make the court swell, and the country pine.[17] The second sort is of those that engage courts in quarrels of

---

1 anticipate   2 tasks   3 irrelevance   4 vainglory, vanity   5 wishfulness
6 steady, uniform   7 notorious   8 bribes   9 secret ways; devious influences
10 compliment   11 attains the victory   12 high evaluation; but also 'illusion'
13 discreet   14 insufficient, insubstantial   15 bandy words, dispute
16 administration of justice   17 dwindle, starve

jurisdiction,* and are not truly *amici curiae*,* but *parasiti curiae*,* in puffing a court up beyond her bounds, for their own scraps[1] and advantage. The third sort is of those that may be accounted the left hands of courts; persons that are full of nimble and sinister* tricks and shifts, whereby they pervert[2] the plain and direct courses of courts, and bring justice into oblique lines and labyrinths. And the fourth is the poller* and exacter of fees; which justifies the common resemblance[3] of the courts of justice to the bush* whereunto while the sheep flies for defence in weather,* he is sure to lose part of his fleece. On the other side, an ancient clerk, skilful in precedents, wary in proceeding, and understanding in the business[4] of the court, is an excellent finger[5] of a court; and doth many times point the way to the judge himself.

Fourthly, for that which may concern the sovereign and estate. Judges ought above all to remember the conclusion of the Roman Twelve Tables;* *Salus populi suprema lex*;* and to know that laws, except they be in order to that end,* are but things captious,[6] and oracles* not well inspired. Therefore it is an happy thing in a state when kings and states[7] do often consult with judges; and again when judges do often consult with the king and state: the one, when there is matter of law intervenient[8] in business of state;* the other, when there is some consideration of state intervenient in matter of law. For many times the things deduced[9] to judgment may be *meum* and *tuum*,* when the reason[10] and consequence thereof may trench to point of estate:* I call matter of estate, not only the parts[11] of sovereignty, but whatsoever introduceth any great alteration[12] or dangerous precedent; or concerneth manifestly any great portion of people. And let no man weakly conceive that just laws and true policy* have any antipathy;[13] for they are like the spirits* and sinews, that one moves with the other. Let judges also remember, that Salomon's throne was supported by lions* on both sides: let them be lions, but yet lions under the throne; being circumspect[14] that they do not check or oppose any points of sovereignty. Let not judges also be so ignorant of their own right, as to think there is not left to them, as a principal part of their office, a wise use and application of laws. For they may remember what the apostle saith of a greater law than theirs; *Nos scimus quia lex bona est, modo quis ea utatur legitime*.*

---

1 petty gains   2 divert   3 comparison   4 proceeding   5 sign-post
6 misleading   7 'estates of the realm' (*SOED*), or civic authorities   8 intervening
9 brought down   10 principle   11 rights, prerogative   12 innovation
13 incompatibility   14 attentive

57. Of Anger

To seek to extinguish Anger utterly is but a bravery[1] of the Stoics.* We have better oracles: 'Be angry, but sin not. Let not the sun go down upon your anger'.* Anger must be limited and confined both in race[2] and in time. We will first speak how the natural inclination and habit[3] to be angry may be attempered* and calmed. Secondly, how the particular motions of anger may be repressed, or at least refrained from doing mischief. Thirdly, how to raise anger or appease anger in another.

For the first; there is no other way but to meditate and ruminate well upon the effects of anger, how it troubles man's life. And the best time to do this, is to look back upon anger when the fit is throughly[4] over. Seneca saith well, that 'anger is like ruin, which breaks itself upon that it falls'.* The Scripture exhorteth us 'To possess our souls in patience'.* Whosoever is out of patience, is out of possession of his soul.* Men must not turn bees;

> ... *animasque in vulnere ponunt.**

Anger is certainly a kind of baseness; as it appears well in the weakness of those subjects in whom it reigns; children, women, old folks, sick folks.* Only men must beware[5] that they carry their anger rather with scorn* than with fear; so that they may seem rather to be above the injury than below it; which is a thing easily done, if a man will give law to himself in it.*

For the second point; the causes and motives of anger are chiefly three.* First, to be too sensible[6] of hurt; for no man is angry that feels not himself hurt; and therefore tender and delicate persons must needs be oft angry; they have so many things to trouble them, which more robust natures have little sense of. The next is, the apprehension and construction[7] of the injury offered to be, in the circumstances thereof, full of contempt: for contempt is that which putteth an edge upon anger, as much or more than the hurt itself.* And therefore when men are ingenious in[8] picking out circumstances[9] of contempt, they do kindle their anger much. Lastly, opinion of the touch* of a man's reputation doth multiply and sharpen anger. Wherein the remedy is, that a

---

1 ostentatious attempt   2 course, scope   3 mental disposition or constitution
4 completely   5 ensure   6 susceptible   7 interpretation
8 have a talent for   9 manifestations

man should have, as Consalvo* was wont to say, *telam honoris cras-siorem*. But in all refrainings of anger, it is the best remedy to win time;* and to make a man's self believe that the opportunity of his revenge is not yet come, but that he foresees a time for it; and so to still himself in the mean time, and reserve* it.

To contain¹ anger from mischief, though it take hold of a man, there be two things whereof you must have special caution. The one, of extreme bitterness of words, especially if they be aculeate* and proper; for *communia maledicta*∗ are nothing so much;* and again, that in anger a man reveal no secrets; for that makes him not fit for society. The other, that you do not peremptorily break off, in any business,² in a fit of anger; but howsoever you shew bitterness, do not act anything that is not revocable.

For raising and appeasing anger in another; it is done chiefly by choosing of times, when men are frowardest³ and worst disposed, to incense them. Again, by gathering (as was touched before) all that you can find out to aggravate the contempt. And the two remedies are by the contraries. The former to take good times, when first to relate to a man an angry business;* for the first impression is much; and the other is, to sever, as much as may be, the construction⁴ of the injury from the point of contempt;* imputing it to misunderstanding, fear, passion, or what you will.

58. OF VICISSITUDE* OF THINGS

Salomon saith, 'There is no new thing upon the earth'.* So that as Plato had an imagination,⁵ that 'all knowledge was but remembrance';* so Salomon giveth his sentence,⁶ that 'all novelty is but oblivion'.* Whereby you may see that the river of Lethe* runneth as well above ground as below. There is an abstruse astrologer* that saith, 'if it were not for two things that are constant (the one is, that the fixed stars ever stand at like distance one from another, and never come nearer together, nor go further asunder; the other, that the diurnal motion perpetually keepeth time), no individual would last one moment'. Certain it is, that the matter* is in a perpetual flux, and never at a stay.⁷ The great winding-sheets,⁸ that bury all things in oblivion, are two: deluges and earthquakes. As for conflagrations and great droughts, they do not

1 restrain   2 dealings, affairs   3 most recalcitrant   4 interpretation
5 conjecture   6 judgement   7 standstill   8 sheets used to wrap corpses

merely[1] dispeople[2] and destroy. Phaëton's car* went but a day. And the three years' drought in the time of Elias* was but particular,[3] and left people alive. As for the great burnings by lightnings, which are often in the West Indies,* they are but narrow.[4] But in the other two destructions, by deluge and earthquake, it is further to be noted, that the remnant of people which hap to be reserved,* are commonly ignorant and mountainous* people, that can give no account of the time past; so that the oblivion is all one* as if none had been left. If you consider well of the people of the West Indies, it is very probable that they are a newer or a younger people than the people of the old world.* And it is much more likely that the destruction that hath heretofore[5] been there, was not by earthquakes (as the Egyptian priest told Solon concerning the island of Atlantis, that 'it was swallowed by an earthquake'),* but rather that it was desolated by a particular deluge. For earthquakes are seldom* in those parts. But on the other side, they have such pouring rivers, as the rivers of Asia and Africk and Europe are but brooks to them. Their Andes likewise, or mountains, are far higher than those with us; whereby it seems that the remnants of generation of men* were in such a particular deluge saved. As for the observation that Machiavel* hath, that the jealousy of sects doth much extinguish the memory of things; traducing Gregory the Great,* that he did what in him lay to extinguish all heathen antiquities; I do not find that those zeals[6] do any great effects, nor last long; as it appeared in the succession of Sabinian,* who did revive the former antiquities.

The vicissitude or mutations in the Superior Globe* are no fit matter for this present argument. It may be, Plato's great year,* if the world should last so long, would have some effect; not in renewing the state of like* individuals (for that is the fume[7] of those that conceive the celestial bodies have more accurate influences* upon these things below than indeed they have), but in gross.[8] Comets, out of question, have likewise power and effect over the gross and mass of things; but they are rather gazed upon, and waited upon[9] in their journey, than wisely observed in their effects; specially in their respective[10] effects; that is, what kind of comet, for magnitude, colour, version* of the beams, placing[11] in the region[12] of heaven, or lasting, produceth what kind of effects.

---

1 entirely 2 depopulate 3 limited to one region 4 limited 5 formerly
6 excesses of zeal; fanaticism 7 smoke, empty fantasy 8 in general terms
9 watched, observed 10 particular 11 position 12 zone

There is a toy[1] which I have heard, and I would not have it given over, but waited upon* a little. They say it is observed in the Low Countries (I know not in what part) that every five and thirty years the same kind and suit[2] of years and weathers comes about again; as great frosts, great wet, great droughts, warm winters, summers with little heat, and the like; and they call it the *Prime*.* It is a thing I do the rather mention, because, computing backwards, I have found some concurrence.[3]

But to leave these points of nature, and to come to men. The greatest vicissitude of things amongst men, is the vicissitude of sects and religions. For those orbs[4] rule in men's minds most. The true religion is 'built upon the rock';* the rest are tossed upon the waves of time. To speak therefore of the causes of new sects; and to give some counsel concerning them, as far as the weakness of human judgment can give stay* to so great revolutions.[5]

When the religion formerly received[6] is rent by discords; and when the holiness of the professors[7] of religion is decayed and full of scandal; and withal[8] the times be stupid, ignorant, and barbarous; you may doubt[9] the springing up of a new sect; if then also there should arise any extravagant and strange spirit to make himself author thereof. All which points held when Mahomet* published his law. If a new sect have not two properties,[10] fear it not; for it will not spread. The one is, the supplanting or the opposing of authority[11] established; for nothing is more popular[12] than that. The other is, the giving licence to pleasures and a voluptuous life. For as for speculative* heresies, (such as were in ancient times the Arians,* and now the Arminians),* though they work mightily upon men's wits, yet they do not produce any great alterations in states; except it be by the help of civil[13] occasions. There be three manner of plantations* of new sects. By the power of signs* and miracles; by the eloquence and wisdom of speech and persuasion; and by the sword. For martyrdoms, I reckon them amongst miracles; because they seem to exceed the strength of human nature: and I may do the like of superlative and admirable holiness of life. Surely there is no better way to stop the rising of new sects and schisms, than to reform abuses; to compound[14] the smaller differences; to proceed mildly,

1 trifle   2 sequence   3 agreement   4 the spheres, or starry orbs
5 changes in affairs   6 accepted   7 those who profess, practise   8 besides
9 suspect, fear   10 characteristics   11 civil power
12 favoured by the common people (and therefore subversive)
13 political, involving many citizens   14 compromise over, settle

and not with sanguinary persecutions; and rather to take off[1] the principal authors by winning and advancing[2] them, than to enrage them by violence and bitterness.

The changes and vicissitude in wars are many; but chiefly in three things; in the seats or stages[3] of the war; in the weapons; and in the manner of the conduct. Wars, in ancient time, seemed more to move from east to west; for the Persians, Assyrians, Arabians, Tartars* (which were the invaders), were all eastern people.[4] It is true, the Gauls were western; but we read but of two incursions of theirs: the one to Gallo-Graecia,* the other to Rome. But East and West have no certain[5] points of heaven; and no more have the wars, either from the east or west, any certainty of observation. But North and South are fixed;* and it hath seldom or never been seen that the far southern people have invaded the northern, but contrariwise.* Whereby it is manifest that the northern tract of the world is in nature the more martial region:* be it in respect[6] of the stars* of that hemisphere; or of the great continents that are upon the north, whereas the south part, for aught that is known, is almost all sea; or (which is most apparent) of the cold of the northern parts, which is that which, without aid of discipline,[7] doth make the bodies hardest, and the courages warmest.

Upon the breaking and shivering[8] of a great state and empire, you may be sure to have wars. For great empires, while they stand, do enervate[9] and destroy the forces of the natives which they have subdued, resting[10] upon their own protecting forces; and then when they fail also, all goes to ruin, and they become a prey. So was it in the decay of the Roman empire; and likewise in the empire of Almaigne,[11] after Charles the Great,* every bird taking a feather; and were not unlike to befall[12] to Spain, if it should break. The great accessions[13] and unions of kingdoms do likewise stir up wars: for when a state grows to an overpower, it is like a great flood, that will be sure to overflow. As it hath been seen in the states of Rome, Turkey, Spain, and others. Look when the world hath fewest barbarous peoples, but such as commonly will not marry or generate, except they know means[14] to live (as it is almost every where at this day, except Tartary), there is no danger of inundations of people:[15] but when there be great shoals[16] of people, which go

---

1 disarm, placate   2 promoting, giving them office   3 theatre of operations
4 nations   5 stable   6 because   7 special training
8 shattering into pieces   9 weaken   10 relying on   11 Germany
12 happen   13 acquisitions   14 know how to find   15 nations   16 masses

on to populate, without foreseeing[1] means of life and sustentation,[2] it is of necessity that once in an age or two they discharge a portion of their people upon other nations; which the ancient northern people were wont to do by lot; casting lots what part should stay at home, and what should seek their fortunes. When a warlike state grows soft and effeminate, they may be sure of a war. For commonly such states are grown rich in the time of their degenerating; and so the prey inviteth, and their decay in valour encourageth a war.

As for the weapons, it hardly falleth under rule and observation:* yet we see even they have returns and vicissitudes. For certain it is, that ordnance[3] was known in the city of the Oxidrakes* in India; and was that which the Macedonians* called thunder and lightning, and magic. And it is well known* that the use of ordnance hath been[4] in China above two thousand years. The conditions of weapons, and their improvement, are: First, the fetching[5] afar off; for that outruns the danger; as it is seen in ordnance and muskets. Secondly, the strength of the percussion; wherein likewise ordnance do exceed all arietations* and ancient inventions. The third is, the commodious[6] use of them; as that they may serve in all weathers; that the carriage may be light and manageable; and the like.

For the conduct of the war: at the first, men rested[7] extremely upon number: they did put the wars likewise upon main force and valour; pointing[8] days for pitched fields,[9] and so trying it out upon an even match: and they were more ignorant* in ranging and arraying their battles.* After[10] they grew to rest upon number rather competent than vast; they grew to advantages of place, cunning diversions, and the like: and they grew more skilful in the ordering[11] of their battles.

In the youth of a state, arms do flourish; in the middle age of a state, learning,[12] and then both of them together for a time; in the declining age of a state, mechanical arts and merchandise. Learning hath his infancy, when it is but beginning and almost childish: then his youth, when it is luxuriant[13] and juvenile: then his strength of years, when it is solid and reduced:[14] and lastly, his old age, when it waxeth dry and exhaust. But it is not good to look too long upon these turning wheels

1 providing 2 sustenance 3 large guns, artillery 4 has existed
5 striking, reaching 6 versatile 7 relied 8 appointing 9 battles
10 afterwards 11 arrangement 12 knowledge, the sciences
13 uncontrolled in growth 14 concentrated, brought within bounds

of vicissitude, lest we become giddy. As for the philology* of them, that is but a circle of tales,* and therefore not fit for this writing.

59. A FRAGMENT OF AN ESSAY ON FAME

The poets* make Fame* a monster. They describe her in part finely and elegantly; and in part gravely and sententiously.[1] They say, look how many feathers she hath, so many eyes she hath underneath; so many tongues;* so many voices; she pricks up so many ears.

This is a flourish.[2] There follow excellent parables;* as that she gathereth strength in going:* that she goeth upon the ground, and yet hideth her head in the clouds:* that in the day-time she sitteth in a watch tower,* and flieth most by night:* that she mingleth things done with things not done:* and that she is a terror to great cities.* But that which passeth all the rest is; they* do recount that the Earth, mother of the Giants that made war against Jupiter and were by him destroyed, thereupon in an anger brought forth Fame; for certain it is that rebels, figured[3] by the giants, and seditious fames and libels, are but brothers and sisters; masculine* and feminine. But now, if a man can tame this monster, and bring her to feed at the hand, and govern her, and with her fly* other ravening fowl* and kill them, it is somewhat worth.

But we are infected with the stile of the poets. To speak now in a sad[4] and a serious manner. There is not in all the politics[5] a place[6] less handled,[7] and more worthy to be handled, than this of fame. We will therefore speak of these points. What are false fames; and what are true fames; and how they may be best discerned; how fames may be sown and raised;* how they may be spread and multiplied; and how they may be checked and laid dead. And other things concerning the nature of fame. Fame is of that force, as there is scarcely any great action wherein it hath not a great part; especially in the war. Mucianus* undid Vitellius, by a fame that he scattered, that Vitellius had in purpose to remove the legions of Syria into Germany, and the legions of Germany into Syria; whereupon the legions of Syria were infinitely inflamed. Julius Caesar took Pompey unprovided, and laid asleep[8] his industry and preparations, by a fame that he cunningly* gave out, how Caesar's own soldiers loved him not; and being wearied with wars, and

1 full of meaning   2 embellishment   3 represented   4 grave
5 political science   6 topic   7 discussed   8 neutralized

laden with the spoils of Gaul, would forsake him as soon as he came into Italy. Livia* settled all things for the succession of her son Tiberius, by continual giving out that her husband Augustus was upon recovery and amendment.[1] And it is an usual thing with the Bashaws,[2] to conceal* the death of the great Turk from the Janizaries* and men of war, to save[3] the sacking of Constantinople and other towns, as their manner is. Themistocles* made Xerxes King of Persia post apace[4] out of Graecia, by giving out that the Grecians had a purpose to break his bridge of ships which he had made athwart[5] Hellespont. There be a thousand such-like examples, and the more they are, the less they need to be repeated; because a man meeteth with them every where. Therefore let all wise governors have as great a watch and care over fames, as they have of the actions* and designs themselves.

1 recuperating from sickness 2 Grandees (the earlier form of *Pasha*) 3 prevent
4 leave hastily 5 across

APPENDIX I

ESSAYS (1597)

OF STUDIES

Studies serve for pastimes, for ornaments, and for abilities. Their chief use for pastime is in privateness and retiring; for ornament is in discourse, and for ability is in judgment. For expert men can execute, but learned men are fittest to judge or censure.

¶ To spend too much time in them is sloth; to use them too much for ornament is affectation; to make judgment wholly by their rules is the humour of a scholar.

¶ They perfect Nature, and are perfected by experience.

¶ Crafty men contemn them, simple men admire them, wise men use them. For they teach not their own use; but that is a wisdom without them, and above them, won by observation.

¶ Read not to contradict, nor to believe, but to weigh and consider.

¶ Some books are to be tasted, others to be swallowed, and some few to be chewed and digested. That is, some books are to be read only in parts; others to be read, but cursorily; and some few to be read wholly and with diligence and attention.

¶ Reading maketh a full man, conference a ready man, and writing an exact man. And therefore if a man write little, he had need have a great memory; if he confer little, he had need have a present wit; and if he read little, he had need have much cunning, to seem to know that he doth not.

¶ Histories make men wise, poets witty; the mathematics subtle, natural philosophy deep; moral grave, logic and rhetoric able to contend.

OF DISCOURSE

Some in their discourse desire rather commendation of wit in being able to hold all arguments, than of judgment in discerning what is true; as if it were a praise to know what might be said, and not what should be thought. Some have certain commonplaces and themes wherein they are good, and want variety; which kind of poverty is for the most part tedious, and now and then ridiculous.

¶ The honourablest part of talk is to give the occasion, and again to moderate and pass to somewhat else.

¶ It is good to vary and mix speech of the present occasion with argument, tales with reasons, asking of questions with telling of opinions, and jest with earnest.

¶ But some things are privileged from jest, namely religion, matters of state, great persons, any man's present business of importance, and any case that deserveth pity.

¶ He that questioneth much shall learn much, and content much, specially if he apply his questions to the skill of the person of whom he asketh, for he shall give them occasion to please themselves in speaking, and himself shall continually gather knowledge.

¶ If you dissemble sometimes your knowledge of that you are thought to know, you shall be thought another time to know that you know not.

¶ Speech of a man's self is not good often; and there is but one case wherein a man may commend himself with good grace, and that is in commending virtue in another, especially if it be such a virtue as whereunto himself pretendeth.

¶ Discretion of speech is more than eloquence, and to speak agreeably to him with whom we deal is more than to speak in good words or in good order.

¶ A good continued speech, without a good speech of interlocution, sheweth slowness; and a good reply or second speech, without a good set speech, sheweth shallowness and weakness: as we see in beasts, that those that are weakest in the course are yet nimblest in the turn.

¶ To use too many circumstances ere one come to the matter is wearisome; to use none at all is blunt.

OF CEREMONIES AND RESPECTS

He that is only real had need have exceeding great parts of virtue, as the stone had need be rich that is set without foil.

¶ But commonly it is in praise as it is in gain. For as the proverb is true, that 'light gains make heavy purses', because they come thick, whereas great come but now and then, so it is as true that small matters win great commendation, because they are continually in use and in note, whereas the occasion of any great virtue cometh but on holidays.

¶ To attain good forms it sufficeth not to despise them; for so shall a man observe them in others, and let him trust himself with the rest. For if he care to express them, he shall leese their grace, which is to be natural and unaffected. Some men's behaviour is like a verse, wherein every syllable is measured. How can a man comprehend great matters, that breaketh his mind too much to small observations?

¶ Not to use ceremonies at all is to teach others not to use them again, and so diminish his respect; especially they be not to be omitted to strangers and strange natures.

¶ Among a man's peers a man shall be sure of familiarity, and therefore it is a good title to keep state. Amongst a man's inferiors one shall be sure of reverence, and therefore it is good a little to be familiar.

¶ He that is too much in any thing, so that he give another occasion of satiety, maketh himself cheap.

¶ To apply one's self to others is good, so it be with demonstration that a man does it upon regard, and not upon facility.

¶ It is a good precept generally in seconding another yet to add somewhat of one's own; as if you will grant his opinion, let it be with some distinction; if you will follow his motion, let it be with condition; if you allow his counsel, let it be with alleging further reason.

OF FOLLOWERS AND FRIENDS

Costly followers are not to be liked, lest while a man maketh his train longer he make his wings shorter. I reckon to be costly not them alone which charge the purse, but which are wearisome and importune in suits. Ordinary following ought to challenge no higher conditions than countenance, recommendation, and protection from wrong.

¶ Factious followers are worse to be liked, which follow not upon affection to him with whom they range themselves, but upon discontentment conceived against some other; whereupon commonly ensueth that ill intelligence that we many times see between great personages.

¶ The following by certain states, answerable to that which a great person himself professeth, as of soldiers to him that hath been employed in the wars, and the like, hath ever been a thing civil, and well taken even in monarchies, so it be without too much pomp or popularity.

¶ But the most honourable kind of following is to be followed as one that apprehendeth to advance virtue and desert in all sorts of persons; and yet where there is no eminent odds in sufficiency, it is better to take with the more passable than with the more able. In government it is good to use men of one rank equally, for to countenance some extraordinarily is to make them insolent and the rest discontent, because they may claim a due. But in favours to use men with much difference and election is good, for it maketh the persons preferred more thankful and the rest more officious, because all is of favour.

¶ It is good not to make too much of any man at first, because one cannot hold out that proportion.

¶ To be governed by one is not good, and to be distracted with many is worse; but to take advice of friends is ever honourable. 'For lookers-on many times see more than gamesters; and the vale best discovereth the hill'.

¶ There is little friendship in the world, and least of all between equals; which was wont to be magnified. That that is, is between superior and inferior, whose fortunes may comprehend the one the other.

OF SUITS

Many ill matters are undertaken, and many good matters with ill minds. Some embrace suits which never mean to deal effectually in them. But if they see there may be life in the matter by some other means, they will be content to win a thank or take a second reward. Some take hold of suits only for an occasion to cross some other, or to make an information whereof they could not otherwise have an apt pretext, without care what become of the suit when that turn is served. Nay some undertake suits with a full purpose to let them fall, to the end to gratify the adverse party or competitor.

¶ Surely there is in sort a right in every suit, either a right of equity, if it be a suit of controversy; or a right of desert, if it be a suit of petition. If affection lead a man to favour the wrong side in justice, let him rather use his countenance to compound the matter than to carry it. If affection lead a man to favour the less worthy in desert, let him do it without depraving or disabling the better deserver.

¶ In suits a man doth not well understand, it is good to refer them to some friend of trust and judgment, that may report whether he may deal in them with honour.

¶ Suitors are so distasted with delays and abuses that plain dealing in denying to deal in suits at first, and reporting the success barely, and in challenging no more thanks than one hath deserved, is grown not only honourable but also gracious.

¶ In suits of favour the first coming ought to take little place. So far forth consideration may be had of his trust, that if intelligence of the matter could not otherwise have been had but by him, advantage be not taken of the note.

¶ To be ignorant of the value of a suit is simplicity, as well as to be ignorant of the right thereof is want of conscience.

¶ Secrecy in suits is a great means of obtaining, for voicing them to be in forwardness may discourage some kind of suitors, but doth quicken and awake others.

¶ But timing of the suits is the principal, timing I say not only in respect of the person that should grant it, but in respect of those which are like to cross it.

¶ Nothing is thought so easy a request to a great person as his letter, and yet if it be not in a good cause it is so much out of his reputation.

OF EXPENSE

Riches are for spending, and spending for honour and good actions. Therefore extraordinary expense must be limited by the worth of the occasion; for voluntary undoing may be as well for a man's country as for the kingdom of heaven. But ordinary expense ought to be limited by a man's estate, and governed with such regard as it be within his compass; and not subject to deceit and abuse of servants; and ordered to the best shew, that the bills may be less than the estimation abroad.

¶ It is no baseness for the greatest to descend and look into their own estate. Some forebear it not upon negligence alone, but doubting to bring themselves into melancholy in respect they shall find it broken. But 'wounds cannot be cured without searching'.

¶ He that cannot look into his own estate had need both choose well those whom he employeth, yea, and change them often. For new are more timorous and less subtle.

¶ In clearing of a man's estate, he may as well hurt himself in being too sudden as in letting it run on too long, for hasty selling is commonly as disadvantageable as interest.

¶ He that hath a state to repair may not despise small things; and commonly it is less dishonourable to abridge petty charges than to stoop to petty gettings.

¶ A man ought warily to begin charges which once begun must continue. But in matters that return not he may be more magnificent.

Of Regiment of Health

There is a wisdom in this beyond the rules of physic. A man's own observation what he finds good of, and what he finds hurt of, is the best physic to preserve health. But it is a safer conclusion to say this agreeth not well with me, therefore I will not continue it, than this I find no offence, of this therefore I may use it. For strength of nature in youth passeth over many excesses, which are owing a man till his age.

¶ Discern of the coming on of years, and think not to do the same things still.

¶ Beware of any sudden change in any great point of diet, and if necessity enforce it, fit the rest to it.

¶ To be free-minded and cheerfully disposed at hours of meat, and of sleep, and of exercise, is the best precept of long lasting.

¶ If you fly physic in health altogether, it will be too strange to your body when you shall need it; if you make it too familiar, it will work no extraordinary effect when sickness cometh.

¶ Despise no new accident in the body, but ask opinion of it.

¶ In sickness respect health principally, and in health action. For those that put their bodies to endure in health, may in most sicknesses which are not very sharp be cured only with diet and tendering.

¶ Physicians are some of them so pleasing and conformable to the humours of the patient, as they press not the true cure of the disease; and some other are so regular in proceeding according to art for the disease, as they respect not sufficiently the condition of the patient. Take one of a middle temper; or if it may not be found in one man, compound two of both sorts, and forget not to call as well the best acquainted with your body as the best reputed of for his faculty.

OF HONOUR AND REPUTATION

The winning of honour is but the revealing of a man's virtue and worth without disadvantage. For some in their actions do affect honour and reputation, which sort of men are commonly much talked of, but inwardly little admired; and some darken their virtue in the show of it, so as they be undervalued in opinion.

¶ If a man perform that which hath not been attempted before, or attempted and given over, or hath been achieved but not with so good circumstance, he shall purchase more honour than by effecting a matter of greater difficulty or virtue, wherein he is but a follower.

¶ If a man so temper his actions as in some one of them he do content every faction or combination of people, the music will be the fuller.

¶ A man is an ill husband of his honour that entereth into any action, the failing wherein may disgrace him more than the carrying of it through can honour him.

¶ Discreet followers help much to reputation.

¶ Envy, which is the canker of honour, is best extinguished by declaring a man's self in his ends, rather to seek merit than fame, and by attributing a man's successes rather to divine providence and felicity than to his virtue or policy.

¶ The true marshalling of the degrees of sovereign honour are these. In the first place are *Conditores*, founders of states. In the second place are *Legislatores*, lawgivers, which are also called second founders, or *Perpetui principes*, because they govern by their ordinances after they are gone. In the third place are *Liberatores*, such as compound the long miseries of civil wars, or deliver their countries from servitude of strangers or tyrants. In the fourth place are *Propagatores* or *Propugnatores imperii*, such as in honourable wars enlarge their territories, or make noble defence against invaders. And in the last place are *Patres patriae*, which reign justly and make the times good wherein they live.

¶ Degrees of honour in subjects are first *Participes curarum*, those upon whom princes do discharge the greatest weight of their affairs, their *Right hands* (as we call them). The next are *Duces belli*, great leaders, such as are princes' lieutenants, and do them notable services in the wars. The third are *Gratiosi*, favourites, such as exceed not this scantling, to be solace to the sovereign and harmless to the people. And the fourth *Negotiis pares*, such as have great place under princes, and execute their places with sufficiency.

OF FACTION

Many have a new wisdom, indeed a fond opinion, that for a prince to govern his estate, or for a great person to govern his proceedings, according to the respects of factions, is the principal part of policy. Whereas contrariwise, the chiefest wisdom is either in ordering those things which are general, and wherein men of several factions do nevertheless agree, or in dealing with correspondence to particular persons one by one. But I say not that the consideration of factions is to be neglected.

¶ Mean men must adhere, but great men, that have strength in themselves, were better to maintain themselves indifferent and neutral; yet even in beginners, to adhere so moderately, as he be a man of the one faction which is passablest with the other, commonly giveth best way.

¶ The lower and weaker faction is the firmer in conjunction.

¶ When one of the factions is extinguished the remaining subdivideth, which is good for a second faction. It is commonly seen that men once placed take in with the contrary faction to that by which they enter.

¶ The traitor in factions lightly goeth away with it, for when matters have stuck long in balancing, the winning of some one man casteth them, and he getteth all the thanks.

OF NEGOTIATING

It is generally better to deal by speech than by letter, and by the mediation of a third than by a man's self. Letters are good when a man would draw an answer by letter back again, or when it may serve for a man's justification afterwards to produce his own letter. To deal in person is good when a man's face breeds regard, as commonly with inferiors.

¶ In choice of instruments it is better to choose men of a plainer sort, that are like to do that that is committed to them, and to report back again faithfully the success, than those that are cunning to contrive out of other men's business somewhat to grace themselves, and will help the matter in report for satisfaction's sake.

¶ It is better to sound a person with whom one deals afar off, than to fall upon the point at first; except you mean to surprise him by some short question.

¶ It is better dealing with men in appetite, than with those which are where they would be.

¶ If a man deal with another upon conditions, the start or first performance is all; which a man cannot reasonably demand, except either the nature of the thing be such, which must go before, or else a man can persuade the other party that he shall still need him in some other thing, or else that he be counted the honester man.

¶ All practice is to discover or to work. Men discover themselves in trust, in passion, at unawares, and of necessity, when they would have somewhat done and cannot find an apt pretext. If you would work any man, you must either know his nature and fashions, and so lead him; or his ends, and so win him; or his weaknesses or disadvantages, and so awe him; or those that have interest in him, and so govern him.

¶ In dealing with cunning persons we must ever consider their ends to interpret their speeches; and it is good to say little to them, and that which they least look for.

APPENDIX II

FROM THE *ESSAYS* (1612)

OF SEDITIONS AND TROUBLES

Shepherds of people had need know the calendars of tempests in state; which are commonly greatest when things grow to equality; as natural tempests are greatest about the *Equinoctia*. And as there are certain hollow blasts and secret swellings of seas before tempests, so are there in states:

> *caecos instare tumultus*
> *Saepe monet, fraudesque et operta tumescere bella.*

Certainly, libels and licentious discourses are amongst the signs of troubles. Virgil, giving the pedigree of fame, saith she was sister to the giants,

> *Illam terra parens ira irritata deorum*
> *Extremam ut perhibent Cæo Enceladoque sororem*
> *Progenuit.*

As if fames and rumors were the relics of seditions past; but they are no less the preludes of seditions to come. But he notes it right, that seditious tumults and seditious fames, differ no more but as masculine and feminine.

Also, that kind of obedience (which Tacitus describeth in an army) is to be held suspected: *Erant in officio, sed tamen qui mallent mandata Imperantium interpretari, quam exequi.* When mandates fall to be disputed and distinguished, and new senses given to them, it is the first essay of disobeying.

Also, as Machiavell well notes, when Princes that ought to be common fathers make themselves as a party, and lean to a side in the estate, it is as a boat that tilts aside before it overthrows. Also, when discords, and quarrels, and factions are carried openly and audaciously, it is a sign the reverence of government is lost. And reverence is that wherewith Princes are girt from God, who threateneth the dissolving thereof, as one of his great judgments: *Solvam cingula regum.*

So when any of the four pillars of government are mainly shaken, or weakened, which are Religion, Justice, Counsel, and Treasure, men had need to pray for fair weather. But let us leave the part of predictions, and speak of the materials, and the causes, and the remedies.

The matter of seditions is of two kinds; much poverty, and much discontent. Certainly, so many overthrown estates, so many votes for troubles. Lucan noteth well the state of the times before the civil war:

Hinc usura vorax, rapidumque in tempore foenus,
Hinc concussa fides, et multis utile bellum.

This same *multis utile bellum* is an assured and infallible sign of a state disposed to troubles and seditions. For discontents, they are the very humours
in the politic body, apt to gather a preternatural heat and to inflame. And let
not Princes measure the danger of them by this, whether they are just or unjust, for that were to imagine people too reasonable; nor yet by this, whether
the griefs whereupon they arise be in true proportion great, or small; for
they are the most dangerous kinds of discontents where the fear is greater
than the feeling.

The causes and motives of sedition are: religion, taxes, alterations of laws
and customs, breaking privileges, general oppression, advancement of unworthy persons, strangers, dearths, and whatsoever in offending people
joineth them in a common cause.

For the remedies, there may be some general preservatives; the cure must
answer to the particular disease. To give moderate liberty for griefs to evaporate, so it be without bravery or importunity, is a safe way; for he that
turneth the humours or maketh the wound bleed inwards endangereth
malign ulcers and pernicious imposthumations. Also, the part of Epimetheus
may become Prometheus in this case: he, when griefs and evils flew abroad,
yet kept hope in the bottom of the vessel.

The politic and artificial nourishing of some degree of hopes is one of
the best antidotes against the poison of discontents; and it is a certain sign
of a wise government, if it can hold by hope where it cannot by satisfaction.

Also the foresight and prevention, that there be no likely or fit head
whereunto discontents may resort, and under whom they may join, is a
known but an excellent point of caution. I understand a fit head to be one
that hath greatness and reputation, that hath confidence with the discontented party, and upon whom they turn their eyes; and that is thought discontent in his particular. Also, the dividing and breaking of any combination
that is adverse to the state is none of the worst remedies. For it is a desperate
case if the true part of the state be full of discord and faction, and the false,
entire and united.

Lastly, let Princes, against all events, not be without some great person of
military value near unto them, for the repressing of seditions in their beginnings. For without that, there useth to be more trepidation in Courts upon
the breaking out of troubles than were fit, and the State runneth the danger
of that which Tacitus saith; *Atque is habitus animorum fuit, ut pessimum facinus auderent pauci, plures vellent, omnes paterentur.* But let such one be an assured one and not popular, and holding good correspondence with the gown
men; or else the remedy is worse than the disease.

Of Friendship

There is no greater desert or wilderness than to be without true friends. For without friendship, society is but meeting. And as it is certain that in bodies inanimate, union strengtheneth any natural motion, and weakeneth any violent motion; so amongst men, friendship multiplieth joys, and divideth griefs. Therefore, whosoever wanteth fortitude, let him worship friendship, for the yoke of friendship maketh the yoke of fortune more light.

There be some whose lives are as if they perpetually played upon a stage, disguised to all others, open only to themselves. But perpetual dissimulation is painful, and he that is all fortune and no nature is an exquisite hireling. Live not in continual smother, but take some friends with whom to communicate. It will unfold thy understanding; it will evaporate thy affections; it will prepare thy business.

A man may keep a corner of his mind from his friend, and it be but to witness to himself that it is not upon facility, but upon true use of friendship that he imparteth himself. Want of true friends, as it is the reward of perfidious natures, so it is an imposition upon great fortunes. The one deserveth it, the other cannot escape it. And therefore it is good to retain sincerity, and to put it into the reckoning of ambition that the higher one goeth, the fewer friends he shall have.

Perfection of friendship is but a speculation. It is friendship, when a man can say to himself, I love this man without respect of utility; I am open-hearted to him; I single him from the generality of those with whom I live; I make him a portion of my own wishes.

Of Religion

The quarrels and divisions for religion were evils unknown to the heathen: and no marvel, for it is the true God that is the jealous God, and the gods of the heathen were good fellows. But yet the bonds of religious unity are so to be strengthened, as the bonds of human society be not dissolved. Lucretius the poet, when he beheld the act of Agamemnon, enduring and assisting at the sacrifice of his daughter, concludes with this verse:

Tantum religio potuit suadere malorum.

But what would he have done if he had known the massacre of France, or the powder treason of England? Certainly he would have been seven times more epicure and atheist than he was. Nay, he would rather have chosen to be one of the madmen of Münster than to have been a partaker of those counsels. For it is better that religion should deface men's understanding than their piety and charity, retaining reason only but as an engine and chariot driver of cruelty and malice.

It was a great blasphemy when the devil said, 'I will ascend, and be like the highest'. But it is a greater blasphemy if they make God to say, 'I will descend, and be like the prince of darkness'; and it is no better when they make the cause of religion descend to the execrable actions of murdering of princes, butchery of people, and firing of states. Neither is there such a sin against the person of the holy Ghost (if one should take it literally) as, instead of the likeness of a dove, to bring him down in the likeness of a vulture or raven; nor such a scandal to their church, as out of the bark of Saint Peter to set forth the flag of a bark of pirates and assassins.

Therefore, since these things are the common enemies of human society, princes by their power, churches by their decrees, and all learning (Christian, moral, or whatsoever sect or opinion) by their Mercury rod, ought to join in the damning to hell for ever these facts, and their supports. And in all counsels concerning religion that counsel of the apostle would be prefixed, *Ira hominis non implet iustitiam Dei*.

APPENDIX III

FROM BACON'S *ANTITHESES OF THINGS* (1623)

NOBILITY

For

They whose virtue is in the stock cannot be bad even if they would.

Nobility is the laurel with which Time crowns men.

We reverence antiquity even in dead monuments; how much more in living ones?

If you regard not nobility of birth, where will be the difference between the offspring of men and brutes?

Nobility withdraws virtue from envy, and makes it gracious.

Against

Seldom comes nobility from virtue; seldomer virtue from nobility.

Noblemen have to thank their ancestors for pardon oftener than for advancement.

New men are commonly so diligent, that noblemen by their side look like statues.

Noblemen look behind them too often in the course; the mark of a bad runner.

YOUTH

For

First thoughts and young men's counsels have more of divineness.

Old men are wiser for themselves, not so wise for others and for the commonwealth.

Old age, if it could be seen, deforms the mind more than the body.

Old men are afraid of everything, except the Gods.

Against

Youth is the seedbed of repentance.

There is implanted in youth contempt for the authority of age; so every man must grow wise at his own cost.

The counsels to which Time is not called, Time will not ratify.

In old men the Loves are changed into the Graces.

HEALTH

For

The care of health humiliates the mind and makes it the beggar of the body.

Against

Often to recover health, is often to renew youth.

Ill health is a good excuse for many

A healthy body is the soul's host, a sick body her gaoler.

Nothing forwards the conclusion of business so much as good health; weak health on the contrary takes too many holidays.

things; which we are glad to use even when well.

Good health makes too close an alliance between the soul and the body.

Great empires have been governed from bed, great armies commanded from the litter.

WIFE AND CHILDREN

For

Love of his country begins in a man's own house.

A wife and children are a kind of discipline of humanity; whereas unmarried men are harsh and severe.

To be without wife or children is good for a man only when he wants to run away.

He who begets not children, sacrifices to death.

They that are fortunate in other things are commonly unfortunate in their children; lest men should come too near the condition of Gods.

Against

He that has wife and children has given hostages to fortune.

Man generates and has children; God creates and produces works.

The eternity of brutes is in offspring; of men, in fame, good deserts, and institutions.

Domestic considerations commonly overthrow public ones.

Some persons have wished for Priam's fortune, who survived all his children.*

HONOURS

For

Honours are the suffrages not of tyrants (as they are said to be), but of divine providence.

Honours make both virtues and vices conspicuous; therefore they are a spur to the one and a bridle to the other.

No man can tell how far his virtue will go unless honours give him a fair field.

Virtue, like all things else, moves

Against

While we seek honours we lose liberty.

Honours commonly give men power over those things wherein the best condition is not to will, the next best not to can.

The rising to honours is laborious, the standing slippery, the descent headlong.

Great persons had need to borrow

violently to her place, calmly in her place; now the place of virtue is honour.

the opinions of the vulgar, to think themselves happy.

NATURE

For

Custom advances in an arithmetical ratio, nature in a geometrical.

As common laws are to customs in states, such is nature to custom in individuals.

Custom against nature is a kind of tyranny, and is soon and upon slight occasions overthrown.

Against

We think according to our nature, speak as we have been taught, but act as we have been accustomed.

Nature is a schoolmaster, custom a magistrate.

FORTUNE

For

Overt and apparent virtues bring forth praise; secret and hidden virtues bring forth fortune.

Virtues of duty bring forth praise; virtues of ability bring forth fortune.

Fortune is like the Milky Way; a cluster of obscure virtues without a name.

Fortune is to be honoured if it be but for her daughters, Confidence and Authority.

Against

The folly of one man is the fortune of another.

The best that can be said of fortune is that, as she uses no choice in her favours, so she does not care to uphold them.

Great men, to decline the envy of their own virtues, turn worshippers of fortune.

PRIDE

For

Pride is unsociable to vices among other things; and as poison by poison, so not a few vices are expelled by pride.

The good-natured man is subject to other men's vices as well as his own; the proud man to his own only.

Against

Pride is the ivy that winds about all virtues and all good things.

Other vices do but thwart virtues; only pride infects them.

Pride lacks the best condition of vice—concealment.

The proud man while he despises others neglects himself.

Let pride go a step higher, and from
contempt of others rise to contempt of self, and it becomes
philosophy.

INGRATITUDE

For	*Against*
The crime of ingratitude is nothing more than a clear insight into the cause of a benefit conferred.*	The crime of ingratitude is not restrained by punishments, but given over to the Furies.
In our desire to show gratitude to certain persons we sacrifice both the justice we owe to others and the liberty we owe to ourselves.	The bonds of benefits are stricter than the bonds of duties; wherefore he that is ungrateful is unjust and every way bad.
Before we are called on to be grateful for a benefit, let us be sure as to the value of it.	This is the condition of humanity: no man is born in so public a fortune but he must obey the private calls both of gratitude and revenge.

UNCHASTITY

For	*Against*
It is owing to jealousy that chastity has been made a virtue.	Unchastity was the worst of Circe's transformations.*
A man must be of a very sad disposition to think love a serious matter.	He that is unchaste is without all reverence for himself, which is the bridle of all vices.
Why make a virtue of that which is either a matter of diet, or a show of cleanliness, or the child of pride?	All who like Paris prefer beauty, quit like Paris wisdom and power.*
Loves are like wildfowl; there is no property in them, but the right passes with the possession.	It was no vulgar truth that Alexander lighted on, when he said that sleep and lust were earnests of death.*

CRUELTY

For	*Against*
None of the virtues has so many crimes to answer for as clemency.*	To delight in blood, one must be either a wild beast or a Fury.
Cruelty, if it proceeds from revenge, is justice, if from danger, prudence.	To a good man cruelty always seems fabulous, and some tragical fiction.

He that has mercy on his enemy has
no mercy on himself.

Bloodlettings are not oftener necessary in medicine than executions
in states.

JUSTICE

For	*Against*
Kingdoms and governments are but accessories to justice; for there would be no need of them if justice could be carried on without.	If to be just be not to do that to another which you would not have another do to you, then is mercy justice.
It is owing to justice that man is a god to man, and not a wolf.*	If everyone has a right to his own, surely humanity has a right to pardon.
Justice though it cannot extirpate vices, yet prevents them from doing hurt.	What tell you me of equal measure, when to the wise man all things are equal?
	Consider the condition of accused persons among the Romans, and conclude that justice is not for the good of the commonwealth.
	The ordinary justice of governments is but as a philosopher in the court—it merely conduces to the reverence of those who govern.

FORTITUDE*

For	*Against*
Nothing is to be feared except fear itself. There is nothing either solid in pleasure, or secure in virtue, where fear intrudes.	A noble virtue, to be willing to die yourself in order to kill another!
He that looks steadily at dangers that he may meet them, sees also how he may avoid them.	A noble virtue, which a man may acquire by getting drunk!
Other virtues free us from the domination of vice, fortitude only from the domination of fortune.	He that is prodigal of his own life is dangerous to other men's.
	Fortitude is the virtue of the iron age.*

TEMPERANCE

For	*Against*
The power of abstinence is not much other than the power of endurance.	I like not these negative virtues; for they show innocence and not merit.
Uniformity, concord, and measured motion, are attributes of heaven and characters of eternity.	The mind grows languid that has no excesses.
Temperance is like wholesome cold; it collects and braces the powers of the mind.	I like those virtues which induce excellence of action, not dullness of passion.
Exquisite and restless senses need narcotics; so do passions.	If you will have the motions of the mind all consonant, you must have them few—for it is a poor man that can count his stock.
	To abstain from the use of a thing that you may not feel the want of it, to shun the want that you may not fear the loss of it,* are precautions of pusillanimity and cowardice.

CONSTANCY

For	*Against*
Constancy is the foundation on which virtues rest.	Constancy is like a surly porter; it derives much useful intelligence from the door.
Wretched is the man who knows not what himself may become.	It is fit that constancy should bear adversity well, for it commonly brings it on.
Human judgment is too weak to be true to the nature of things, let it then at least be true to itself.	The shortest folly is the best.
Even vices derive a grace from constancy.	
If inconstancy of mind be added to the inconstancy of fortune, in what darkness do we live?	
Fortune is like Proteus; if you persevere she returns to her shape.	

MAGNANIMITY

For	Against
If the mind do but choose generous ends to aim at, it shall have not only the virtues but the deities to help.	Magnanimity is a poetical virtue.
Virtues induced by habit or by precepts are ordinary; those imposed by a virtuous end are heroical.	

LEARNING

For	Against
If books were written about small matters, there would be scarce any use of experience.	In colleges men learn to believe.
In reading a man converses with the wise, in action generally with fools.	What art ever taught the seasonable use of art?*
Sciences which are of no use in themselves are not to be deemed useless, if they sharpen the wit and put the thoughts in order.	To be wise by rule and to be wise by experience are contrary proceedings; he that accustoms himself to the one unfits himself for the other.
	Art is often put to a foolish use, that it may not be of no use at all.
	Almost all scholars have this— when anything is presented to them, they will find in it that which they know, not learn from it that which they know not.

LOQUACITY

For	Against
He that is silent betrays want of confidence either in others or in himself.	Silence gives to words both grace and authority.
All kinds of constraint are unhappy, that of silence is the most miserable of all.	Silence is the sleep which nourishes wisdom.
Silence is the virtue of a fool. And therefore it was well said to a man that would not speak, 'If	Silence is the fermentation of thought.
	Silence is the style of wisdom.
	Silence aspires after truth.

you are wise you are a fool; if you
are a fool, you are wise.'*

Silence, like night, is convenient for
treacheries.

Thoughts are wholesomest when
they are like running waters.

Silence is a kind of solitude.

He that is silent lays himself out for
opinion.

Silence neither casts off bad
thought nor distributes good.

LOVE

For	*Against*
See you not that all men seek themselves? But it is only the lover that finds himself.	The stage is much beholden to love, life not at all.
There is nothing which better regulates the mind than the authority of some powerful passion.	Nothing has so many names as love; for it is a thing either so foolish that it does not know itself, or so foul that it hides itself with paint.
If you are wise, seek something to desire; for to him who has not some special object of pursuit all things are distasteful and wearisome.*	I hate those men of one thought.
Why should not one be content with one?	Love is a very narrow contemplation.

FLATTERY

For	*Against*
Flattery proceeds more from manners than malice.	Flattery is the style of slaves.
To suggest what a man should be, under colour of praising what he is, was ever a form due in civility to the great.	Flattery is the refuse of vices.
	The flatterer is like the fowler that deceives birds by imitating their cry.
	The unseemliness of flattery is matter of comedy, its mischief of tragedy.
	Nothing so hard to cure as the ear.

Revenge

For	Against
Revenge is a kind of wild justice.	He that did the first wrong made a beginning of mischief, he that returned it made no end.
He who requites violence with violence, sins against the law but not against the man.	The more natural revenge is, the more need to restrain it.
The fear of private revenge is a useful thing; for laws too often sleep.	He that is ready to return an injury was behindhand more in time perhaps than in will.

Suspicion

For	Against
Distrust is the sinews of wisdom, but suspicion is a medicine for the joints.	Suspicion discharges faith.*
His faith is justly suspected whose faith suspicion shakes.	The distemper of suspicion is a kind of civil madness.
Suspicion loosens a frail faith, but braces a strong one.	

The Words of the Law

For	Against
The interpretation which departs from the letter is not interpretation but divination.	The sense according to which each word is to be interpreted must be gathered from all the words together.
When the letter is departed from, the judge becomes the law-giver.	The worst tyranny is the torturing of the law.

For Witnesses against Arguments

For	Against
He who relies on arguments decides according to the merits of the pleader, not of the cause.	If witnesses are to be believed in spite of arguments, it is enough if the judge be not deaf.
He who believes arguments more than witnesses, ought to give more credit to the wit than the senses.	Arguments are the antidote against the poison of testimony.
	It is safest to believe those proofs which seldomest lie.

Arguments might be trusted, if
    men never acted absurdly.
Arguments, when opposed to testi-
    mony, may make a fact seem
    strange, but cannot make it seem
    not a fact.

EXPLANATORY NOTES

Abbott	*Bacon's Essays*, ed. E. A. Abbott, 2 vols. (London, 1876).
Guicciardini, *Ricordi*	Francesco Guicciardini, *Selected Writings*, ed. C. and M. Grayson (London, 1965)
Henry VII, ed. Vickers	*The History of the Reign of King Henry VII*, ed. Brian Vickers (Cambridge, 1998)
Kiernan	*The Essayes or Counsels, Civill and Morall*, ed. Michael Kiernan (Oxford, 1985)
Melchionda	*Gli 'Essayes' di Francis Bacon. Studio Introduttivo, Testo Critico e Commento*, ed. Mario Melchionda (Florence, 1979)
Montaigne	*Essais*, in *Œuvres complètes*, ed. A. Thibaudet and M. Rat (Pléiade edn.; Paris, 1939)
OED	*Oxford English Dictionary*
PMLA	*Publications of the Modern Language Association of America*
'Promus'	'The Promus of formularies and elegancies by Francis Bacon', ed. Mrs H. Pott (London, 1883)
Reynolds	*The Essays or Counsels, Civil and Moral*, ed. S. H. Reynolds (Oxford, 1890)
SOED	*Shorter Oxford English Dictionary*
TOA	*Francis Bacon*, ed. Brian Vickers (The Oxford Authors; Oxford, 1996)
Vickers (ed.), *Essential Articles*	Brian Vickers (ed.), *Essential Articles for the Study of Francis Bacon* (Hamden, Conn., 1968; London, 1972)
Vickers, *Renaissance Prose Works*	Brian Vickers, *Francis Bacon and Renaissance Prose* (Cambridge, 1968) *The Works of Francis Bacon*, ed. J. Spedding, R. L. Ellis, and D. D. Heath, 14 vols. (London, 1857–74; repr. New York, 1968; London, 1996)
Wright	*Bacon's Essays and Colours of Good and Evil*, ed. W. A. Wright (London, 1862)

1. OF TRUTH

3 *What is Truth?*: John 18: 38, before Pilate delivered up Christ for execution. 'Jesus answered, . . . for this cause came I into the world, that I should bear witness unto the truth. . . . Pilate saith unto him, What is truth?'

that kind: the Sceptics.

discoursing wits: rambling minds. Bacon may be referring to the sceptical treatise by Franciscus Sanchez, *Quod nihil scitur* (1576).

One . . . Grecians: Lucian of Samosata (*c.* AD 120–80), in his dialogue *Philopseudes* ('The lover of lies'), 1.

carbuncle: precious stone of a red, fiery colour, supposed to shine in the dark.

vinum daemonum: 'the wine of demons'. A fusion of remarks by St Augustine on the *vinum erroris* in Terence (*Confessions*, 1. 16. 26), and St Jerome, that *Daemonum cibus est carmina poetarum* ('the song of the poets is the food of demons': *Epistles*, 146). Bacon probably follows Henry Cornelius Agrippa, who in *De incertitudine et vanitate scientiarum declamatio* (1530) quotes in successive sentences the two patristic authorities whom Bacon conflates.

4 *truth*: here in the sense of right reason.

days: the six days of creation. For the 'light of the sense', or eyesight, see Gen. 1: 2–5; for the 'light of reason' see Gen. 1: 26–7.

illumination . . . Spirit: a genitive: 'the divine spirit illuminates the works of creation'.

The poet . . . sect: Lucretius (*c.*94–55 BC) described the Epicurean philosophy favourably in *De rerum natura*, from which Bacon quotes the opening of book 2.

yet: despite belonging to that inferior sect. (The Epicureans, who believed that the world was created by chance, not by a divine act, and that the goal of philosophy was to avoid pain, were traditionally dismissed as atheists and hedonists.)

turn . . . poles: as a planet moves upon its axis, with constancy.

Montaigne: *Essais*, 2. 18, 'Du démentir' (Pléiade edn., pp. 649–50); in fact quoting Plutarch, 'Life' of Lysander, 4.

5 *peal*: of the bell; here, the summons announcing the Day of Judgement.

foretold: Luke 18: 8.

2. OF DEATH

See M. Walters, 'The Literary Background of Francis Bacon's Essay "Of Death"', *Modern Language Review*, 35 (1940), 1–7.

fear . . . dark: Seneca, *Epistles*, 87. 15.

wages of sin: Rom. 6: 23.

books of mortification: Catholic treatises on mortifying the flesh in this world to avoid punishment in the next, which often included discussions of the 'Four Last Things' (death, judgement, heaven, and hell).

natural: guided only by nature, not by the grace of Christian revelation.

Pompa . . . ipsa: 'it is the trappings of death that scare us more than death itself': freely quoted from Seneca, *Epistles*, 24. 14. The idea is developed at length by Montaigne, *Essais*, 1. 20, 'Que philosopher, c'est apprendre à mourir' (Pléiade edn., pp. 79–95).

5 *Honour aspireth to it*: the 1612 edition, and the Latin translation of 1638, add the phrase 'delivery from *Ignominy* chuseth it'. But perhaps Bacon omitted it here since the next phrase duplicates it.

pre-occupateth: anticipates death (by committing suicide): cf. Seneca, *Epistles*, 24. 23 and 70. 5–8.

Otho: Marcus Salvius Otho, emperor AD 69: Tacitus, *Histories*, 2. 49.

6 *Cogita . . . potest*: 'reflect how long you have been doing the same thing. The desire to die may be felt, not only by the sensible man or the brave or unhappy man, but even by the man who is merely surfeited': *Epistles*, 77. 6, adapted.

Livia . . . vale: 'farewell, Livia, and forget not our married life': Suetonius, 'Life' of Augustus, 99. Augustus was emperor 31 BC–AD 14.

Iam . . . deserebant: 'Tiberius was now losing his vigour and vitality, but not his dissimulation': *Annals*, 6. 50. Tiberius was emperor AD 14–37.

Ut . . . fio: 'as I suppose, I am on the point of becoming a god': Suetonius, 'Life' of Vespasian, 23. Vespasian was emperor AD 69–79.

Feri . . . Romani: 'strike, if it be for the benefit of the Roman people': Plutarch, 'Life' of Galba, 20. Servius Sulpicius Galba was emperor AD 68–9.

Adeste . . . agendum: 'be ready, in case anything remains for me to do': Dio Cassius, 76. 17. Septimius Severus was emperor AD 193–211.

bestowed . . . cost: made too much fuss about. This is the burden of Montaigne's complaint about Seneca in *Essais*, 3. 12, 'De la phisionomie' (Pléiade edn., pp. 1027–9).

qui . . . naturae: 'who considers the end of life among the gifts of nature': Juvenal, *Satires*, 10. 358 (inaccurately quoted).

Nunc dimittis: Luke 2: 29: '[Lord,] now lettest thou [thy servant] depart [in peace]'.

Extinctus . . . idem: 'he, too, [disliked in life] will win affection when his light is quenched': Horace, *Epistles*, 2. 1. 14.

3. OF UNITY IN RELIGION

In this essay Bacon is especially concerned with unity within the Church of England, a topic on which he had written two earlier treatises, the *Advertisement touching the Controversies of the Church of England*, *c*.1593 (TOA 1–19; *Works*, viii. 74–95), and *Certain Considerations touching the Better Projection and Edification of the Church of England*, 1604 (*Works*, x. 103–27). In the 1612 volume this essay is simply called 'Of Religion'; in the Latin translation, *De Unitate Ecclesiae*. In revising the 1612 version for the 1625 volume, Bacon (unusually) deleted several passages: see above, p. 144–5 and Kiernan, 11–16.

jealous God: Exod. 20: 5, 34: 14.

7 *schisms*: divisions within the church over religious doctrine.

scandals: discredits to religion caused by its adherents.

solution of continuity: 'the separation from each other of normally continuous parts of the body by external or internal causes' (*SOED*).

corrupt humour: diseased component (the four constituent humours, whose balance was thought essential to bodily health, were: red bile, yellow bile, choler, melancholy).

Ecce in deserto . . . in penetralibus: Christ's warning to his disciples against the 'false Christs and false prophets' who will declare a second coming: 'Wherefore if they shall say unto you, "Behold, he is in the desert", go not forth; "behold, he is in the secret chambers", believe it not': Matt. 24: 26 (Vulgate).

conventicles: religious meetings (corresponding to the *desertum*).

Doctor . . . Gentiles: St Paul.

If . . . mad: 1 Cor. 14: 23.

to sit . . . scorners: Ps. 1: 1.

master of scoffing: François Rabelais (*c.*1490–1553), in the library catalogue of the Abbey St Victor: *Pantagruel*, ch. 7.

morris-dance: a grotesque dance performed on feast-days (derived from the Moriscos or Moors).

cringe: servile bow, distortion (in the Latin translation, *gestus deformitatem*).

Is it . . . me: 2 Kings 9: 18–19.

Peace . . . party: such zealots are not seeking peace but more partisan followers.

Laodiceans: inhabitants of Laodicea, reproved in Rev. 3: 16 for being 'lukewarm' in their religious faith.

8 *He . . . against us*: Matt. 12:30 (which actually reads 'with me . . . against me').

He . . . with us: Mark 9: 40.

In . . . sit: 'let there be variety in the garment, but not division': St Augustine, *Enarratio in Psalmos xliv, xxiv*, quoting John 19: 23–4 and Ps. 45: 14, a saying frequently applied to the mystic marriage between Christ and the Church.

frail men: humankind being weak.

Devita . . . scientiae: 'avoid profane novelties of terms, and oppositions of science falsely so called': 1 Tim. 6: 20 (Vulgate).

terms: definitions (the subject or predicate in a logical proposition).

9 *for all colours . . . dark*: cf. the expression 'in the dark all cats are grey', and Ruth Tarselius, ' "All colours will agree in the dark": A Note on a feature in the style of Francis Bacon', in Vickers (ed.), *Essential Articles*, 293–9.

Nebuchadnezzar's image: Dan. 2: 31–43.

9 *dissolve*: annul—used of laws (Lat. *dissolvere*).

two swords: Luke 22: 38.

third sword . . . Mahomet's: of a holy war, within Christendom.

dash . . . second: oppose the first commandment, enjoining duty to God, against the second, enjoining duty to men. (See Exod. 32: 19 for Moses shattering the Decalogue's stone tablets.)

Tantum . . . malorum: 'to such ill actions religion could persuade a man': Lucretius' comment on the Greek myth telling of Agamemnon's sacrificing Iphigenia (*De rerum natura*, 1. 101–2).

massacre in France: the Catholics' massacre of *c*.13,000 Protestants on Saint Bartholomew's Eve and after, August 1572.

powder treason of England: on 5 November 1605 (the Catholic conspiracy of Guy Fawkes).

Epicure and atheist: Epicurean and unbeliever (according to Christian standards). Lucretius followed Epicurus, who denied both that the gods concerned themselves on man's behalf, and that the human soul was immortal.

Anabaptists: a sect of radical Protestants who refused to recognize civil authority, would not allow their children to be baptized, asserted the equality of all men under divine illumination, and used violence to obtain its ends (unsuccessfully).

I will . . . Highest: Isa. 14: 12–14. These words are in fact spoken by the evil king of Babylon, but early patristic writers argued that the devil was the speaker.

10 *dove*: Matt. 3: 16. The form in which the Holy Spirit appeared at the baptism of Christ: an emblem of peace and divine protection.

bark: ship (as in the traditional image of the 'bark of Peter').

Assassins: Muslim fanatics, sent out (during the Crusades) to murder Christian leaders.

Mercury rod: the staff with which Mercury guides souls to the underworld, an emblem of protection and authority. Cf. Virgil, *Aeneid*, 4. 242–4, and Homer, *Odyssey*, 24. 1–5.

the same: those actions and opinions producing disaster to society.

Ira . . . Dei: 'the wrath of man worketh not the righteousness of God': Jas. 1: 20.

a wise father: not traced.

4. OF REVENGE

Revenge: for the destructive effects of duelling in Jacobean England see Bacon's *Charge touching duels* (TOA 304–13; *Works*, xi. 399–409). Despite Bacon's condemnation of the practice, 'the essay's tone' is one of 'detached exploration' (Kiernan, 186).

wild: uncultivated (as against civilized laws).

It . . . offence: Prov. 19: 11.

two for one: two punishments against one: that inflicted by his enemy, and that which the law inflicts as a punishment for his illegal act of revenge.

11 *Some . . . cometh*: cf. Aristotle, *Rhetoric*, 2. 3, 1380^{b}20 ff.; also Guicciardini, *Ricordi*, no. 202: 'Those who take their revenge in such a way that the victim does not realize whence it comes, can be said to do so merely to satisfy hatred and spite. It is more generous to do so openly so that everyone knows whence it comes, and it may then be interpreted as being done less from hatred and desire for revenge than for honour, that is, so as to be known as a man who will not suffer offence' (p. 51).

arrow . . . dark: cf. Ps. 91: 5, 'Thou shalt not be afraid for the terror by night, Nor for the arrow that flieth by day'.

Cosmus: Cosimo I de' Medici, Duke of Florence 1537–69; source untraced.

Shall we . . . also?: Job 2: 10.

Caesar . . . Henry the Third: the assassination of Julius Caesar ultimately brought the prosperous rule of Augustus; that of Publius Helvius Pertinax in AD 193 led to the efficient rule of Septimius Severus; while the murder of Henry III in 1589 led to the reign of the heroic Henry IV and the Edict of Nantes (1598), guaranteeing tolerance to the Huguenots.

5. OF ADVERSITY

Seneca: *Epistles*, 66. 29.

command over nature: self-command, in restraint of natural impulse.

the other: *Epistles*, 53. 12 (paraphrased). This saying was too 'high' (lofty), 'heathens' not having access to Christian revelation.

strange fiction: a myth recorded in Apollodorus, *Bibliotheca*, 2. 5. 10. In the classical sources the 'pitcher' or vessel, in which Hercules sailed, was made of gold, not clay.

12 *lively work*: vivid pattern or picture.

discover: reveal. Cf. Guicciardini, *Ricordi*, no. 164: 'Men's good fortune is often their greatest enemy, for it causes them to become wicked, frivolous, insolent. Thus it is a better test of a man to withstand good fortune than adversity' (p. 42).

6. OF SIMULATION AND DISSIMULATION

Dissimulation: concealment (under a feigned semblance). Bacon's treatment of this topic overlaps that of Guicciardini in his *Ricordi*, nos. 104–5 (pp. 28–9).

Tacitus: *Annals*, 5. 1.

Mucianus: commander of Syrian troops; cf. *Histories*, 2. 76.

13 *half lights*: in part; or 'by twilight' (the Latin translation has 'tanquam in crepusculo').

  Tacitus: Annals, 3. 70; *Agricola*, 39.

  without hold . . . is: without revealing himself (a 'hold' is a grip in wrestling).

  close . . . open: as the confined air in a room gives way to the colder air from outside.

  in that kind: in the same way that a confessor does.

  mysteries are due to secrecy: people who can keep a secret earn others' confidences.

  futile: unable to hold their tongue; Lat. *futilis*, 'easily pouring out'.

  set it down: take note, as of an important truth.

14 *face give . . . leave*: that his facial expression does not reveal beforehand what the tongue has to say, or does not contradict what he has said.

  equivocations: using a word in more than one sense, intending to deceive.

  oraculous speeches: obscure hints, often deceptive.

  take a fall: be thrown (another metaphor from wrestling).

  freedom of thought: reserving judgement.

15 *spoil . . . mark*: prevent the arrow's direct ('round') flight to its target.

  temperature: temperament (ideally, a balance between the humours).

  to . . . opinion: have a reputation for frankness.

7. OF PARENTS AND CHILDREN

  memory: 'exemption from oblivion' (Dr Johnson).

  noblest works . . . images of their minds . . . bodies have failed: cf. Plato, *Symposium*, 208 B–209 A.

  raisers of their houses: founders of a family or dynasty.

  work: serving to perpetuate the family.

  children and creatures: that is, both 'kin' and 'created beings', corresponding to 'kind' and 'work' earlier.

  A wise . . . mother: Prov. 10: 1. Bacon explains this obscure sentence in the *De Augmentis* as meaning that 'a wise and prudent son is of most comfort to the father, who knows the value of virtue better than the mother. . . . But the mother has more sorrow at her son's ill fortune . . . both because the affection of a mother is more gentle' and perhaps because she feels she may have spoiled him (*Works*, v. 40).

16 *keep . . . not their purse*: withhold money.

  of the lump: lot (here lineage).

  the blood happens: as the family traits come out.

  optimum . . . consuetudo: 'choose what is best: custom will make it pleasant and easy': Pythagoras, according to Plutarch, 'De exilio', 8 (*Moralia*, 602 C).

8. OF MARRIAGE AND SINGLE LIFE

hostages: pledge or security (which Fortune can damage).

which: who. (The 1625 edition omits part of the 1612 text here: 'which have sought eternity in memory, and not in posterity'.)

17 *vetulam ... immortalitati*: 'he preferred his old wife to immortality': *Odyssey*, 5. 135, perhaps via Cicero, *De oratore*, 1. 44, or Plutarch's 'Gryllus' (*Moralia*, 985 F, 989 A), in a Latin translation.

quarrel: motive (here: reason for marrying at any age).

he ... answer: Thales, according to Diogenes Laertius, 1. 26, and Plutarch, 'Table-Talk', 3. 6. 3 (*Moralia*, 654 C).

9. OF ENVY

On a remarkable stylistic feature of the Essay, the fact that no fewer than 21 of its 76 head clauses begin with the explanatory 'For', see Ruth Tarselius, ' "All colours will agree in the dark": A Note on a feature in the style of Francis Bacon', in Vickers (ed.), *Essential Articles*, 293–9. Reynolds (p. 62) observes that Bacon uses 'envy' in two senses: in the private sphere it has its ordinary meaning, and sometimes 'malevolence'; in the public sphere it means 'discontent, disaffection'. For a partial source see Aristotle, *Rhetoric*, 2. 10 (on envy), and Cicero, *Tusculan Disputations*, 3. 9. 19–21.

18 *fascinate*: to 'cast a spell over with a look'. In Renaissance occultism 'fascination' was thought to begin through the eye, before overpowering the imagination. In his 'Table-Talk' (5. 7; *Moralia*, 680 C–681 E) Plutarch discusses at length 'people who are said to cast a spell and to have an evil eye'. This power derives from 'effluences', the 'most active stream of such emanations' issuing from the eye. So 'envy, which naturally roots itself more deeply in the mind than any other passion, contaminates the body too with evil ... When those possessed by envy to this degree let their glance fall upon a person, their eyes, which are close to the mind and draw from it the evil influence of the passion, then assail that person as if with poisoned arrows ...'.

into the eye: thought to be the strongest of the senses, hence most vulnerable to external influences.

Scripture: Mark 7: 22.

influences: a 'stream' from the stars.

evil aspects: angular relationships between the planets or zodiacal signs and the Earth; some of which were supposed to be inauspicious.

ejaculation ... eye: Renaissance optics and psychology believed that the eye perceived by emitting beams of light; so here envy is thought of as being physically transmitted.

spirits: vital powers (within the body, 'spirit' was thought to be an extremely fine liquid, easily vaporized). The 'outward parts' are the bodily surface.

18 *virtue*: in Bacon this word often has the sense of Latin *virtus* and Italian *virtù*, 'innate strength'.

19 *Non ... malevolus*: 'no one is inquisitive without wishing for the worst': Plautus, *Stichus*, 1. 3. 54.

new men: those who have newly acquired rank, were not born to it (Lat. *novi homines*).

deceit of the eye: optical illusion.

old men: cf. Aristotle, *Rhetoric*, 2. 10: 'We also envy those who have what we ought to have, or have got what we did have once. Hence old men envy younger men ...' (1388ª19 ff.).

Narses ... Agesilaus ... Tamberlanes: Narses (*c*.478–*c*.578) was an outstanding Byzantine general, who reclaimed Italy from the Ostrogoths. Agesilaus, 444–360 BC, King of Sparta, had one leg shorter than the other: Plutarch, 'Life' of Agesilaus, 2. 2. Tamberlane, Mongol conqueror, *c*.1336–1405, was lame according to some sources.

vain-glory: vanity, ambition. Cf. Aristotle, *Rhetoric*: 'Ambitious men are more envious than those who are not ... Indeed, generally, those who aim at a reputation for anything are envious on this particular point' (1387ᵇ31 ff.).

cannot want work: always have occasion to feel envy.

Hadrian: Publius Aelius Hadrianus, emperor AD 117–38.

near kinsfolks: cf. Aristotle, *Rhetoric*: 'We feel [envy] towards equals ... in birth, relationship, age, disposition, distinction, or wealth' (1387ᵇ23 ff.); 'we envy those who are near us in time, place, age, or reputation. Hence the line "Ay, kin can even be jealous of their kin" ' (1388ª5 ff.).

fellows in office: companions sharing the same rank.

pointeth at: directs attention to (contemptuously). Cf. Aristotle, *Rhetoric*: 'We also envy those whose possession of or success in a thing is a reproach to us: these are our neighbours and equals; for it is clear that it is our own fault we have missed the good thing in question; this annoys us, and excites envy in us' (1388ª17 ff.).

sacrifice: Abel's offering (Gen. 4: 3–5).

no body to look on: no spectators to see his disgrace, and so justify his envy.

20 *comparing ... kings*: Cf. Aristotle, *Rhetoric*, on the envy we feel towards 'our fellow-competitors': 'We compete with those who follow the same ends as ourselves ... who are after the same things; and it is therefore these whom we are bound to envy beyond all others. Hence the saying, "Potter against potter" ' (1388ª9 ff.).

per saltum: 'by a leap'.

travels: travails, labours. Cf. Plutarch, 'On inoffensive self-praise', *Moralia*, 544 D: men 'seldom or never envy such as have bought [glory] very dear, with many travails and great dangers'.

quanta patimur: 'how much we suffer!'

21 *that*: i.e. by crafty disclaimers.

disavow fortune: disown it, as having favoured him more than he deserved.

lot: spell; Lat. *sors*, which gave its name to the practisers of witchcraft, sorcerers. According to Renaissance witchcraft theory, a maleficent spell could only be removed by being transferred to some other person or animal.

Sedition: see Essay 15, below.

handled: discussed earlier.

22 *Invidia . . . agit*: 'envy keeps no holidays'.

devil: 'the word *devil* means *slanderer*, i.e. one that slanders God to men, and . . . slanders men to God' (Abbott, 2. 139).

The envious . . . night: Matt. 13: 25 (although the biblical text refers not to an envious man but to 'his enemy').

10. OF LOVE

syren: mythical creatures, half-woman, half-bird, whose song lured sailors to destruction (Homer, *Odyssey* 12. 39). Cf. Bacon, *De Sapientia Veterum*, 31: 'The Sirens, or Pleasure' (*Works*, vi. 762–4).

fury: in Greek myth, winged woman with snakes for hair, goddess of vengeance.

great spirits: outstanding rulers and statesmen.

Marcus Antonius: infatuated by Cleopatra (as in Plutarch and Shakespeare).

half-partner: joint ruler (with Octavius Caesar).

Appius Claudius: judge and one of the decemvirs (body of ten men administering Rome and its laws), whose lust for Virginia caused her murder and a people's revolt in 449 BC; cf. Livy, 3. 33.

Satis . . . sumus: 'each of us is enough of an audience for the other': Seneca, *Epistles*, 7. 11 (who quotes the saying to prove that the opinion of the multitude is of no account).

23 *phrase*: diction (as well as in the thought).

said: by Plutarch, 'How to tell a Flatterer from a Friend', 11 (*Moralia*, 48 E–F): the flatterer can appeal to 'Self-love, whereby every man being the first and greatest flatterer of himself, he can be very well content to admit a stranger to . . . confirm that good self-conceit and opinion of his own'.

have intelligence: have an understanding with; conspire.

that . . . wise: a sentence first found in Publilius Syrius and in Plutarch's 'Life' of Agesilaus, but given great currency by Erasmus' *Adagia*.

poet's relation: poetic narrative of the choice of Paris, who preferred beauty (Venus) to wisdom (Pallas) and power (Juno), as in Ovid, *Heroides*, 16. 163–6.

true . . . ends: constant in pursuing their own interests.

martial men: soldiers. Cf. Aristotle, *Politics*, 2. 9, 1269^{b}27 ff.

11. OF GREAT PLACE

23 *great place*: public eminence (the Latin translation renders it *De Magis-tratibus & Dignitatibus*).

24 *Cum . . . vivere*: 'when you are no longer what you have been, you see no reason why you should wish to live': Cicero, *Ad familiares*, 7. 3.

   the shadow: the obscurity of home (as against the openness of public life). The Latin translation reads *umbram et otium*.

   the puzzle of business: the confused bustle of public life.

   Illi . . . sibi: 'death comes heavily on him who dies well-known to the world, a stranger to himself': Seneca, *Thyestes*, 2. 401–3.

   can: be able (an unusual usage).

   vantage and commanding ground: superior position, able to do good.

   theatre: spectacle (a life of good works).

   rest: in heaven (as God rested on the seventh day of Creation).

   Et . . . nimis: 'and God turned to look upon the works which his hands had made, and saw that all were very good': Gen. 1: 31. Cf. also Augustine, *Confessions*, 13. 36. 51.

25 *first institution*: beginning. Cf. Machiavelli, *Discorsi*, 3. 1.

   direct in chief: rule through intermediaries. Cf. Plutarch, 'Precepts of Statecraft', *Moralia*, 812 C.

   taking . . . offering: gifts and bribes.

26 *importunity*: allowing oneself to be pressurized or manipulated by others.

   respects: considerations, or 'favours' (to the wrong people).

   To respect . . . bread: Prov. 28: 21.

   anciently: by various classical writers, including Plutarch (*Lives*), and in the later proverb found (e.g.) in Erasmus' *Adagia*, '*Magistratus virum indicat*'.

   Omnium . . . imperasset: 'an unanimous verdict would have judged him fit to rule, if he had never ruled': *Histories*, 1. 49. Proclaimed emperor in AD 68, Galba was so unpopular that he was murdered within a year.

   Solus . . . melius: 'Vespasianus was the only emperor that was improved by empire' (ruling power): *Histories*, 1. 50. Emperor AD 69–79, Vespasianus' rule brought peace and prosperity.

   sufficiency: ability, administrative competence.

   honour: celebrity, fame (in Renaissance ethics, properly the reward for or recognition of virtuous behaviour for the public good).

   in nature . . . in their place: Renaissance astronomy and physics distin-guished linear motion (often caused by attraction) from circular motion (as in a planet's orbit).

12. OF BOLDNESS

   trivial grammar-school text: a trite or elementary text, as taught in the *trivium* or three beginning subjects of education (grammar, logic, rhetoric) between the ages of 10 and 16.

Demosthenes: the greatest Athenian orator (?384–322 BC); the anecdote is recorded in Pseudo–Plutarch, 'Lives of the ten Orators', *Moralia*, 845 B, and often in Cicero, e.g. *De oratore*, 3. 56. 213, *Brutus*, 38. 142.

action: the five 'parts' of rhetoric were *inventio, dispositio, elocutio, memoria*, and *actio* (or *pronuntiatio*), the last stage teaching the rhetorical gestures to be used in delivering a speech.

that: that which. In his 'Life' of Demosthenes, 11. 1–2, Plutarch records that he had by nature a soft voice, a stammer, and short breath, all of which defects he overcame by training.

noble: the intellectually more demanding processes of composition.

27 *taken*: enthralled. Cf. Aristotle, *Rhetoric*, 3. 1, 1404ᵃ1–9.

popular: democratic (or demagogic). Reynolds (p. 85) cites Herodotus, 5. 97, on how Aristagoras 'failed to persuade Cleomenes to attack Persia and give aid to the Ionian revolt; but when he came to Athens he carried the people with him by his boundless promises and assurances of easy success'.

Mahomet's miracle: proverbial in the sixteenth century already.

in bashfulness . . . spirits . . . stay: in shy people the vital spirits fluctuate wildly (as in blushing); in bold people they are less volatile or expressive.

13. OF GOODNESS AND GOODNESS OF NATURE

28 *Philanthropia*: love of mankind.

humanity: Latin *humanitas* was sometimes used to translate *philanthropia*, but weakly. Cf. Aulus Gellius: 'Those who have spoken Latin and have used the language correctly do not give the word *humanitas* the meaning which it is commonly thought to have, namely, what the Greeks call φιλανθρωπια, signifying a kind of friendly spirit and good-feeling towards all men without distinction; but they gave to *humanitas* about the force of the Greek παιδεια; that is, what we call *eruditionem institutionemque in bonas artes*, or "education and training in the liberal arts". Those who earnestly desire and seek after these are most highly humanized. For the pursuit of that kind of knowledge, and the training given by it, have been granted to man alone of all the animals, and for that reason it is termed *humanitas*, or "humanity" ' (*Noctes Atticae*, 13. 17. 1, tr. J. C. Rolfe (London, 1960), ii. 457).

habit . . . inclination: categories used by Aristotle in *Metaphysics*, 5. 20; *Nicomachean Ethics*, 2. 1, 6. 13, 10. 9; *Eudemian Ethics*, 2. 2; *Politics*, 7. 13.

no excess: Bacon places goodness outside the scheme of Aristotle's *Nicomachean Ethics*, in which each virtue occupies a mid-point between excess and deficiency.

Turks: in the Middle Ages and Renaissance they were major opponents of the Church, and thus proverbial for inhumanity.

Busbechius: Ogier Ghiselain de Busbecq (1522–92), a diplomat at the Turkish court, whose letters, published in 1589, include many anecdotes of the Turks' kindness to animals.

28 *errors*: Cf. Aristotle, *Nicomachean Ethics*, 6. 13.

Machiavel: in *Discorsi*, 2. 2. (Bacon distorts Machiavelli's point, which is that Christianity makes men indifferent to worldly affairs by proposing more worthy goals.)

bondage . . . fancies: gratifying their passing whims.

29 *Aesop's cock*: actually, in a fable by Phaedrus (3. 12).

He sendeth . . . unjust: Matt. 5: 45.

Sell . . . me: Mark 10: 21; Matt. 19: 21.

a habit of goodness: Aristotle, *Nicomachean Ethics*, 6. 13.

right reason: in Renaissance ethics, the faculty that should control human behaviour.

loading part: taking the side which increases other people's burdens.

Lazarus' sores: Luke 16: 21.

Timon: in his extreme misanthropy he invited anyone who so wished to hang themselves from a tree in his garden. See Plutarch's 'Life' of Timon, 70. 2, and Shakespeare, *Timon of Athens*, 5. 2. 205–12.

errors: sports, deformities. Cf. Suetonius, 'Life' of Augustus, 65.

knee timber: growing crooked (like the human knee), and so more resistant.

citizen of the world: this concept, first formulated by Cicero (*De legibus*, 1. 23. 61), defines someone receptive to the whole of human life.

no island . . . lands: compare Donne's *Devotions* (1624): 'No Man is an *Island*, intire of itselfe; every man is a peece of the *Continent*, a part of the *maine*' (Meditation 17).

the noble tree: the incense tree (see Pliny, *Natural History*, 12. 14) which, like the pelican, was an emblem of self-sacrifice for the good of others.

30 *St Paul's perfection*: Rom. 9: 3, 'For I could wish that myself were accursed from Christ for my brethren, my kinsmen according to the flesh'.

14. OF NOBILITY

the Switzers: the Swiss, who by this time had thirteen cantons, both Protestant and Catholic.

The united provinces: Holland, Belgium, Flanders.

presseth: oppresses (since the nobility is a closed class).

too great . . . for justice: being above the law.

31 *act of power*: created by royal decree.

15. OF SEDITIONS AND TROUBLES

This essay is found in the MS collection preceding the 1612 edition, but was not printed there: see p. xix above. The detail with which Bacon analyses civil disturbances shows the fear with which they were generally regarded throughout Europe in the sixteenth and seventeenth centuries.

Shepherds: rulers, governors.

things . . . equality: when the various levels of society gain equal power.

Equinoctia: in the spring and autumn equinoxes, when the days and nights are equal in length, storms are more likely.

Ille . . . bella: Virgil, *Georgics*, 1. 464–5: the sun 'often warns us that dark tumults threaten, and deceits and hidden wars are swelling'.

Illam . . . Progenuit: *Aeneid*, 4. 178–80: 'Mother Earth (as they relate), irritated by anger against the gods, brought forth [Rumour] last as sister to Cœus and Enceladus'.

32 *conflata . . . premunt*: *Histories*, 1. 7 (adapted): 'when envy is once roused, good actions are as much assailed as bad'.

Erant . . . exequi: *Histories*, 2. 39 (adapted): 'They were on duty, but none the less preferred to interpret the orders of their generals rather than to follow them'.

Machiavel: *Discorsi*, 3. 27, on the danger of factions.

common parents: as if the parents of everyone in a state.

entered league: joined with. The Holy League, formed in 1576 by a group of Catholics to defend their faith and to destroy the Protestants, was expelled by King Henry III (1574–89) from Paris in 1585.

accessary . . . cause: participating in some activity, but not as principal.

carried: carried on.

primum mobile: in Ptolemaic astronomy, the 'first mover' or outermost of the ten planetary spheres, from which the rest derive their motion, was supposedly set in motion by the Creator. For many Renaissance writers it was a favourite metaphor for the King's orderly rule of the state.

old opinion: ancient theory. Bacon did not fully accept either the Ptolemaic or the Copernican system, holding both unproven.

particular: in the stars, the planet's individual motion; in the state, the (violent) actions of powerful men seeking their own gain.

liberius . . . meminissent: *Annals*, 3. 4 (adapted): 'More freely than if they had remembered their governors'.

33 *orbs . . . frame*: the system is disordered.

Solvam . . . regum: a fusion of two texts, Job 12: 18, and Isa. 45: 1, 'I will loosen the girdles of kings', a threat that presages the break-up of society.

Materials . . . Motives: Bacon is using the Aristotelian categories of 'material cause' and 'efficient cause' (*Posterior Analytics*, 2. 1, 94^{a-b}; *Metaphysics*, 4. 2, 1013). Material causes, described in the two following paragraphs, are situations generally existing (poverty, discontent); efficient causes, described in the fourth paragraph, are events taking place at a given point in time.

Hinc . . . bellum: *Pharsalia*, 1. 181–2: 'Hence devouring usury and interest rapidly compounded, hence shaken credit, and war profitable to many'.

33 *of the belly*: from hunger, in the 'mean people' or labouring classes.

Dolendi . . . item: Pliny, *Epistles*, 8. 17: 'There is an end to suffering, but not to fearing'.

34 *Causes and Motives*: synonymous: 'efficient causes'.

innovation: any alteration to established rituals or beliefs in the period 1520 to 1690 was (rightly) feared as likely to create disturbances.

strangers: grievances arising out of the success of foreigners in trade.

counsel . . . rule: individual discretion, no general rule.

sumptuary laws: laws against extravagance in dress and behaviour.

live lower and gather more: satisfied with a lower level of subsistence, such people save more.

multiplying of nobility: the vast increase in numbers of the aristocracy in the sixteenth and seventeenth centuries created many social problems.

upon the foreigner: for the benefit of foreign trading-partners (or 'at the expense of').

whatsoever . . . lost: cf. Aristotle, *Politics*, 1. 10, 1258^{b}1–2, and Montaigne, *Essais*, 1. 22, 'Le Profit de l'un est dommage de l'aultre' (p. 120).

35 *as in a spring tide*: abundantly (as tides are fullest at the new moon).

materiam . . . opus: Ovid, *Metamorphoses*, 2. 5: 'The workmanship will surpass the material'.

mines above ground: the Dutch, despite their lack of raw materials, were celebrated for their industry both in manufacturing and in transportation, which became as profitable as gold mines.

ingrossing: monopolizing, buying 'in the gross' in order to corner the market. Many statutes were passed in the sixteenth century forbidding buying in order to resell, but they failed to prevent the practice.

great pasturages: enclosures, by which small farmers were denied use of common agricultural land, which was fenced off for sheep pastures to support the increasingly profitable export trade in wool. Bacon brought a bill into the 1597 parliament against the depopulation caused by enclosures: *Works*, ix. 82.

troubling of the waters: as in the pool of Bethesda, which could cure paralytics: John 5: 2 ff.

poets: Homer, *Iliad*, 1. 396–406 (where in fact it is Thetis, not Pallas, who sent for Briareus).

turneth . . . back: obstructs, preventing the fluid (e.g. blood) from escaping.

endangereth: risks producing malignant tumours.

Epimetheus: Epimetheus is after-thought, Prometheus fore-thought. In this version of the fable Jupiter takes revenge for Prometheus' gift of fire to the human race by creating Pandora with her box or jar of calamities, which Epimetheus opens. Cf. *De Sapientia Veterum*, 26 (*Works*, vi. 745 ff.).

36 *greatness*: high standing in society.

Sulla . . . dictare: Suetonius, 'Caesar', 77: 'Sulla did not know his letters, he could not dictate' (with a pun on 'act the dictator').

legi . . . emi: Tacitus, *Histories*, 1. 5: '[He] selected his soldiers, and did not buy them'.

si . . . militibus: Flavius Vopiscus, *Scriptores Historiae Augustae*, 20. 20: 'If I live, the Roman empire shall have no more need of soldiers'.

37 *Atque . . . paterentur*: *Histories*, 1. 28: 'And such was the condition of their minds, that a few dared the evilest deeds, more desired them, all permitted them'.

holding . . . correspondence: bearing a proportion, corresponding.

16. OF ATHEISM

the Legend: the *Legenda aurea*, a collection of Saints' lives and miracles compiled in Latin by Jacobus de Voragine in the thirteenth century, which had a great influence on Renaissance religion and art.

Talmud: the collection of Jewish civil and ceremonial law.

Alcoran: the Koran, the sacred book of Islam.

universal frame: the universe.

second causes scattered: God is the first cause: the works of man are second (or efficient) causes, seemingly 'scattered' or unconnected to the divine plan.

the school: the earliest atomists (not properly a 'school', since they lived at different times) who believed that matter had been created out of the random combination of small particles. In both classical and Christian times their denial of a divine creation caused all atomists to be judged atheistical. Leucippus (*c*.470–360 BC) was the first of the atomists; Democritus (*c*.460–370 BC) and Epicurus (*c*.342–270 BC) were important philosophers.

four mutable elements: according to Heraclitus (followed by Aristotle), earth, air, fire, water. Aristotle added a fifth element, ether, supposedly the substance from which the heavenly bodies are composed. Cf. *On the heavens*, 1. 4, 270^{a}13 ff.

The fool . . . God: Ps. 14: 1; 53: 1.

for . . . maketh: for whose advantage it is to believe.

38 *appeareth . . . more*: nowhere else it is so evident.

charged: for this accusation see Cicero, *De natura deorum*, 1. 44. 123.

blessed natures: Epicurus conceived the gods ('blessed natures') as happy in their own existence, not caring about man (ibid. 123, 139).

Non . . . profanum: 'it is not profane to deny the gods of the vulgar, but it is profane to apply the opinions of the vulgar to the gods': according to Diogenes Laertius, 10. 123.

he: Epicurus denied that the gods rule over and care for mankind.

38 *Indians of the west*: the South American Indians, according to Acosta, *Naturall and Morall Historie of the East and West Indies* (Eng. tr., 1604), 5. 3.

   Diagoras . . . Bion: Diagoras of Melos (late fifth century BC), and *Bion*, Bio the Borysthenite (*c*.325–*c*.255 BC), both avowed atheists. Cf. Cicero, *De natura deorum*, 1. 1. 2, 23. 63, 42. 117; 3. 37. 89; Diogenes Laertius, 4. 54–7.

   Lucian: Lucian of Samosata (born *c*. AD 120), rather a mocker than an atheist.

   Non . . . sacerdos: 'one can no longer say the priest is as [bad as] the people, for the people are not [so bad] as the priests': Pseudo St Bernard, *Sermo ad Pastores*.

39 *raising*: elevating (to a divine level).

   melior natura: 'a better nature': Ovid, *Metamorphoses*, 1. 21.

   Quam . . . superavimus: 'rate ourselves as highly as we may, Conscript Fathers, yet we cannot match the Spaniards in numbers, the Gauls in bodily strength, the Carthaginians in craft, the Greeks in art, nor our own Italians and Latins in the home-bred and native patriotism characteristic of this land and nation. But our piety, our religion, and our recognition of the one great truth of the Divine government of all things—these are the points wherein we have surpassed all nations and peoples': Cicero, *De haruspicum responsis*, 9. 19.

17. OF SUPERSTITION

In a letter to Tobie Matthew (*c*.1608) Bacon wrote that 'superstition is far worse than atheism; by how much it is less evil to have no opinion of God at all, than such as is impious towards his divine majesty and goodness' (*Works*, xi. 10).

   the reproach of the Deity: Seneca, *Epistles*, 123. 16.

   Plutarch: 'De superstitione', 10 (*Moralia*, 169 F).

   Saturn: according to the ancient mythographers Saturn, fearing a prophecy that he would be deposed by his children, ate them as fast as they were born, only Jupiter escaping. Cf. Ovid, *Fasti*, 4. 197 ff.

   natural piety: the links of affection joining mankind.

40 *Augustus Caesar*: emperor 31 BC–AD 14, whose reign was unusually 'civil' or peaceful.

   primum-mobile: the tenth heaven or outer sphere in classical cosmology, which transmitted motion to the other nine.

   arguments are fitted to practice: logical reasoning is (erroneously) adapted to experience, instead of governing it. So the wise men champion the foolish instead of enlightening them.

   gravely: authoritatively. (In fact, it was meant as a witticism.)

   council of Trent: ecumenical Council of the Roman Catholic Church, which met three times between 1545 and 1563 to correct abuses and codify dogma in response to the Protestant Reformation. See Paolo Sarpi, *Istoria del Concilio Tridentino* (London, 1619), ii. 83.

engines of orbs: skilful devices (made with 'ingenium' or intelligence) representing planetary orbits.

eccentrics . . . phaenomena: the Ptolemaic philosophy of nine planetary spheres revolving concentrically around the earth did not 'save' (that is account for) all the 'phaenomena' of observed (irregular) planetary movement, so it had to evolve theories of additional types of rotation, imagining the planets moving in circles (epicycles) whose centres themselves moved in circles (eccentrics) at a little distance from the earth.

axioms and theorems: scientific propositions. So, the metaphor argues, the scholastic philosophers had to 'frame' or contrive similarly fictitious principles to account for inconsistencies within the Church.

taking an aim . . . human: conjecturing, trying to understand religion purely in terms of human reason, not divine revelation.

18. OF TRAVEL

The title of the Latin version is *De Peregrinatione in Partes Externas*, namely Europe. Cf. Bacon's 'Advice to the Earl of Rutland on his travels' (TOA 69–80; *Works*, ix. 16–20).

41 *exercises or discipline*: forms of instruction and study.

go hooded: be closed off from life (metaphor from falconry).

armories: arsenals, storage-places for military and naval equipment and weapons.

magazines: public storage-houses (e.g. for grain).

exchanges; burses: meeting-places where merchants transact business.

cabinets and rarities: museums, collections of rare objects.

put . . . little room: benefit most quickly.

42 *the life*: their actual way of living.

healths: toasts (a common cause of quarrels).

country manners: those of his own country (like Lat. *patrius*).

19. OF EMPIRE

Empire: rule, especially by a king or emperor.

43 *representations*: imaginations, delusions; in the Latin version, *phantasmata*.

that . . . inscrutable: Prov. 25: 3.

erecting . . . order: establishing a fraternity, especially religious.

Nero: Suetonius, 'Nero', 20; Dio Cassius, 63. 1.

Domitian: Suetonius, 'Domitian', 19.

Commodus: Aelius Lampidius, *Scriptores Historiae Augustae*, 11. 10 ff.; Herodian, 1. 15 ff.; Dio Cassius, 72. 10, 22.

Caracalla: Dio Cassius, 77. 10, 17.

43 *Alexander*: Plutarch, 'Of Isis and Osiris', 466 D.

Diocletian: Roman emperor AD 284–305, who in fact abdicated because of ill-health rather than melancholy.

Charles the Fifth: Holy Roman emperor (1519–58) and King of Spain, who abdicated in 1556 in favour of his son, Philip II, and spent the two remaining years of his life in ascetic contemplation.

temper: mixture, temperament: mingling the constituent parts into one balanced whole.

distemper: disorder, alteration; interchanging contraries without mingling them.

answer: Philostratus, *Life of Apollonius of Tyana*, 5. 28.

44 *try masteries*: compete with, as to who shall be master.

Sunt . . . contrariae: in fact Sallust, *Bellum Jugurthinum*, 113. 1: 'The desires of kings are commonly vehement and contradictory'.

solecism: lack of congruence, violating the norms (of syntax; or government).

approaches: massing forces on the frontier.

During: between 1519 and 1556. Bacon re-uses here his discussion of the balance of power from 'Considerations Touching a War with Spain' of 1624: cf. *Works*, xiv. 469–505, especially 477, and V. Luciani, 'Bacon and Guicciardini', *PMLA* 62 (1947), 96–113, at 104–7.

take up . . . interest: accept ('borrow') a present peace at the cost of future loss.

league: made in 1480; Guicciardini, *Storia d'Italia*, 1. 1.

schoolmen: cf. *Works*, xiv. 477–8, quoting Aquinas, *Summa Theologica*, 2. 2. 40. 1.

infamed: infamous. Cf. Tacitus, *Annals*, 4. 3.

husband: Augustus, with poisoned figs. Cf. Dio Cassius, 56. 30.

destruction: in 1553, to favour her own son.

otherwise: in other ways. Roxolana supported Bajazet, her younger son, against his elder brother Selymus.

queen: Isabella. See e.g. Marlowe's *Edward II*.

45 *strange*: impure, 'not of one's kin or family' (*SOED*).

Crispus: executed in AD 326, at the instigation of his stepmother Fausta, Constantine's second wife.

Demetrius: falsely accused by his brother Perseus, and executed by his father, 179 BC: Livy, *History*, 40. 24, insists on his innocence.

Second: in fact, the Fifth: Livy, 40. 54–6.

Selymus: who had his father poisoned by his own physician.

three sons: who openly rebelled against their father between 1173 and 1189.

Anselmus: St Anselm, appointed archbishop of Canterbury in 1093, and who clashed with two kings.

Becket: murdered by four of King Henry II's knights in Canterbury Cathedral in 1170.

state: estate of the realm (here: the clergy).

dependance . . . authority: depends on a foreign power (i.e. the Pope).

collation: the presentation of a clergyman to a benefice or living.

noted: cf. *Works*, vi. 242; and *Henry VII*, ed. Vickers, 201.

46 *vena porta*: the gate-vein, a large vein which was thought to distribute chyle to the liver: similarly, the merchants concentrate the resources of a country in order to redistribute them.

hundred: a division of a county in England originally supposed to consist of a hundred families.

wins . . . shire: gains in a small matter but loses in a larger.

janizaries: an elite Turkish corps, formed in 1326. Bacon's source here and elsewhere is Richard Knolles, *The generall historie of the Turks* (1603).

pretorian bands: originally an imperial bodyguard, instituted by Augustus.

Princes are like . . . but no rest: cf. Seneca, *Consolatio ad Polybium*, 7. 3: 'On the day that Caesar dedicated himself to the wide world, he robbed himself of himself; and even as the planets, which, unresting ever pursue their courses, he may never halt or do anything for himself'.

memento . . . Dei: 'remember that you are a man'; 'Remember that you are a God', or 'God's lieutenant'.

20. OF COUNSEL

in other: dealing with stewards, tutors, agents, financial advisers.

they: the counsellors.

47 *Counsellor*: Isa. 9: 6.

Salomon: Prov. 20: 18 (paraphrased).

Salomon's son: in 1 Kings 12: 1–19 Rehoboam rejects the advice of his father's counsellors to be lenient to the Israelites, who rebel at his harshness.

Jupiter . . . Metis . . . Pallas: according to Hesiod (*Theogony*, 886–900) Metis is 'counsel' and Pallas Athena 'wisdom'. Cf. *De Sapientia Veterum*, ch. 30, 'Metis; or Counsel' (*Works*, vi. 761–2).

delivered . . . armed . . . head: gave birth, out of his own head, to Pallas Athena, dressed in armour.

council of state: the king's main advisory body (the Privy Council in Britain).

48 *cabinet councils*: secret councils, held in 'cabinets' (private apartments), often of *ad hoc* advisers, 'recommended chiefly by flattery and affection', as Bacon put it in a manuscript draft which he did not publish (Kiernan, 216). For other contemporary disapproval of this innovation see Melchionda, 485.

48 *plenus . . . sum*: 'I am full of cracks': Terence, *Eunuchus*, 1. 2. 23–5 (cf. the contemporary term, 'to leak' a confidential matter).

which . . . persons: not more than one or two people should know the secret.

grind with a hand-mill: manage affairs himself without helpers.

Henry the Seventh: cf. *Works*, vi. 40; ed. Vickers, 19.

the fable: of Metis and Jupiter above. Kings should call back the fruits of counsel, which they own as children.

bereaved of his dependances: deprived of his dependencies, and so power.

over-greatness . . . combination: excessive power in one, or a rigorous alliance between several.

non . . . terram: 'he will not find faith on the earth': Luke 18: 8.

49 *Principis . . . suos*: 'it is a ruler's greatest excellence to know his subjects': Martial, *Epigrams*, 8. 15. 8.

inferior sort: of lower social standing.

secundum genera: generally, according to types.

optimi . . . mortui: 'the best counsellors are the dead' (a saying of Alphonso of Aragon, 1416–58).

order or act of council: decree to be put into action.

in nocte consilium: 'night is the season for counsel': a proverb (found in Erasmus' *Adagia* and elsewhere).

Commission of Union: in 1604 a committee was formed to discuss the implications of uniting the Kingdoms of England and Scotland. Bacon had written a detailed memorandum on the issue in 1603, 'A Brief Discourse touching the happy union of the Kingdoms of England and Scotland' (*Works*, x. 90–9, 241).

hocagere: 'do this', or 'mind this', i.e. 'concentrate on the business in hand'. Cf. Plutarch, 'Life' of Coriolanus, 25.

50 *tribunitious*: violent, turbulent, like the Tribunes in early Rome (cf. Livy, 3. 19, 4. 2; Shakespeare, *Coriolanus*).

upper end: with the president at the end of a table, those counsellors near him can 'sway' or control business.

take the wind of him: gain the advantage.

placebo: the first word of the Vesper hymn for the dead (Vulgate Ps. 114: 9), *Placebo Domino in regione vivorum . . .*: (Ps. 116: 9), 'I shall walk before the Lord in the land of the living'. Here, 'I shall please you', words of flatterers or time-servers who tell their superior what they know he wants to hear.

21. OF DELAYS

On the associative structure of argument in this essay see Vickers, *Renaissance Prose*, 228–31.

Sibylla's offer: this old woman offered to sell Tarquin at an enormous price nine books containing the oracles of the Gods. When the King refused she burnt three, then another three, but he finally bought the last three at the original price for all nine. Cf. Aulus Gellius, *Noctes Atticae*, 1. 19.

the common verse: popular saying, found in Erasmus' *Adagia* and elsewhere: *Fronte capillata, post haec occasio calva*, 'Take Time (Occasion) by the forelock, for she is bald behind'.

51 *shone on ... back*: illuminated from behind. Cf. Plutarch's 'Life' of Pompeius, 32–6.

buckling: putting on armour, preparing to do battle.

Argos: in classical mythology Argos, who had a hundred eyes, was set to watch over Io. Cf. Aeschylus, *Prometheus Bound*, 567 ff.

Briareus: a giant with a hundred hands, who helped Jupiter to combat the Titans. Cf. Homer, *Iliad*, 1. 403.

Pluto: Perseus was able to slay the gorgon Medusa by wearing Pluto's helmet, which made him invisible.

politique: astute. Cf. Homer, *Iliad*, 5. 845.

22. OF CUNNING

pack the cards: shuffle the cards deceitfully.

their own alley: on their own ground, in familiar surroundings (a metaphor from bowls).

Mitte ... videbis: 'send them both naked to those they know not, and you will see [who they are]': a saying of Aristippus recorded by Diogenes Laertius, 2. 73.

set ... shop: display their tricks.

Jesuits: one of their rules for modesty was not to look directly at the person you talk to, but with a lowered gaze.

52 *a counsellor*: probably Sir Francis Walsingham (?1530–90), appointed to a leading post on the Privy Council in 1573, its sole secretary from 1577 on, famous for his cunning.

took himself up: corrected himself (so using the rhetorical figure *aposiopesis*, breaking off an utterance uncompleted).

And ... king: Neh. 2: 1.

Narcissus: Tacitus, *Annals*, 11. 29–30.

53 *two ... secretary's place*: probably Sir Robert Cecil and Sir Thomas Bodley in 1596; Cecil got the post.

The turning ... pan: saying of obscure origin, meaning 'to turn a situation round to one's own advantage'.

glance and dart: allude, as if reluctantly.

Se ... spectare: 'he had no divergent aims; but his one object was the safety of the Emperor': Tacitus, *Annals*, 14. 57. Said by Tigellinus, a debased crony of the emperor Nero, commenting on the death in AD 62 of Nero's sometime tutor and adviser, Sextus Afranius Burrus.

53 *in Paul's*: St Paul's Cathedral, London, a popular meeting-place. Cf. Jonson, *Every man out of his humour* (1599), 3. 1, set in 'The middle aisle of St Paul's'.

54 *resorts and falls*: sources (springs) and outcomes; or, beginnings and endings.

sink . . . main: penetrate to the important part.

find out pretty looses: make an impressive display (from 'looses', discharging arrows).

wits of direction: intellects fitted to manage affairs.

Prudens . . . dolos: 'the wise man giveth heed to his own steps; the fool turneth aside to deceits': Prov. 14: 8, 15.

23. OF WISDOM FOR A MAN'S SELF

Wisdom . . . Self: selfishness, egoism.

wise: the epithet traditionally applied to the ant in Prov. 6: 6; 30: 24–5, here used ironically.

society: the claims of other people. The Latin version is *amorem reipublicae*.

right earth: truly base (earth was the lowest of the four elements in Aristotelian philosophy).

affairs: in the Latin translation, *negotia publica*.

proportion: harmony, correspondence (continuing the cosmological analogy).

55 *set a bias . . . bowl*: cause the bowl to swerve from its straight course: i.e. manipulate affairs to their own advantage.

model: pattern (that is, for self-profit).

sell: trading their master's disadvantage for their own profit.

rats: Pliny, *Natural History*, 8. 28.

crocodiles . . . devour: according to the old belief that crocodiles weep in order to disarm their prey.

sui . . . rivali: 'lovers of themselves, without rivals': *Ad Quintum fratrem*, 3. 8.

24. OF INNOVATIONS

Innovations: in Renaissance political theory, which was often conservative, changes in the structure or government of a state were usually regarded with fear or suspicion. Bacon adopts a carefully balanced position.

as . . . perverted: corrupted as it is by the sin of Adam and Eve.

natural motion: like the fall of a heavy body, continually accelerating.

forced motion: like the flight of an arrow, continually less rapid.

56 *piece*: agree, match together. Aldis Wright (p. 319) compares Matt. 9: 16, 'No man putteth a piece of new cloth unto an old garment, for . . . the rent is made worse'.

suspect: a person or thing suspected (liable to be dangerous).

Scripture: Jer. 6: 16 (paraphrased).

25. OF DISPATCH

Dispatch: speed in settling business.

57 *for the time*: at this point; or, 'in proportion to the time taken'.

false periods: divisions which profess to include all the relevant topics, but do not.

a wise man: Sir Amyas Paulet, with whom Bacon went to France in 1576: cf. *Works*, vii. 136, for this apophthegm.

Spartans . . . Spaniards: both proverbial for prudence and caution. For the Spartans, cf. Thucydides, 1. 70, 84. Bacon quotes the proverb elsewhere, more appropriately, in Italian (*Works*, x. 351).

divide: distinguish (in rhetoric the process of *partitio*, dividing up the main points to be considered).

58 *middle*: the 'debate or examination'.

ashes . . . dust: cf. Pliny, *Natural History*, 17. 5, and Bacon, *Works*, ii. 525, 546.

26. OF SEEMING WISE

Having . . . thereof: Paul, in 2 Tim. 3: 5.

magno . . . nugas: 'trifles with great effort': Terence, *Heautontimoroumenos* (*The Self-Tormentor*), 4. 1. 8 (line 621).

prospectives: optical glasses which make surfaces appear three-dimensional.

Respondes . . . placere: 'you answer, with one eyebrow hoisted to your forehead and the other bent down to your chin, that you do not approve of cruelty': *In Pisonem*, 6. 14.

take by admittance . . . good: accept as valid something that they cannot prove.

59 *Hominem . . . pondera*: 'a madman who breaks up weighty matter with verbal niceties'. Bacon misattributes the quotation: it is Quintilian's judgement on Seneca's style (*Institutio oratoriae*, 10. 1. 130).

Plato: Protagoras, 337 A–C.

affect . . . object: try to gain credit by objecting.

inward: beneath the surface (his poverty hidden).

27. OF FRIENDSHIP

Bacon replaced the 1612 essay on friendship (Appendix II) with this completely new text, at the urging of his friend Sir Tobie Matthew. As Bacon wrote to him in March 1622: 'It is not for nothing that I have deferred my essay *De Amicitia*, whereby it hath expected the proof of your great friendship towards me' (*Works*, xiv. 344); and in June 1623: 'For the essay of friendship, while I took your speech of it for a cursory request I took my promise for a compliment. But since you call for it I shall perform it' (xiv. 429). See also Kiernan, p. lxxix, n. 82. Bacon's classical sources probably include Aristotle, *Nicomachean Ethics*, books 8 and 9; *Eudemian Ethics*, 7; *Magna Moralia*, 2. 11–17; *Rhetoric*, 2. 4; and Cicero, *De amicitia*.

59 *Whosoever . . . god*: Aristotle, *Politics*, 1. 2, 1253^{a}3 ff., 25 ff. But Bacon's interpretation is unfair.

feignedly: pretended. Bacon's strictures only apply to Numa, in fact.

Epimenides: teacher and miracle-worker of Crete ('Candia') (*c*.600–500 BC), supposed to have acquired prophetic powers after having fallen asleep in a cave for 57 years.

Numa: king of the Romans (*c*.715–673 BC), who regularly withdrew from society for mystic meditation with the goddess Egeria. But, according to Plutarch, he feigned this 'conference with the gods' to make his countrymen accept religion (Kiernan, 227).

Empedocles: philosopher and poet (*c*.493–*c*.433 BC), who claimed divine powers.

Apollonius of Tyana: a wandering ascetic in the early Christian era, whose miraculous powers were celebrated in Philostratus' *Life* of him.

tinkling cymbal: 1 Cor. 13: 1.

Magna . . . solitudo: 'great city, great solitude': Erasmus' *Adagia*, from Strabo (who applied it to Babylon).

60 *fullness . . . heart*: tension, emotional upset (in Renaissance physiology, usually located in the heart).

sarza: sarsaparilla, a medicinal plant from tropical America used to regulate the digestion.

steel: one of the new chemical treatments advocated by Paracelsus.

flower of sulphur: 'amorphous sulphur in a fine powder' (*SOED*).

civil shrift: non-clerical penance for guilt.

participes curarum: 'partners in care': Dio Cassius, 58. 4. 3. But, as Reynolds (p. 193) observes, there is 'no authority for Bacon's statement that this is "the Roman name". He seems to have been misled by his double habit of reading Greek authors in a Latin version, and of quoting from memory afterwards.' Here Bacon used Xylander's sixteenth-century Latin version of a passage describing the titles which Tiberius conferred on Sejanus, as in fact part of a plan to overthrow a feared rival. This forced application shows how phrases entered in, and quoted from a commonplace book can become false to their original context.

61 *for . . . setting*: Plutarch's 'Life' of Pompey, 14 f.

Julius Caesar: Plutarch's 'Life' of Julius Caesar, 64.

heir . . . nephew: heir in succession after Augustus.

Cicero's Philippics: 13. 11.

Maecenas: Dio Cassius, 54. 6. 5.

friends: Tacitus, *Annals*, 1. 3; Dio Cassius, 58. 4 ff. 14; 75. 15. 2.

haec . . . occultavi: 'these things, for the sake of our friendship, I have not hidden from you': Tacitus, *Annals*, 4. 40, and 74 for the altar to Friendship.

Septimius Severus: Dio Cassius, 76. 2. 7; Herodian, 3. 12. 3 f.

words: Dio Cassius, 75. 15. 2.

Trajan: Marcus Ulpius Trajanus, emperor AD 98–117, a great benefactor of learning.

Marcus Aurelius: emperor AD 169–80, whose *Meditations* was one of the most admired works of moral philosophy by a pagan.

an half piece: either a work of art left incomplete; or (Reynolds) 'the old practice of cutting silver pennies into halves to make up for the deficiency of smaller coins'.

nephews: the word also meant 'grandsons'.

Comineus: Philippe de Commines (*c*.1446–*c*.1511), French diplomat and historian, in his *Mémoires*, 5. 3, 5.

62 *Pythagoras*: according to Diogenes Laertius, 8. 18, and Plutarch, 'On the Education of Children', 12 (*Moralia*, 17 E): 'Eat not thy heart; that is to say, offend not thine own soul, nor hurt and consume it with pensive cares'.

truth of operation: efficacy.

stone: the alchemists' 'Philosopher's stone', supposedly able to cure all diseases.

bodies: inanimate bodies.

discourse . . . meditation: rather by conversation than by continuous thought.

63 *cloth of Arras*: embroidered wall-hanging tapestry made in Arras, France.

put abroad: spread out, the pattern appears in full outline ('in figure'); or, 'according to the design' (Melchionda).

that speech . . . in packs: Plutarch's 'Life' of Themistocles, 29; recorded more accurately (as juxtaposing not speech and thought, but the perfect and imperfect expression of thought by language) in Bacon's *Apophthegms* (*Works*, vii. 153).

whetteth: sharpens (cf. Horace, *Ars poetica*, 304–5).

Heraclitus: pre-Socratic philosopher (fl. *c*.500 BC); the saying is recorded in Plutarch's 'Life' of Romulus. Compare Bacon's application of this 'enigma' (obscure saying) in *Advancement of Learning* (TOA 125).

infused and drenched: soaked, submerged or confused by the passions and habit.

friend . . . flatterer: Bacon alludes to the essay in Plutarch's *Moralia* (48 E ff.), 'How a man may discern a flatterer from a friend'.

63 *calling . . . account*: self-criticism, stringently applied.

    them: their 'errors and absurdities'.

    saith: Jas. 1: 23–4 (paraphrased).

64 *said over . . . letters*: repeated the alphabet, until his anger calmed down. The letters *j* and *u* were not generally included until after 1630.

    all in all: all things in all respects.

    put you in way for: give you good chance of.

    say: as did Pythagoras, according to Porphyry's *Life*, 33; cf. also Aristotle, *Nicomachean Ethics*, 9. 4, 1166ᵃ31, *Magna Moralia*, 2. 15, 1213ᵃ12 f., and *Eudemian Ethics*, 7. 12, 1245ᵃ30; Diogenes Laertius, 7. 23, and Cicero, *De amicitia*, 21. 80.

    their time: their appointed time.

    in his desires: so far as his desires are concerned.

65 *face . . . comeliness*: modesty of decorum.

    How many . . . himself?: Cicero, *De amicitia*, 16. 57.

28. OF EXPENSE

This topic was of acute interest to landowners, especially the aristocracy, suffering under a huge inflation rate: 'the cost of living rose by about 80 per cent between 1550 and 1600', hence 'competent estate management became increasingly important as the pressure of inflation built up. Careful scrutiny and strict control of leases . . . could make crucial differences to the fortunes of noble families': D. M. Loades, *Politics and the Nation 1450–1600* (London, 1974), 344, 340.

    for honour: according to one's social status.

    voluntary undoing: freely giving away one's substance.

    kingdom of heaven: poverty was valued in the ascetic life, as being more likely to earn a place in heaven. Cf. Essay 13, 'Of Goodness and Goodness of Nature', p. 28, which also juxtaposes worldly and other-worldly attitudes to money.

    less than the estimation abroad: smaller than generally imagined.

    in respect . . . broken: in case they find themselves bankrupt.

    turn . . . certainties: establish a scale of fixed expenses (so denying his employees any chance of cheating).

66 *return not*: are 'extraordinary', as discussed at the beginning.

29. OF THE TRUE GREATNESS OF KINGDOMS AND ESTATES

Bacon first set down his ideas on this topic in a speech delivered to the House of Commons in February 1607, and further developed in a treatise 'Of the True

Greatness of the Kingdom of Britain' (*Works*, vii. 39–40, 47–64), planned and written in 1608 (*Works*, xi. 73–4) but not published until 1734. An earlier (less warlike) version was included in the 1612 *Essays* (TOA 301–3; *Works*, vi. 586–8). The revised and expanded English text first appeared in a Latin translation in the *De Augmentis* (8, 3), with the title *De proferendis Imperii finibus*, 'Of extending the bounds of Empire' (*Works*, i. 793–802; English translation, v. 79–88). The 'true greatness' in the English title, as the second paragraph makes clear, means 'expansive power', or 'the power and forces' of a state to acquire and hold new territory by warfare, a dynamic activity not employed (or needed?) by large but static states. On other occasions (e.g. *Works*, xiii. 20) he recommended the pursuit of peace. For a useful study of Bacon's thinking on these issues see Markku Peltonen, 'Politics and science: Francis Bacon and the True Greatness of States', *Historical Journal*, 35 (1992), 279–305, also in his *Classical Humanism and Republicanism in English Political Thought 1570–1640* (Cambridge, 1995), ch. 4.

As Melchionda shows (p. 518) the paired phrase, 'Kingdoms and Estates', which occurs 19 times in the *Essays*, means 'Monarchies and Republics', corresponding to the similar terms *principati e repubbliche*, frequently used by Machiavelli.

    speech: saying, recorded by Plutarch, 'Life' of Themistocles, 2. 4.

    fiddle: meaning: (*a*) 'play the instrument', (*b*) cheat.

    metaphor: by being transferred to politics (the Latin term for metaphor is *translatio*).

67 *negotiis pares*: equal to the business, just. Cf. Tacitus, *Annals*, 6. 39, 16. 18.

    compared: in Matt. 13: 31, Mark 4: 30–2.

    stem: stalk, bearing leaves; a race or family.

    artillery: any engines of war (the term was retained after the invention of gunpowder).

    sheep . . . skin: Bacon is alluding to the text of Matt. 7: 15.

    Virgil: *Eclogues*, 7. 51–2.

    answered: Plutarch, 'Life' of Alexander, 31. 5.

68 *said*: Plutarch, 'Life' of Lucullus, 27. 4.

    greatness . . . military men: cf. Machiavelli, *Discorsi*, 2. 18, and *The Prince*, ch. 10.

    trivially said: a classical common place (found in Diogenes Laertius, Cicero, Plutarch, Tacitus), which Bacon probably took from Machiavelli, *Discorsi*, 2. 10: 'Money is not the sinews of war, although it is generally so considered'.

    Solon: this saying, found in the same passage in Machiavelli, derives from Lucian's dialogue 'Charon'.

    militia: originally 'citizen army' (not professional).

    otherwise . . . themselves: weak for other reasons.

68 *rest*: rely. On the dangers of relying on mercenaries see *Discorsi*, 1. 43, 2. 20, and *The Prince*, chs. 12, 13.

blessing: 'grace given by God': see Gen. 49: 9, 14.

between burthens: loaded down.

excises: taxes on home commodities, especially food, drink, and clothing, which were as high as 50 per cent in the Low Countries at this time.

subsidies: contributions to the royal budget voted by Parliament.

staddles: young trees left standing in a plantation after the removal of the underwood.

69 *helmet*: only one man in a hundred fit to be a soldier.

infantry . . . an army: cf. Machiavelli, *Discorsi*, 2. 18.

middle people: yeomanry (see below).

spoken: *History of Henry VII*: *Works*, vi. 93–5; *Henry VII*, ed. Vickers, 65–7.

of a standard: up to a reasonable standard, proportional to their undertakings.

hirelings: hired labourers. Bacon is referring to current economic conditions: 'while the cost of living rose by about 80 per cent between 1550 and 1600, wages had risen by only 50 per cent. At the same time the expanding population, and the necessity for landlords to exploit their estates more efficiently, were multiplying the numbers of the rural poor . . . Outright depopulation was not common, but the numbers of cottagers and wage labourers increased; and they tended to become poorer as those with secure tenures or long leases flourished': D. M. Loades, *Politics and the Nation*, 344–5.

Terra . . . glebae: *Aeneid*, 1. 531, 'A land powerful in arms and richness of soil'.

free servants: as Melchionda makes clear (p. 524), these are paid servants wearing livery supplied by their masters, a practice which was frequently condemned in *Henry VII*: *Works*, vi. 80, 85–6, 219–20, 224; ed. Vickers, pp. 53, 57–8, 177–8, 182.

yeomanry: farmers owning their land, ranking one grade below gentlemen, and who often served in the army as foot soldiers.

tree: Dan. 4: 10–26.

great enough . . . boughs: cf. Machiavelli, *Discorsi*, 2. 3; and Bacon, *Works*, x. 96.

nice: fastidious, particular. Cf. Machiavelli, *Discorsi*, 1. 6.

windfall: anything blown down by the wind.

70 *monarchy*: in the sense of 'absolute dominion'.

jus civitatis: right of citizenship.

jus commercii . . . honorum: the all-important legal rights of commerce, marriage, receiving property by will, voting, holding office.

colonies: Roman colonies were set up by the state, not by private individuals, and modelled on the government of Rome.

constitutions: institutions (naturalization and colonization).

highest: many Spanish generals were foreigners.

Pragmatical Sanction: a royal proclamation, issued by Philip IV in 1622, offering tax incentives to those who married and bore many children, especially male.

within-door arts: crafts practised in a building or factory.

delicate manufactures: skilled occupations.

rid those manufactures: perform those artisanal activities.

abolished: slavery was abolished in Europe in the late medieval period, but persisted in the Americas.

71 *habilitations*: trainings, means of attaining ability.

intention and act: endeavour, putting into practice.

Romulus: Plutarch, 'Life' of Romulus, 28; Livy, 1. 16. 6–8.

sent a present: bequeathed (the advice to become soldiers).

oracle of time: prediction proved true by history.

sect: religion (Islam).

borderers: who live in one country and work in another.

politique ministers: official representatives of the state.

72 *tacit conformity*: as if the foreign country had the same political system, which would justify interfering in its internal affairs.

Romans: the second Macedonian war, 200–197 BC. Cf. Livy, 33. 32–3.

Athenians: the Peloponnesian wars. Cf. Thucydides, 1. 19.

slothful peace: the idea that peace is dangerous to a country, bringing idleness and diseases, goes back to the ancient Romans, especially Cato and Livy. See e.g. Brian Vickers, 'Leisure and idleness in the Renaissance: the ambivalence of *otium*', *Renaissance Studies*, 4 (1990), 1–37 and 107–54.

always on foot: on permanent service.

the law: the power of arbitrating, the supremacy.

abridgment: epitome, a short cut to dominion.

Consilium ... potiri: *Ad Atticum*, 10. 8, 'Pompey's plan is quite Themistoclean; for he thinks that the mastery of the sea means the mastery of the war'.

left that way: given up that course.

Actium: where the fleet of Augustus defeated Antony's, September 31 BC.

Lepanto: where the fleet of the Holy League, led by Don John of Austria, crushed the Turkish fleet in 1571.

set ... rest: risked everything (a metaphor from gambling).

take ... little: can give or refuse battle when it suits him.

73 *accessary*: a consequence of, dependent.

no soldiers: such honorary titles as knighthood, originally conferred for bravery on the battlefield, but subsequently a civic honour which could also be purchased by a payment into the royal coffers. (When Bacon received his knighthood from James I in 1603, he was one of 300 ennobled that day.)

scutcheon: coat of arms or shield, which sometimes recorded military honours.

hospitals: the earliest hospitals in Europe, founded in the Middle Ages, were for wounded soldiers.

garlands personal: crowns granted to individuals: the Romans awarded them to soldiers who had saved the lives of their comrades, or first mounted the wall of a besieged town (cf. Shakespeare, *Coriolanus*, 1. 9. 57 ff.).

style of Emperor: the 'title' of *imperator*, with which Roman soldiers saluted their generals after a victory.

Triumph: a triumphal procession awarded for outstanding victories: an institution that attracted much interest in the Renaissance with the rediscovery of Roman customs, as in the *Trionfi* of Petrarch and the 'Triumph of Caesar' by Mantegna, now in Hampton Court, London.

Scripture: Matt. 6: 27; Luke 12: 25.

74 *observed*: as they ought to be, according to Bacon's design for the establishment of a science of politics.

30. OF REGIMENT OF HEALTH

this: that is, the following observation.

observation . . . hurt of: Plutarch, 'Advice about keeping well' (*Moralia*, 136 E f.).

safer . . . one: Machiavelli, *Discorsi*, 1. 26.

studies: concerns. Cf. Bacon's *Historia Vitae et Mortis*: *Works*, ii. 171–2.

fretting inwards: suppressed, corrosive.

fly . . . altogether: completely avoid medicine.

75 *respect*: concentrate on recovering.

Celsus: Aulus Cornelius Celsus, AD 14–37, a physician and author of *De medicina*.

spoken: *De medicina*, 1. 1; cf. Bacon, *Works*, ii. 153.

masteries: superiority, to overcome difficulties.

conformable to the humour: readily adapting treatment to the bodily state, however imbalanced.

31. OF SUSPICION

heart: seat of courage.

suspicious: see *Henry VII*, *Works*, vi. 243; *Henry VII*, ed. Vickers, 202–3.

composition: combination of character traits (a metaphor from alchemy).

76 *Sospetto . . . fede*: 'suspicion licenses faith'.

discharge itself: free itself from suspicion by good behaviour.

32. OF DISCOURSE

Discourse: both formal and informal speech. In addition to this essay, see *Advancement of Learning* (TOA 265 ff.) and the fragmentary 'Short Notes for Civil Conversation' (*Works*, vii. 109). Reynolds (p. 236) suggests that the essay may be in part a response to Cicero, *De officiis*, 1. 37. 132: 'There are rules for oratory laid down by rhetoricians; there are none for conversation; and yet I do not know why there should not be'. But it was a common topic in Italian courtesy-manuals. The 1597 version (Appendix I) lacks this element.

wit: mental agility. (In Renaissance psychology 'wit' is the associative faculty, 'judgment' the discriminative one.)

should be thought: that is, the truth.

common places and themes: prepared topics.

want variety: cf. Plutarch, 'On the education of children', *Moralia*, 7 B–C.

present occasion . . . arguments: topics of immediate but ephemeral interest with substantial, more general ones.

77 *vein*: inclination. Cf. Cicero, *De officiis*, 1. 38. 136.

Parce . . . loris: 'spare, child, the whip, and rein the horses hard': Ovid, *Metamorphoses*, 2. 27.

take them off: stop them performing. Cf. Cicero, *De officiis*, 1. 37. 135.

galliards: lively French court dances, where evidently some dancers 'hogged the stage'.

self: cf. Cicero, *De officiis*, 1. 37. 134.

coming home: affecting, being directed towards.

78 *continued*: sustained speech, monologue.

interlocution: alternate speaking, conversational exchanges.

the turn: in turning, manoeuvring.

33. OF PLANTATIONS

Plantations: colonies. The first English settlements in Roanoke, off the coast of Virginia, were short-lived, from 1585 to 1587 (a search party in 1590 found only four survivors). Bacon had drawn up in 1606 'Certain Considerations Touching the Plantation in Ireland' (*Works*, xi. 116–26), in which he had expressed scepticism about plans for overseas colonies. But he soon changed his mind, developing an interest in colonizing ventures and subscribing to the re-founded Virginia Company of London (1610) and several similar enterprises (for Newfoundland, the North-West

Passage, and East India). Kiernan (p. 239) describes this essay as 'essentially a gloss upon the Virginia plantation before 1623', when a bitter internal dispute led to the dissolution of the Company and the imposition of royal control.

78 *world was young*: cf. Lucretius, 5. 818 ff.

pure soil: uncultivated, unoccupied—that is, 'not actually possessed of any Christian Prince nor inhabited by Christian people', as laid down in the earliest Letters Patent, to Humphrey Gilbert in 1578, and to Ralegh in 1584 (Reynolds, 241). Cf. Bacon, *Works*, xiii. 50 f.

people . . . displanted: where populations are not displaced.

drawing: withdrawing. For complaints about crude profit motives see e.g. Thomas Harriot, *True Report of the New Found Land of Virginia* (1588), in D. B. Quinn (ed.), *The Roanoke Voyages, 1584–1590*, 2 vols. (London, 1955), i. 320, 323.

scum of people: several of the early colonies were peopled with criminals (Reynolds, 242–3; Kiernan, 240).

certify: send reports, as did a group of thirty men (described in the official report as 'that scum of men') in 1610, who, having stolen a ship, turned pirates but failed, subsequently defaming the Company in England when their food ran out (Kiernan, 240).

79 *artichokes of Hierusalem*: a species of sunflower (Ital. *girasole*) with an edible root.

meat: food of all kinds.

meal: 'the edible grain or pulse, now usu. other than wheat, ground to a powder' (*SOED*).

in proportion: according to the size of the individual farmer's land.

prejudice . . . tobacco: the financial yields from Virginia tobacco were so great that farmers neglected all other crops (Kiernan, 242–3).

one: a suitable commodity.

brave: fine. Cf. Harriot, *True Report*, 331–2.

bay-salt: coarse-grained salt extracted from sea-water ponds by the sun's heat.

Growing silk: a vegetable fibre, resembling silk. Cf. Harriot, *True Report*, 325–6.

sweet woods: various South American and West Indian lauraceous trees.

Soap-ashes: alkaline salts with corrosive qualities (e.g. caustic soda).

mines: gold mines. (The fruitless search for precious metals in the early colonies damaged their proper development: Melchionda, 541.)

80 *carriage*: the cost and bother of transport.

defence . . . not amiss: it is right to help them defend themselves.

spread into generations: grow with the human propagation.

destitute: abandon (as happened with several early settlements, notably Roanoke).

guiltiness of blood: responsibility for the death of.

34. OF RICHES

baggage: hindrance. In his 'Promus of formularies and elegances' (1594) Bacon had noted *Divitiae impedimenta virtutis*. Cf. Guicciardini, *Ricordi*, no. 65: 'The man who called baggage trains "impediments" could not have expressed it better; the one who invented the saying "more trouble than moving camp" put it very well' (p. 20).

81 *Where . . . eyes?*: Eccles. 5: 11.

Riches . . . man: Prov. 18: 11.

sold: deceived, ruined. Cf. Juvenal, 10. 12–18.

friarly: like a monk, with his vow of poverty.

In . . . quaeri: 'in striving to increase his wealth, it was apparent that he sought not prey for his avarice, but an instrument for his goodness': *Pro Rabirio Postumo*, 3. 5.

Qui . . . insons: 'he that maketh haste to be rich shall not be innocent': Prov. 28: 20.

poets feign: Lucian, *Timon*, 20 ff.

Plutus: the Greek god of wealth.

Pluto: the Greek god of the underworld.

stoop: personally apply themselves to managing their own estates (agriculture).

a nobleman: probably George Talbot, 6th Earl of Shrewsbury (*c*.1522–90).

82 *husbandry*: here in the general sense of branches of 'productive activity' (*SOED*).

one: Lampone, a rich Greek merchant, according to Plutarch, 'That aged men ought to govern the commonwealth' (*Moralia*, 787 A).

overcome . . . bargains: make his own deals.

in . . . alieni: 'in the sweat of another man's face': a parody of God's punishment of Adam for his disobedience, 'in the sweat of thy face shalt thou eat bread' (Gen. 3: 19).

plough upon Sundays: violates religious principles.

scriveners and brokers: intermediaries between lender and borrower.

value: represent as trustworthy; or overvalue (to increase their own commission).

privilege: monopoly on foreign trade.

sugar man . . . Canaries: owner of a sugar plantation on the Canary Islands.

82 *logician*: Peter Ramus (1515–72), the French scholar whose proposed 'reforms' of logic and rhetoric included dividing dialectic into two parts, invention and judgement.

gains certain: safe returns on investments.

83 *coemption of wares*: ingrossing, hoarding goods.

party . . . intelligence: if the person concerned has inside knowledge.

feeding humours: pandering to whims, appetites.

executorships: the administrator of a will received a fee.

testamenta . . . capi: 'he seized testaments [of men without heirs] and wards as if with nets': *Annals*, 13. 42.

penny-wise: as in the proverb, 'Penny wise, pound foolish'.

riches have wings . . . themselves: Prov. 23: 5.

sacrifices without salt: see Lev. 2: 13 and Mark 9: 49, texts which Bacon elsewhere interpreted as meaning 'that God is not pleased with the body of a good intention, except it be seasoned with that spiritual wisdom and judgment, as it be not easily subject to be corrupted and perverted: for salt, in the scripture, is a figure both of wisdom and lasting' (*Works*, xi. 249).

painted sepulchres: Christ described the hypocritical Pharisees as 'whited Sepulchres' (Matt. 23: 27).

putrefy: rot (salt was used to preserve meat and fish).

liberal . . . of his own: distributes generously what belongs rather to others than to himself (presumably since many wills, including Bacon's own, contained bequests which the estate could not cover).

35. OF PROPHECIES

divine prophecies: those involving God's chosen people and the Messiah.

natural: made naturally, from known data, as opposed to 'hidden causes'.

Pythonissa: the name used in the Vulgate (drawing on Greek traditions involving Apollo and the python) for the witch of Endor, whom Saul petitioned to call back the ghost of Samuel. Cf. 1 Chron. 10: 13.

Saul: 1 Sam. 28: 3–25.

At . . . illis: 'the house of Aeneas shall reign in all lands, and his children's children, and their generations': Virgil, *Aeneid*, 3. 97–8, itself an adaptation of *Iliad*, 20. 307–8. Bacon used Eobanus Hessus' Latin translation of the *Iliad* (Basel, 1540).

84 *Venient . . . Thule*: 'in far-off years there shall come the ages when ocean shall loosen the bounds of the world, and the huge earth shall lie revealed, and Tiphys shall disclose new worlds; and Thule shall no longer be the limit of all lands': *Medea*, 2. 375–9.

Polycrates: tyrant of Samos, lured to his death by the Persians. Cf. Herodotus, 3. 124–5.

Philip of Macedon: Plutarch's 'Life' of Alexander the Great, 2. 3.

Philippis . . . videbis: 'you shall see me again at Philippi', Plutarch's 'Life' of Brutus, 36. 3; Appian, *Bellum civile*, 4. 134; cf. Shakespeare, *Julius Caesar*, 4. 3. 283 f.

Tu . . . imperium: 'thou, too, Galba, shalt have thy taste of empire': Tacitus, *Annals*, 6. 20; Suetonius, 'Life' of Galba, 4, tells it of Augustus, not Tiberius.

Vespasian's time: Tacitus, *Histories*, 5. 13; said to refer to Vespasian.

Domitian: Suetonius, 'Life' of Domitian, 23.

Henry the Sixth: cf. *Henry VII*, *Works*, iv. 245; *Henry VII*, ed. Vickers, 204; and Shakespeare, *3 Henry VI*, 4. 6. 65–76.

in France: Bacon spent from 1576 to 1579 in the train of Sir Amyas Paulet, ambassador to the French Court.

Queen Mother: wife of King Henry II of France (1547–59).

a course at tilt: a joust with a lance; tournament.

beaver: front part of a helmet, which had openings for the eyes.

hempe: a coarse fibre, sometimes woven (or spun) into a rope.

principial: initial, a word coined by Bacon (*OED*).

85 *Britain*: 'Britain, after the OE period, was for long used only as a historical term, but in 1604 James I & VI was proclaimed 'King of Great Britain' (*SOED*).

eighty-eight: 1588, when the Spanish Armada was outsailed and outgunned by the English navy, and subsequently destroyed by bad weather.

Baugh . . . May: the Bass Rock; the isle of May—both islands in the Firth of Forth, Scotland.

Regiomontanus: Johannes Müller of Königsberg (1436–76), German astronomer, who is said to have written four lines in German foretelling great revolutions in 1588. But these were enlarged and latinized by Gaspar Bruschius in 1553, and applied to a quite different prediction (Reynolds, 262).

octogesimus . . . annus: 'the wonderful year 88', when a supposedly inauspicious conjunction of the planets was prophesied to bring terrible disasters.

Cleon's dream: in Aristophanes' *Knights* (197 ff.) Demosthenes expounds the oracle's prediction that Cleon will be overcome by a serpent as referring to a sausage-seller (who indeed triumphs over him).

severe laws: Henry VIII, Edward VI, and Elizabeth all passed laws against fantastical prophecies, especially those involving 'any figure, casting of nativity, or by calculation, prophesying, witchcraft, conjuration, &c'.

Seneca's verse: from *Medea*, quoted above.

then: before the world had been explored.

86 *Atlanticus*: in *Timaeus*, 24 E–25 D, Plato records the tradition of a huge sunken island in the Atlantic. His dialogue *Critias* (sometimes known in Renaissance Latin translations as *Atlanticus*) describes this lost island.

great: the decisive argument.

36. OF AMBITION

Ambition: cf. Guicciardini, *Ricordi*, no. 32: 'Ambition is not to be condemned, nor should one revile the ambitious man's desires to attain glory by honourable and worthy means. Such men as these do great and outstanding things, and anyone who lacks this urge is a cold spirit and inclined rather to idleness than to effort. Ambition is pernicious and detestable when its sole end is power. This is usually true of those princes who, when they set it up as an idol to achieve what will lead them to power, set aside conscience, honour, humanity, and all else' (p. 13).

choler: yellow bile, the source of anger, one of the four 'humours' from which the body was thought to be composed. Health depended on their balanced circulation. The analogy with ambition is positive at this point.

retrograde: moving backwards, as the planets sometimes seem to do when viewed from the Earth (thought by astrologers to be an inauspicious omen).

seeled: blindfolded. The eyelids of the bird (usually a falcon) were stitched together by thread, to make it fly higher.

Tiberius . . . Sejanus: see Dio Cassius, 58. 9; Tacitus, *Annals*, 6. 48; and Ben Jonson, *Sejanus*, Act 5.

87 *popular*: loved by the people (a source of instability).

figure . . . ciphers: the only number amid zeros.

37. OF MASQUES AND TRIUMPHS

88 *Triumphs*: chivalric exercises, discussed in the final paragraph.

serious observations: as are the other Essays.

daubed with cost: put on at great expense. In the currency of those days putting on a masque cost between £700 and over £3,000.

Dancing to song: that is, in the main masque.

broken music: a consort or small group containing both wind and string instruments.

ditty . . . device: text or words (Lat. *dicta*) of the song matching the masque's plot or theme.

Acting in song: sung recitative, as in the operas produced in Florence from the 1590s on.

dancing: singing while dancing, as in the popular 'jig'.

high and tragical: in the high style, with dignity.

against another: with the voices repeating separate phrases antiphonally, as in the music written by Gabrieli and Monteverdi for St Mark's Cathedral, Venice.

figure: shape (a pyramid, for example, or spelling out a name).

alterations: scene-changes, for which the machinery (only possible at this time in some specially adapted private halls, not in the open-air public theatres) was often noisy.

masquers: the performers, some of whom were professional.

come . . . scene: descend from the stage to the hall, for a dance in which the leading members of the audience took part.

motions: movements, gestures which will attract the onlookers' attention.

chirpings or pulings: singing like birds or in a thin, child-like voice (the 'trebles' that Bacon disliked).

sharp: vivacious, cheerful (in a major key). In a letter of 1594–5 Bacon wrote that 'in music, I ever loved easy airs, that go full all the parts together, and not these strange points of accord and discord' (*Works*, viii. 356–7).

oes: the plural of the letter 'o'; *oes* or *spangs* were spangles, sequins, circular pieces of glittering metal sewn onto costumes.

lost: invisible from a distance, lacking adequate lighting.

vizards: masks: at the end of the show the masquers often removed their masks and presented themselves to the leading spectators.

anti-masques: grotesque episodes, with music and dancing, as contrast to the stately main masque.

Ethiops: blacks (as in Jonson's *Masque of Blackness*, 1605).

turquets: 'little Turks', a word coined by Bacon (*OED*).

89 *strange changes*: unexpected transitions, discords suitable to the anti-masque.

jousts . . . tourneys: sporting encounters between armed knights on horseback with blunted lances and swords, respectively.

barriers: combats within a fenced-off area, fought on foot with short swords and lances.

38. OF NATURE IN MEN

Nature: inclination, innate drives.

return: rebound (having been suppressed).

arrest . . . time: slow down nature's workings.

say . . . letters: repeat the alphabet.

90 *Optimus . . . semel*: 'he is the best liberator of his mind who has burst the chains binding his breast, and has done with grieving': Ovid, *Remedia amoris*, 293–4.

90 *ancient rule*: Aristotle, *Nicomachean Ethics*, 2. 9, 1109^{b}4 ff.

   understanding it: that is. Cf. *Nicomachean Ethics*, 2. 6, 1107^{a}9 ff.

   induce . . . both: get used to the same (bad) habits in both. Cf. Cicero, *De oratore*, 1. 33. 149 f.

   Aesop's damsel: in this (post-Aesopic) fable, a cat which had been turned into a girl actually revealed her true nature not at the 'board' (dining-table) but in the bridal chamber.

   multum . . . mea: 'my soul has long been a sojourner' (Ps. 120: 6, Vulgate). In the Authorized Version it reads 'My soul hath long dwelt with him that hateth peace' (Geneva Bible, similarly).

39. OF CUSTOM AND EDUCATION

Machiavel: *Discorsi*, 3. 6.

91 *Clement . . . Gerard*: four (Catholic) assassins: Jacques Clement assassin-ated King Henry III of France in 1589; François Ravillac killed King Henry IV of France in 1610; John Jaureguy wounded, but failed to kill Prince William of Orange in 1582; Baltazar Gerard finally murdered him in 1584. The Latin translation of the *Essays* (1638) adds 'or Guy Fawkes'.

   men of the first blood: those committing their first murder.

   votary resolution: taking a vow to perform something.

   dead images: lifeless statues.

   Indians: the Gymnosophists: see Cicero, *Tusculan Disputations*, 5. 17. 27–8.

   Sparta: see Montaigne, *Essais*, 2. 32.

   queching: uttering a sound; or perhaps 'flinching'. Cf. Cicero, *Tusculan Disputations*, 2. 14. 34; 5. 27. 77.

   an Irish rebel: Brian O'Rourke, in 1597; the incident also appears in the play *Sir John Oldcastle*, part 1 (1600).

   Deputy: Lord-Lieutenant of Ireland.

   with: a band made of twisted twigs, as opposed to the 'halter', a type of rope used to hang criminals, or lead animals.

   engaged: held fast, as in a vice. Bacon's source was Giles Fletcher, *Russe Commonwealth* (1591).

   pliant: adaptable. Cf. Montaigne, 'De l'institution des enfans', *Essais*, 1. 26 (Pléiade edn., p. 152).

92 *collegiate*: in company (as in a college).

   misery . . . desired: some commentators see here a reference to the Jesuits' educational system: Bacon admired its efficiency, but deplored its aims (*Works*, iii. 276–7). To others it is a complaint about the gap between methods and goals in contemporary moral education.

40. OF FORTUNE

occasion fitting virtue: circumstances coupled with merit.

Faber . . . suae: 'each man is the maker of his own fortune': a saying combined from several classical sources, including Plautus, *Trinummus*, 2. 2. 84 (line 363).

Serpens . . . draco: 'a serpent must eat another serpent before it can become a dragon': Erasmus, *Adagia*.

deliveries: ways of behaving; free use of the limbs.

Cato Major: Marcus Porcius Cato (234–149 BC), exemplar of Roman austerity and virtue.

In . . . videretur: 'in this man there was such strength of body and mind that no matter where [in what level of society] he was born he would have made himself a fortune': paraphrase of *Histories*, 39. 40.

falleth upon: settles on (as an explanation).

versatile ingenium: 'adaptable nature'.

blind: (according to the traditional iconographical representation).

93 *Poco di matto*: (Ital.) 'A bit of a fool', corresponding to the English proverb, 'Fortune favours fools'.

enterpriser . . . remover: adventurer or restless person, always on the move.

virtues: here, great achievements.

Caesarem . . . ejus: 'you carry Caesar and his fortune': Plutarch, 'Life' of Caesar, 38.

Sulla . . . Felix . . . Magnus: 'fortunate', not 'great'. Spoken at the end of a triumph: Plutarch, 'Life' of Sulla, 6. 3 f.

Timotheus: Athenian general, referred to by Plutarch in the same passage.

slide: smoothness of movement. In his 'Life' of Timoleon (36) Plutarch compared the 'singular grace' of Homer's verses, 'easily made', with the wars of Timoleon, in which, 'besides equity and justice, there [was] also great ease and quietness', thus proving that credit should be given not to Fortune but to his 'most noble and fortunate courage'.

much: mostly—that is, *virtù* (human endeavour) is the crucial factor, not fortune.

41. OF USURY

Money-lending had long been accepted throughout Europe (not just in Jewish hands) as a standard commercial practice in the financing of new businesses, with the shareholders receiving a form of interest. However, traditional ethical attitudes, going back to Aristotle, disapproved of the unnaturalness of making money 'breed' of itself. The Church officially endorsed this disapproval, also invoking the Christian concept of charity against taking advantage of an individual in need. The accepted interest rate in Elizabeth's reign was 10 per cent, but in 1623 parliament reduced it to 8 per cent. Bacon, like most courtiers and noblemen in this period, lived a life based on credit and died heavily in debt. For Bacon's proposals to control usury, drafted in 1623 and very similar to this essay, see *Works*, xiv. 410, 413–20; Reynolds, 292–5; and Kiernan, 124, 266–9.

93 *tithe*: one-tenth of the annual income or produce was supposed to be paid to the Church. The maximum rate of usury under Henry VIII and Elizabeth I was 10 per cent.

sabbath-breaker: church laws forbade working on Sundays, but interest accumulated daily.

94 *Ignavum . . . arcent*: 'they drive the drones, a lazy herd, from the hives': *Georgics*, 4. 168.

the first law: God's commandment to Adam and Eve.

In . . . alieni: 'in the sweat of thy face shalt thou eat bread': Gen. 3: 19; not 'in the sweat of another man's face'.

orange-tawny bonnets: the Jews in the Venetian Ghetto were compelled to wear a distinguishing dress, red and yellow (dark orange) turbans.

do judaize: follow Jewish customs. In fact, despite popular stereotypes and prejudice, Jews were in a minority as money-lenders, and not only in England.

against nature: this argument goes back to Aristotle, *Politics*, 1. 10, 1258^{b}2 ff. See also Shakespeare, *The Merchant of Venice*, 1. 3. 94–137, and 'A Devillish Usurer' in Sir Thomas Overbury's *Characters*.

concessum . . . cordis: 'a concession because of the hardness of heart': Matt. 19: 8.

vena porta: 'gate-vein', i.e. the multi-branched vein distributing chyle to the liver.

sit at . . . rent: be a tenant paying a high rent.

the box: the 'bank' or pot in gambling.

95 *mortgaging or pawning*: loaning of property or land as security for a debt and depositing objects as security for payment.

take pawns without use: take securities in pledge (and lend money upon them) without exacting interest.

forfeiture: yielding up a property as a penalty for not paying the interest due. Compare Shylock in *The Merchant of Venice*, 4. 1. 206 ff.

idle: pointless; a statute passed in 1551 prohibiting usury failed, encouraging the revival of even worse abuses.

sent to Utopia: dismissed as imaginary, unreal.

grinded: blunted; cf. earlier the (traditional) metaphor for usury as 'gnawing'.

to seek for: at a loss for, have difficulty finding money. The high profits of commerce can support a higher interest rate.

96 *to take . . . penalty*: from taking a proportion of the interest rate (state tax).

purchase: 'the annual return or rent from land' (*SOED*), so that 'sixteen year's purchase' is the purchase price calculated as the revenue for that period.

mislike: dislike. Banks were not yet established in England, and were regarded with distrust as centres of financial power.

answered . . . matter: guaranteed a small fee (known as 'the King's profit').

colour: 'represent as one's own' (*SOED*): lending money they have themselves borrowed, under pretence that it is their own.

42. OF YOUTH AND AGE

This essay owes something to Aristotle's juxtaposition of these two states of life in *Rhetoric*, 2. 12–13, 1389ᵃ2–90ᵃ25.

old in hours . . . lost no time: mature, experienced. Cf. Guicciardini, *Ricordi*, no. 145: 'Rest assured that, although man's life is short, yet there is plenty of time for those who know how to make capital of it and not to consume it in vain' (p. 38).

97 *heat*: an excess of one of the four humours.

meridian: mid-point (of the sun's course; here of life).

Julius Caesar, and Septimius Severus: Julius Caesar fought the Gallic war in his mid-forties, and became dictator in 46 BC, aged 56. Septimius Severus was proclaimed emperor in AD 193, aged 47.

Juventutem . . . plenam: 'he spent a youth full of errors, nay more, of madnesses': paraphrase of A. Spartianus, 'Life' of Severus, *Scriptores Historiae Augustae*, 2.

Augustus Caesar . . . Cosmus . . . Gaston de Fois: Octavius (63 BC–AD 14), first Roman emperor, held power by his early thirties; Cosimo I de' Medici (1537–69) became Duke of Florence at the age of 17; Gastone III 'Fébus', Count of Foix and Viscount of Béarn (1331–90), was an outstanding military and political leader at an early age.

invent . . . judge: terms from logic: to have ideas, then to evaluate them.

fitter . . . counsel: cf. Plutarch, 'That aged men ought to govern the commonwealth', *Moralia*, 789 E.

degrees: intermediate stages. Cf. Aristotle, *Rhetoric*: 'Young men have strong passions . . . are hot-tempered and quick-tempered . . . All their mistakes are in the direction of doing things excessively and vehemently . . . they overdo everything' (1389ᵃ3 f., 9 f., 1389ᵇ3 ff.).

object too much . . . adventure too little: cf. Aristotle, *Rhetoric*: Old men 'are sure about nothing and under-do everything. They "think", but they never "know", and because of their hesitation they always add a "possibly" or a "perhaps", putting everything this way and nothing positively' (1389ᵇ17 ff.).

actors: protagonists, here: 'directors'. Cf. Plutarch, *Moralia*, 790 D ff.

extern accidents: outside events (unpredictable).

97 *moral*: in ethics. Cf. Aristotle, *Rhetoric*: Young men 'love honour . . . more
    than they love money . . . They look at the good side rather than the bad . . .
    They trust others readily . . . They would always rather do noble deeds
    than useful ones', showing the dominance of 'character' and 'excellence'
    over 'reasoning' (1389ᵃ12 ff.).

    politic: politics, but also implying 'prudential self-concern'. Cf. Aristotle,
    Rhetoric: Old men are 'distrustful', 'not generous', 'cowardly', and 'are too
    fond of themselves; this is one form that small-mindedness takes. Because
    of this, they guide their lives too much by consideration of what is useful
    and too little by what is noble—for the useful is what is good for oneself, and
    the noble what is good absolutely' (1389ᵇ21 ff.).

    rabbin: the rabbinical scholar Isaac Abravanel (1437–1508), commenting on
    Joel 2: 28.

98 *Hermogenes*: a rhetorician of the second century AD, who produced several
    books between the ages of 18 and 20 but at 24 completely lost his memory.
    Cf. Philostratus, *De vitis sophistarum*, 2. 7.

    luxuriant: exuberant in growth, over-abundant (originally: producing
    foliage without fruit). Cf. Quintilian, *Institutio oratoriae*, 11. 1. 31.

    Idem . . . decebat: 'he remained the same, when the same was not becoming':
    paraphrase of *Brutus*, 95. Hortensius was Cicero's early rival.

    Ultima . . . cedebant: 'his end did not match his beginning': the phrasing is
    from Ovid, *Heroides*, 9. 23, but Bacon is thinking of Livy, *Histories*, 38.
    52–3.

43. OF BEAUTY

In this essay Bacon discusses not so much aesthetics as human beauty and its relationship to other qualities, beginning and ending with virtue. As he wrote in
the *Antitheta Rerum*, 'Virtue is nothing but inward beauty; beauty is nothing but
outward virtue' (*Works*, iv. 473). The corollary, for many Renaissance theorists,
was that ugly people must be evil. For the background see A. P. McMahon,
'Francis Bacon's Essay "Of Beauty" ', *PMLA* 60 (1945), 716–59.

    behaviour . . . virtue: manners, outer appearance, not inner worth.

    *Augustus Caesar, Titus Vespasianus, Philip le Bel . . . Edward the Fourth . . .
    Alcibiades . . . Ismael the Sophy*: for Augustus Caesar see Suetonius,
    'Augustus', 79. Titus Vespasianus, emperor AD 69–79, had 'a goodly pres-
    ence and countenance': Suetonius, 'Vespanianus', in a passage not found in
    modern editions. 'Philip le Bel' or Philip IV, King of France from 1285 to
    1314. Edward the Fourth, King of England from 1461 to 1483. Alcibiades,
    Athenian statesman and general (c.450–404 BC): cf. Plutarch, 'Life' of
    Alcibiades, 1. Shah Ismael reigned from 1500 to 1524.

    high . . . spirits: men of great courage.

    colour: complexion. Contemporary art theory, influenced by rhetoric, de-
    bated whether the highest artistic gift was *disegno* (design, composition) or
    colore.

decent and gracious motion: graceful, appropriate bearing or movement (the rhetorical concept of decorum).

nor . . . life: not even the true likenesses when seen for the first time.

strangeness . . . proportion: Kiernan (p. 273) cites Cicero, *De inventione*, 2. 1. 3: Nature never makes 'anything perfect and finished in every part . . . She bestows some advantage on one . . . but always joins it with some defect'.

Apelles: the same passage in Cicero tells how Zeuxis (not Apelles) painted a composite portrait of Venus using the best features of five beautiful maidens; cf. also Pliny, *Epistles*, 35. 36. 2.

Durer: Albrecht Dürer (1471–1528), German painter and engraver, whose *De Symmetria Partium in Rectis Formis Humanorum Corporum* (1532) contains elaborate diagrams of correct bodily proportions.

99 *pulchrorum . . . pulcher*: 'the autumn of beautiful persons is beautiful': Plutarch, 'Life' of Alcibiades, 1. 5, and Erasmus, *Adagia*. Bacon had noted it in the 'Promus' of 1594.

but by pardon: except by permission (not by right).

makes a dissolute youth: tempts youth to self-indulgence, laxity of morals.

vices blush: out of shame at their evil.

44. OF DEFORMITY

Deformed persons: for the tradition that Bacon was alluding to Robert Cecil (1563–1612), see Reynolds, 309–11, and Kiernan, 274. This essay was first published after Cecil's death in 1612.

Scripture: Rom. 1: 31; 2 Tim. 3: 3 (but not applied to deformed persons).

100 *Agesilaus . . . Socrates*: Agesilaus, Spartan king (444–360 BC), had one leg shorter than the other; cf. Plutarch's 'Life'. Zanger, a hunchback, was son of the Ottoman ruler, Soliman the Magnificent. Aesop was traditionally ugly and deformed. Pedro de la Gasca (*c.*1493–1567) was ugly and disproportioned, while Socrates pronounced himself ugly.

45. OF BUILDING

The country-house whose construction Bacon describes here is on the grand scale, showing the *Essays'* connection with the 'Advice to Princes' tradition. It uses the old-fashioned courtyard plan, suitably fitted out for the 'progress' or country tour of the monarch and his retinue. As Kiernan shows (pp. 276–84), in some respects the building resembles Bacon's family house at Gorhambury.

100 *enchanted palaces*: as in Renaissance epic, Ariosto's *Orlando Furioso*, Spenser's *Faerie Queene*.

Momus: Greek god of fault-finding, who blamed Athena's house for not having wheels with which to escape unpleasant neighbours.

101 *lurcheth*: swallows up (medieval Latin: *lurcare*, to swallow food greedily), merchandise being dearer.

101 *Lucullus*: Plutarch, 'Life' of Lucullus, 39. 4.

Vatican: the residence of the Pope, a vast assemblage of private and state apartments, chapels and courtyards.

Escurial: El Escorial, the huge palace outside Madrid, built by Philip II of Spain in 1563–83.

Hester: Esther 7: 8, 'the place of the banquet of wine'.

not only returns: not just the wings, where the building turns back from the front, but extended on either side of the central tower at a lower elevation. The tower, extending over two storeys, is about ninety foot high.

preparing place: changing room for the performers in the 'masques and triumphs'.

102 *at the first*: beginning from the tower.

open newel: central staircase built around an open well; a recent innovation in English houses (*c*.1605).

images of wood: carved wood figures, painted to look like brass; probably heraldic.

room: space on the ground floor.

outside: (the turrets, not the staircases). Reynolds suggests that Bacon may have had in mind the Great Court of his Cambridge college, Trinity.

But: 'let there be' (understood).

side alleys . . . to graze: the lawn to be surrounded by stone paths, with two central paths intersecting and dividing it into quarters, the turf being cropped by grazing sheep.

row of return: side wing and front.

works: designs in the stained glass windows.

chambers of presence: reception rooms, where the king or lord receives his guests.

ordinary entertainments: the family's normal common rooms.

double house: having rooms back and front.

thorough lights: through lights, windows placed on both sides of the room.

103 *sides*: two sides (neither on the back of the main building nor on the façade of the structure that closes the court).

place of . . . estivation: summer house.

infirmary: the first appearance of this word in English (*OED*).

antecamera, and recamera: ante-room and retiring room.

ground story . . . gallery: at the end of the courtyard facing the garden, a portico.

crystalline: windows of clear, not coloured glass.

fine avoidances: inconspicuous (or invisible) outlet pipes.

green court plain: wholly turfed courtyard.

tarrasses: terraces; open spaces (above the cloisters that surround this courtyard).

104 *offices*: buildings for the household administration.

46. OF GARDENS

Bacon was closely associated with gardens all his life. Every house that he owned, rented, or built, had extensive gardens, and he was responsible for re-designing and developing the gardens of his 'law school', Gray's Inn, where he had rooms for many years. For his alterations to the gardens of the Bacon family house at Gorhambury see the notes in his personal diary of 1608, the 'Commentarius Solutus' (*Works*, xi. 76–7). The garden described here, with its 'royal ordering' like the palace in the previous essay, is meant for a Prince. But Bacon does not follow the fashions for 'state and magnificence', elaborate struc-tural and visual effects, preferring 'use' or usefulness (which, he believes, con-stitutes 'the true pleasure of a garden'), and an environment pleasant to the senses all the year round. 'What is fresh in the essay is the aim of combining landscape architecture and horticulture for as much of the year as the gardener's art will allow' (Kiernan, 286). Kiernan has established that Bacon corrected the proofs of this essay himself (pp. cv–cvi).

God . . . Garden: Gen. 2: 8.

gross handy-works: mere manual contrivances, omitting nature.

germander: plants of the genus *Teucrium*, e.g. chickweed.

flags: the long slender leaves of such plants as lilies or 'sword-flags'.

stooved: heated by a stove (in a hothouse). The uncorrected copies read 'stirred' (Kiernan, 139).

crocus vernus: probably the yellow and white spring saffron, since the yellow crocus was not introduced into England until 1629 (Wright, 361).

bugloss: name of several boraginaceous plants, e.g. borage, lungwort.

105 *genitings, quadlins*: early summer apples.

barberries: shrub with sweet-smelling yellow flowers and red berries.

cornelians: fruit of the cornel-tree, used in some parts of England for tarts.

services: small, long brown berries of the service-tree (or sorb), edible when over-ripe.

medlars: fruit of the medlar-tree, edible when over-ripe.

ver perpetuum: 'perpetual spring' (cf. Virgil, *Georgics*, 2. 149). Bacon altered the text here, his first version having been more expansive: 'Thus, if you will, you may have the *Golden Age* againe, and a Spring all the yeare long' (Kiernan, cv, 140 n.).

place: location (in this case, London).

red: while in the bud, growing.

Bartholomew-tide: 24 August.

105 *which [yield]*: an insertion proposed by Spedding and Aldis Wright; the 1625 text reads simply 'which'. The 1629 edition changed it to 'with' (Kiernan, 140).

dust: particles of pollen from the vine's small greenish-yellow flowers.

bent: a rushlike grass, used for chimney ornaments.

burnet: small purplish-brown flower that yields a penetrating scent when crushed.

106 *thirty acres*: as Kiernan (p. 291) notes, these were truly 'royal' dimensions, ten times the size of Henry VIII's Hampton Court garden, four times as big as Lord Burghley's Great Garden at Theobalds. This scale would have made it the largest garden in England, bigger even than Robert Cecil's Hatfield House.

heath or desert: part left uncultivated, wild.

alleys . . . sides: Bacon disapproves of paths cutting across a garden.

in front upon: towards the garden's entrance.

covert alley: covered walk (made here from trellises and vines).

carpenter's work: wooden construction.

knots . . . earth: herbs planted in intricate geometric designs or abstract patterns, sometimes using coloured sands.

107 *images cut out*: the classical art of topiary (the training and clipping of shrubs into ornamental shapes) was enthusiastically revived in the Renaissance. Bacon was unusual in disliking it.

pyramides: plants cut in this shape.

mount: raised central area, giving a unique perspective on the garden below.

ascents: paths leading uphill, circling the mount at various levels, so giving a clear view over the garden.

banqueting-house: for light meals, or after-dinner desserts.

chimneys . . . cast: ornamental fireplaces.

pools: here, stagnant pools.

admit . . . curiosity: is capable of elaborate design.

fair spouts: well-functioning pipes.

equality of bores: of the same size as the spouts filling the basin.

108 *canopies*: over-arching spouts.

kept with cutting . . . course: kept pruned, to restrain excessive growth.

alleys, private: secluded walks (perhaps covered by pergolas).

going wet: to avoid walking on wet grass.

47. OF NEGOTIATING

109 *Negotiating*: a modern equivalent might be 'business dealings'.

third . . . self: by a third party, rather than in person.

disavow: disown words wrongly imputed to you.

expound: disclaim wrong interpretations by explaining your real meaning.

110 *help . . . sake*: improve upon the facts, so as to please their employer.

upon conditions: conditionally (expecting a return in service or reward).

go before: be performed first (without guarantees of a return).

he: the first agent.

in trust . . . passion . . . at unawares: by trusting someone; in anger; un-expectedly.

48. OF FOLLOWERS AND FRIENDS

train: retinue (punning on 'peacock tail').

111 *export honour . . . return*: deduct good reputation, bringing envy in return.

inquire . . . house: cf. Juvenal, 3. 113.

exchange tales: trade information about households.

no . . . sufficiency: when neither is clearly superior.

take with: have to do with; or perhaps 'employ'.

all . . . favour: all depends on the patron's good grace.

112 *one*: servant or employee.

their: that of their master.

of the last impression: affected by the most recent opinion. Cf. *Advancement of Learning* (TOA 258).

vale . . . hill: the valley gives the best view of the hill: important people are more transparent to those below them.

wont to be magnified: friendship, especially between men, was much celeb-rated both in classical myth and history (Orestes and Pylades, Damon and Pythias, *et al.*) and philosophy. See Diogenes Laertius, 8. 10, Aristotle, *Nicomachean Ethics*, 9. 8, and Seneca, *De Beneficiis*, 6. 33. 3.

49. OF SUITORS

In the Jacobean court, as in many governmental hierarchies then and now, a per-son's main chance of success in a dispute or project (to gain office, say, or a wealthy sinecure) lay in winning the support of some influential figure who could affect the outcome of the affair. As a result, men of influence were pestered with suitors who requested their help and gave them valuable presents or bribes. Bacon had much unhappy experience on both sides of this relationship. Reynolds notes several points of contact with Bacon's letter and 'Advice' to George Villiers (later Duke of Buckingham): *Works*, xii. 15, 27–30.

112 *ill matters and projects*: evil cases and schemes.

undertaken: taken on (by a patron).

putrefy: corrupt. Private citizens who continually lobby men in public office will damage their moral standards.

112 *embrace*: the Latin version is more explicit: 'receive, and eagerly promise aid'.

life . . . mean: that the matter will succeed in some other way.

entertainment: 'diversion, something which withdraws attention from the main subject' (Wright).

suit of controversy: one in a chancery suit or law court, in which a suitor seeks his patron's help to influence the judge's decision (Reynolds).

suit of petition: one seeking help in obtaining some office for which there were other competitors.

depraving and disabling: misrepresenting or damaging.

113 *reporting . . . barely*: giving a frank account of the outcome, or perhaps 'chance of success'.

suits of favour: petition (already mentioned).

his: the first petitioner.

party: person presenting the suit.

Iniquum . . . feras: Quintilian, *Institutio oratoriae*, 4. 5. 16: 'ask for too much, if you want enough'.

hath . . . favour: enjoys the goodwill of whoever will grant the request.

general contrivers: all-purpose devisers of litigations and petitions.

50. OF STUDIES

114 *for ability*: to make men able.

retiring: retirement (for individual study).

ornament . . . discourse: effectiveness in conversation and in society. In classical and Renaissance rhetoric, 'ornament' could also refer to a soldier's weapons or kit, and thus to effective communication, not mere display.

judgment . . . business: evaluating and organizing the practicalities of life.

plots and marshalling: planning and executing.

sloth: laziness (that is, avoiding one's duties to society in the *vita activa*).

humour of a scholar: style of one living in a university; remote from the active life.

directions . . . large: instructions that are too general, vague.

contemn: despise (presumably as irrelevant to cunning practices).

simple: innocent (but also 'stupid').

teach not their own use: a course of study can convey the content and methods of a discipline, but not its application.

without . . . above them: external to, and transcending the scope of any discipline.

by deputy: by proxy (someone hired for that purpose).

distilled books: epitomes, which Bacon, like many Renaissance scholars, regarded as damaging to scholarly inquiry.

distilled waters: juices distilled from radishes, sage, and other plants, for medicinal purposes.

Abeunt . . . mores: 'studies affect our behaviour': Ovid, *Heroides*, 15. 83; 'Promus', no. 1121.

115 *stone and reins*: bladderstone, disorders of the kidneys.

differences: distinctions—which proliferated in scholastic thought: cf. *Advancement of Learning* (TOA 141, 157).

cymini sectores: quibblers, splitters of cummin seeds: Dio Cassius, 70. 3. 3; 'Promus', no. 891.

lawyers' cases: law reports.

51. OF FACTION

Faction: the grouping together of politicians holding a common attitude, often in opposition to the government. It must be remembered that Bacon was writing before the establishment of separate political parties.

not wise: Bacon agrees with Machiavelli (*Discorsi*, 3. 27) on the dangers of a ruler continually trying to exploit rival political groups.

policy: both 'astuteness' and 'politics'.

with correspondence to: according to, suiting the interests of.

mean . . . rising . . . adhere: men of low rank advancing socially or politically must stick together.

Lucullus: Lucius Licinius Lucullus (*c.*117–56 BC), leader of the opposition to Pompey's bid for power; Pompey responded by making a faction with Julius Caesar. Cf. Plutarch, 'Life' of Lucullus, 38. 2, 42. 4 ff.

Optimates: a conservative group from 'the best' families.

brake: broke up, quarrelled (Caesar defeated Pompey at Pharsalus).

116 *lightly . . . it*: easily comes off the gainer.

casteth: decides (as in a 'casting vote').

Padre commune: 'father to all men'.

refer: direct (as if naturally belonging to).

tanquam . . . nobis: 'just like one of us': Gen. 3: 22.

League of France: the Catholic league, formed in 1576 between Henry III and the Guise.

factions . . . in princes: terms also used to describe planetary motion, as in the following sentence, and Essay 11, 'Of Great Place', p. 26.

high . . . violently: cf. Machiavelli, *Discorsi*, 3. 27.

primum mobile: 'first mover', the outside sphere in Ptolemaic cosmology, moved by God. See Essay 15, 'Of Seditions and Troubles', p. 32.

52. OF CEREMONIES AND RESPECTS

116 *Ceremonies and Respects*: formal and respectful behaviour, good manners. Bacon provides his own version of themes much treated in the Renaissance conduct-book, such as Della Casa, *Galateo* (1558), or especially Castiglione, *Il Cortegiano* (1528), with its emphasis (e.g. 1. 26) on 'sprezzatura', a combination of natural, spontaneous, graceful behaviour with a calculated downplaying or dissimulating any conscious exertion.

real: sincere, straightforward, lacking social graces.

foil: 'a thin leaf of metal placed under the stone to improve its colour and lustre' (Reynolds).

117 *Isabella*: queen of Spain, according to a contemporary book of sayings.

commendatory: recommending a person's suitability (e.g. for employment).

For if he labour . . . unaffected: advice very close in spirit to Castiglione, as Melchionda indicates (pp. 605–6).

times and opportunities: for making compliments.

118 *He . . . reap*: Eccles. 11: 4.

53. OF PRAISE

Praise . . . virtue: in traditional ethics and rhetoric (the branch known as epideictic), from the Greeks to the Renaissance, praise was the right response to virtue, blame to vice.

species . . . similes: 'outward appearances resembling virtues': Tacitus, *Annals*, 15. 48.

swoln: inflated. A recurrent metaphor in Bacon for the uneven survival of merit.

Nomen . . . fragrantis: 'a good name is like a sweet-smelling ointment': Eccles. 7: 1, adapted.

arch-flatterer: self-love.

out of countenance: discomforted, embarrassed.

spreta conscientia: 'self-knowledge disdained': someone accepts flattery even when conscious of his own weakness.

laudando praecipere: 'to teach by praising': Pliny, *Epistles*, 3. 18.

what they are . . . should be: as Melchionda (p. 609) observes, in praising the use of ideal behaviour-types here Bacon reverses his endorsement in the *Advancement of Learning* of Machiavelli and all realistic observers of human nature who 'write what men do, and not what they ought to do' (TOA 254). The discrepancy shows the extent to which the *Essays* resemble the traditional conduct-book.

pessimum . . . laudantium: 'the worst kind of enemies, the adulators': Tacitus, *Agricola*, 41.

Grecians: perhaps Theocritus, *Idyll*, 9. 30, 12. 23–4, where the 'push' or pustule is said to be the result of having bestowed praise untruly.

119 *He . . . curse*: Prov. 27: 14.

he: that man (so praising his own profession).

civil business: civic (as opposed to ecclesiastical) affairs.

I . . . fool: 2 Cor. 11: 23.

magnificabo . . . meum: 'I will magnify my apostolate': Rom. 11: 13, adapted.

54. OF VAIN-GLORY

Vain-Glory: vanity.

prettily devised: cleverly imagined. In fact the fabulist was Laurentius Abstemius (L. Bevilacqua), whose fables were included in Renaissance editions of Aesop.

glorious: boastful; cf. the *Miles Gloriosus* or 'boastful soldier' in classical comedy.

bravery . . . comparisons: boasting depends on a person elevating himself, devaluing others.

not effectual: ineffective (the reality beneath the boasting).

There . . . lies: cf. Livy, 35. 49. 4: 'if anyone had been ignorant before what cause had brought Antiochus and the Aetolians together, it could now be clear from the speeches of their delegates and of boasts of strength which they did not possess they filled one another's minds, and in turn were filled, with groundless hopes'. Bacon referred to it again in his *Apophthegms* (*Works*, vii. 171–2): 'It was an easy matter to perceive what it was that had joined Antiochus and the Aetolians together; that it appeared to be by reciprocal lying of each, touching the other's forces.'

120 *somewhat . . . nothing*: in contradiction to the normal law, that 'nothing will come of nothing'.

brings on substance: acquires a (spurious) reality (for 'nothing succeeds like success').

as iron sharpens iron: Prov. 27: 17; 'Promus', no. 549.

upon charge and adventure: subject to expense and risk.

ballast . . . sail: have a steadying, rather than a propulsive, effect.

flight: ascent, as of an arrow, with its 'feathers'; also referring to Virgil's description of Fame, cited in the fragmentary Essay 'Of Fame', p. 132.

Qui . . . inscribunt: 'those who write books on scorning glory, sign their names [on the title-page]': Cicero, *Tusculan Disputations*, 1. 15. 34.

Socrates, Aristotle, Galen: none of whom, however, attacked glory. Bacon elsewhere accuses Socrates of false modesty (TOA 222), Aristotle of confuting every author he named in order to promote his own authority (TOA 193–4, 204), and Galen of various faults. Bacon was presumably following his stated policy of opening the path for new work by attacking undue reverence towards antiquity (TOA 143–4).

120 *at the second hand*: this sentence has given much difficulty to editors. I suggest that Bacon is alluding to the well-known principle from classical philosophy that 'virtue is its own reward', and drawing the consequence that virtue has therefore never been indebted to humanity 'at the second hand' for a reward or recognition, which would in any case be inferior.

Plinius Secundus: Pliny the Younger (*c*. AD 61–115), quoted below.

Omnium . . . ostentator: 'a boaster with a certain art [of setting forth to advantage] all he had said or done': *History*, 2. 80.

In . . . less: *Epistles*, 6. 17.

idols of parasites: they are worshipped by those who prey on them: as in Terence's *Eunuchus*, where Thraso, the foolish Miles Gloriosus, is flattered and exploited by Gnatho (Kiernan, 303).

55. OF HONOUR AND REPUTATION

121 *winning*: obtaining. Wright (p. 344) notes that Bacon's unpublished MS of 1612 reads 'The *true* winning of honour', which gives better sense.

circumstance: 'all the surroundings and accompaniments of an action' (Wright, 359).

failing . . . can honour him: cf. Suetonius, 'Life' of Augustus, 25.

broken: made to break, shine.

upon another: by comparison with, at the expense of a rival (cf. Shakespeare, *1 Henry IV*, 3. 2. 132–52).

facets: little faces.

bow: special accomplishment.

Omnis . . . emanat: Q. Cicero, *De petitione consultatus*, 5. 17: 'All reputation derives from one's servants'.

conditores imperiorum: 'founders of empires'.

Romulus, Cyrus, Caesar, Ottoman, Ismael: Romulus was the legendary founder of Rome; Cyrus the founder of the Persian monarchy; Julius Caesar established the basis for the Roman empire; Othman or Osman (1259–1326) founded the Turkish dynasty; while Ismael, the 'Sophy' of Persia, became sovereign in 1503, aged 18.

perpetui principes: 'perpetual princes'.

Lycurgus, Solon, Justinian, Eadgar, Alphonsus of Castile . . . Siete partidas: Lycurgus reformed the Spartan government and *mores*, seventh century BC; Solon reformed the Athenian constitution and laws, sixth century BC; Justinian, Roman emperor AD 527–65, codified Roman law; Eadgar, King of England, 959–75, codified English law; Alphonsus of Castile, King of Castile and Leon (1252–84), formulated this law code in 'Seven parts'.

liberatores . . . salvatores: 'liberators, saviours'.

122 *Augustus Caesar, Vespasianus, Aurelianus, Theodoricus . . . Henry the Seventh . . . Henry the Fourth*: Augustus Caesar's defeat of Antony inaugurated a

long period of peace for the Roman empire. Vespasianus delivered the empire from the civil wars following the death of Nero. Aurelianus, emperor in AD 270, was the victor in many battles. Theodoricus liberated Italy from foreign dominion, AD 493. Henry VII put down several rebellions, while Henry IV ended the long wars between Catholics and Protestants, signing the Edict of Nantes in 1598.

propagatores . . . imperii: 'enlargers or defenders of empire'.

patres patriae: 'fathers of their country', an honorific title given to many Roman emperors, e.g. in Suetonius, 'Life' of Tiberius, 67.

participes curarum: 'sharers of care', confidants. But cf. note on Essay 27, 'Of Friendship', p. 60.

duces belli: 'leaders of war'.

negotiis pares: 'equals in business'.

M. Regulus: Roman general (d. 250 BC) who, although captured, rejected peace terms that would have brought his release.

the two Decii: father and son, who, in 340 BC and 295 BC respectively, sacrificed themselves in battle for Rome.

56. OF JUDICATURE

Bacon's training, from the age of 15, was in the law, a profession with which he never lost contact. This Essay, written for the 1612 volume, and only slightly changed in 1625, is concerned more with the duties of judges (the Latin title is *De officio Judiciis*) than the administration of justice, and should be read alongside those professional works deriving from Bacon's own duties as a senior legal official, such as the 'Charge on opening the Court of the Verge', 1611 (*Works*, xi. 265–75), the 'Speech on taking his seat in Chancery' (*Works*, xiii. 182–93), the Speeches to Justice Hutton, Sir John Denham, and Sir William Jones (*Works*, xiii. 201–7), and the 'Speech to the judges before the Circuit', 1617 (*Works*, xiii. 211–14).

jus dicere . . . not jus dare: to interpret the words of the law as a whole, not unduly pressing a single point or idiosyncratic version.

novelty: innovation. Bacon thought that caution should be observed in amending the laws.

reverend . . . plausible: more worthy of respect than courting applause.

Cursed . . . landmark: Deut. 27: 17.

foul sentence: wrong, corrupt verdict. The damage so arising is much greater in the English legal system, in which adjudged cases stand as precedents.

123 *Fons . . . adversario*: 'a just man falling down in his cause before his adversary is a troubled fountain and a corrupt stream': Prov. 25: 26, paraphrased.

may have reference: may be seen as referring (i.e. does so refer).

parties that sue: those who take a case to court.

123 *causes*: motives, but also 'legal cases'.

There . . . wormwood: Amos 5: 7. Wormwood is a bitter plant, prescribed as a drug to expel intestinal worms.

force and fraud: violence and injurious deceit. According to classical philosophy, these were the two principal destroyers of justice: cf. Cicero, *De officiis*, 1. 13. 41.

contentious suits: legal actions arising out of malice or quarrelsomeness.

as God . . . hills: Isa. 40: 3–4, and Luke 3: 5.

violent prosecution: rather than the obvious meaning, a 'prosecution using violent methods', Melchionda (p. 619) suggests that Bacon means an unjustified, oppressive prosecution of a private citizen by the state.

great counsel: Kiernan suggests the sense 'disparity of counsellors' (p. 308), but the phrase could also mean 'prestigious advocates', or 'very able defence lawyers', whose skills can gain an unjust advantage (Melchionda, 619).

Qui . . . sanguinem: 'he who blows his nose vigorously, makes it bleed': Prov. 30: 33.

torture: punning on the original sense, turn or twist.

have care . . . rigour: lest punishments meant as extreme deterrents become rigidly or mechanically applied in less serious cases.

Pluet . . . laqueos: 'he shall rain snares upon them': Ps. 11: 6.

of long: for a long time. (For this whole sequence compare Shakespeare, *Measure for Measure*.)

Judicis . . . rerum: 'it is the duty of the judge [to consider] both the deed and the circumstances of the deed': Ovid, *Tristia*, 1. 1. 37.

in justice: in the administration of justice, or 'giving sentence'.

overspeaking: one who talks too much and does not listen.

well-tuned cymbal: source of harmony (from Ps. 150: 5).

to find: to establish by his own efforts.

from the bar: from the barrister responsible.

124 *direct the evidence*: elicit relevant testimony.

give the rule: pronounce the verdict.

they: the judges.

represseth . . . modest: 'God resisteth the proud, but giveth grace to the humble': Jas. 4: 6, paraphrased.

pressing: insistent, importunate behaviour (as in cross-questioning).

ministers: officers of the court.

foot-pace: walking-area near the judge's bench.

precincts and purprise: the whole area or enclosure of the court.

Grapes . . . thistles: 'do men gather grapes of thorns, or figs of thistles?': Matt. 7: 16.

catching . . . polling: grasping and stripping, plundering (hence the term 'catch-pole').

sowers of suits: who bring unjustified legal cases.

125 *quarrels of jurisdiction*: disputes (often lengthy) as to which court should try a case.

amici curiae: 'friends of the court'.

parasiti curiae: 'parasites of the court'.

sinister: left-handed, hence 'inauspicious'.

poller: court official who extracted fees (often excessive and unnecessary).

bush: here, a bramble.

weather: bad weather.

Twelve Tables: the earliest code of Roman laws, c.451 BC (engraved on tablets in the Forum).

Salus . . . lex: 'the welfare of the people is the highest law': in fact from Cicero, *De legibus*, 3. 3. 8.

in order to that end: ordained for that purpose.

oracles: sources of (supposedly) infallible truth.

business of state: national affairs.

meum and tuum: 'mine and yours': the basic principle of ownership in private law.

trench to point of estate: extend in effect to matters concerning national interests.

true policy: wise government, political practices.

spirits: the 'animal spirits' in the blood.

Salomon's throne . . . lions: 1 Kings 10: 19–20.

Nos . . . legitime: 'we know that the law is good, if only a man use it lawfully': 1 Tim. 1: 8 (Vulgate).

57. OF ANGER

For a partial source see Aristotle, *Rhetoric*, 2. 2, on anger.

126 *Stoics*: see e.g. Seneca's treatise *De ira*, which indeed argues that anger should be wholly suppressed.

Be angry . . . anger: Eph. 4: 26.

attempered: regulated, moderated. Cf. Aristotle, *Rhetoric*, 2. 3, on 'growing calm' as 'a settling down or quieting of anger' (1380^a5 ff.).

ruin . . . that it falls: falling brickwork or masonry; *De ira*, 1. 1.

To . . . patience: Luke 21: 19.

out of patience . . . soul: cf. Cicero, *De officiis*, 1. 38. 136 f.

animasque . . . ponunt: 'and lay down their lives in the wound': Virgil, *Georgics*, 4. 238.

126 *Anger . . . sick folks*: Aristotle, *Rhetoric*, 1379ᵃ16 ff.; Seneca, *De ira*, 1. 13, 16; Plutarch, 'On the Control of Anger', *Moralia*, 457 B.

scorn: contempt (as being beneath them).

give law . . . in it: set himself rules to be observed in such cases.

causes . . . chiefly three: cf. Aristotle, *Rhetoric*: 'There are three kinds of slighting—contempt, spite, and insolence' (1378ᵇ12 ff.).

contempt . . . hurt itself: sharpens, stimulates; for 'putteth an edge upon' cf. Aristotle, *Rhetoric*, 1378ᵃ31 f.

touch: offending. Cf. Aristotle, *Rhetoric*, 1378ᵇ22 ff.

127 *Consalvo*: Gonzalo Fernandez Cordoba (1453–1515), distinguished Spanish general, to whom is credited the saying: 'The honour of a gentleman should be made of a stronger cloth'. Cf. 'Promus', no. 392: 'Tela honoris tenerior', and Bacon's *Charge touching Duels* (TOA 311).

win time: cf. Aristotle, *Rhetoric*, 1380ᵇ6 ff.

reserve: hold back (till later).

aculeate: pointed, stinging; specially applicable to the person.

communia maledicta: 'general curses'.

nothing so much: not serious.

good times . . . angry business: favourable moment to inform about a matter that will arouse anger.

from the point of contempt: away from any insinuation of contempt.

58. OF VICISSITUDE OF THINGS

Vicissitude: change, mutation. One of Bacon's sources is Machiavelli, *Discorsi*, 2. 5, describing how 'the changes of religion and of language, together with the occurrences of deluges and pestilences, destroy the record of things'.

There . . . earth: Eccles. 1: 9–10, paraphrased.

that . . . remembrance: cf. *Phaedo*, 72 E; *Meno*, 81 C–D.

that . . . oblivion: Eccles. 1: 9–11.

Lethe: the river in Hades: to drink its water produced oblivion.

astrologer: perhaps Telesio, whom Bacon quotes elsewhere to similar effect (*Works*, iii. 98–100).

the matter: matter generally (as in 'the air').

128 *Phaëton's car*: the chariot which Phaëton stole from his father Helios, the sun-god, but was unable to control, soon crashed: Ovid, *Metamorphoses*, 2. 35–328. Editors suggest an allusion to Plato, *Timaeus*, 22 C–D, which interprets the myth as referring to cosmic conflagrations.

Elias: 1 Kings 17: 1, 18: 1.

West Indies: in the Renaissance this term referred to the Americas as a whole, the continent as well as islands.

hap . . . reserved: happen to be spared.

mountainous: cf. Machiavelli, *Discorsi*, 2. 5: 'the few that escape [inundations] are chiefly ignorant mountaineers, who, having no knowledge of antiquity themselves, cannot transmit any to posterity'. See also Bacon, *New Atlantis* (TOA 468).

all one: just the same (i.e. total).

newer . . . old world: see *New Atlantis* (TOA 469), where the primitive nature of their civic and political institutions is cited as one proof, another being that they have survived from a later Flood.

earthquake: Plato, *Timaeus*, 25 C–D.

seldom: actually, Bacon's main source of knowledge for the Americas, Joseph de Acosta's *Naturall and Morall Historie of the East and West Indies* (1590; English trans. 1604), reports frequent earthquakes in the Andes (a word meaning 'mountains').

generation of men: the human race.

Machiavel: *Discorsi*, 2. 5, describing the early Christians' persecution of 'the heathen religion', so extreme that they 'destroyed all its institutions and all its ceremonies, and effaced all record of the ancient theology', and would have extinguished the Latin language if there had been an alternative.

Gregory the Great: Pope 590–604, who, according to Machiavelli, persecuted with great obstinacy 'all ancient memorials, burning the works of the historians and of the poets, destroying the statues and images and despoiling everything else that gave but an indication of antiquity' (ibid.).

Sabinian: Pope 604–6, who succeeded Gregory and severely criticized him.

Superior Globe: according to Aristotelian–Ptolemaic cosmology, the concentric spheres surrounding the Earth.

Plato's great year: the 'great year', described in *Timaeus*, 39 D, was the space of time taken by all the stars to return to the places they occupied at the creation of the world; variously estimated as 10,000 to 36,000 years. There are similar discussions in Cicero, *De natura deorum*, 2. 20. 51–2, and Augustine, *De civitate dei*, 12. 13. 2.

state of like: the condition of the same individuals.

influences: powers by which, astrologers believed, planets affected human life.

version: direction; but perhaps also 'conversion', rotation.

129 *given over . . . waited upon*: not overlooked, but observed.

Prime: 'the beginning of a period or cycle' (*SOED*); perhaps named by analogy with a lunar cycle of nineteen years.

built . . . rock: Matt. 16: 18.

give stay: check, hinder; or perhaps 'estimate, comprehend'.

Mahomet: Muhammad (AD ?570–632), founder of Islam, whose 'law' is embodied in the Koran.

129 *speculative*: theoretical (matters of thought, not practice).

   Arians: followers of Arius, a fourth-century thinker who taught that Christ was the first creature, but neither eternal nor equal with God.

   Arminians: followers of Jacobus Arminius (1560–1609), a Dutch Reformed theologian who emphasized free will, opposing Calvinist notions of pre-destination and the elect.

   manner of plantations: modes of disseminating.

   signs: omens; miracles as evidence of supernatural power or authority.

130 *Tartars*: 'the combined forces of central Asian peoples, including Mongols and Turks, who under the leadership of Genghis Khan (1202–27) overran much of Asia and Eastern Europe' (*SOED*).

   Gallo-Graecia: Galatia, in central Asia Minor, conquered by the Gauls *c.*278 BC.

   fixed: the two poles.

   contrariwise: cf. Machiavelli, *Istorie Fiorentine*, 1. 1.

   northern tract . . . martial region: cf. Lucan, *Pharsalia*, 8. 363–6.

   stars: astrology divided the world up into regions, each supposedly influenced by the stars overhead.

   Charles the Great: Charlemagne (724–814), King of the Franks and Holy Roman emperor, vastly extended his empire, but it was subsequently divided up among his three grandsons.

131 *it hardly . . . observation*: this topic is difficult to analyse and generalize.

   Oxidrakes: according to Philostratus, *Life of Apollonius of Tyana*, 2. 14, and Raleigh, *History of the World* (1614), 4. 2. 21.

   Macedonians: in ancient times, inhabitants of Northern Greece, Bulgaria, and present-day Macedonia.

   well known: cf. Montaigne, 'Des Coches', *Essais*, 3. 6 (Pléiade edn., p. 886).

   arietations: assault using the aries or battering-ram.

   ignorant: cf. *Iliad*, 2. 362–8; 4. 296–305.

   ranging and arraying their battles: setting their bodies of troop in order of battle, according to terrain and tactics.

132 *philology*: perhaps 'stories to which the subject has lent itself'; or 'literary documentation'.

   circle of tales: perhaps a pun on the Greek phrase for the complete educational system, *enkyklos paideia*, which the Romans rendered as 'encyclopedia'.

59. A FRAGMENT OF AN ESSAY ON FAME

poets: As in Virgil, *Aeneid*, 4. 173–90, passages noted in 'Promus', nos. 1080–2. In the translation by C. Day Lewis:

Rumour, the swiftest traveller of all the ills on earth,
Thriving on movement, gathering strength as it goes; at the start
A small and cowardly thing, it soon puffs itself up,
And walking upon the ground, buries its head in the cloud-base.
The legend is that, enraged with the gods, Mother Earth produced
This creature, her last child, as a sister to Enceladus
And Cœus—a swift-footed creature, a winged angel of ruin,
A terrible, grotesque monster, each feather upon whose body—
Incredible though it sounds—has a sleepless eye beneath it,
And for every eye she has also a tongue, a voice and a pricked ear.
At night she flits midway between earth and sky, through the gloom
Screeching, and never closes her eyelids in sweet slumber:
By day she is perched like a look-out either upon a roof-top
Or some high turret; so she terrorizes whole cities,
Loud-speaker of truth, hoarder of mischievous falsehood, equally.
(*The Eclogues, Georgics and Aeneid of Virgil* (London, 1960), 224–5.)

Fame: rumour.

feathers . . . tongues: the traditional iconography, as in *2 Henry IV, Induction*: 'Enter RUMOUR, painted full of tongues'.

parables: specific attributes, often interpreted allegorically, as by Bacon himself on many occasions.

gathereth . . . going: the more rumours are disseminated, the stronger they grow.

ground . . . clouds: rumours readily circulate, but are intangible.

sitteth . . . watch tower: is constantly alert.

flieth . . . night: rumour flourishes in darkness and secrecy.

things not done: cf. *2 Henry IV, Induction*, lines 6 ff.: 'Upon my tongues continual slanders ride, | . . . Stuffing the ears of men with false reports'.

terror . . . cities: the disturbances produced by false rumours are greatest where the population is most dense.

they: the poets.

masculine: cf. Essay 15, 'Of Seditions and Troubles', p. 32.

fly: let fly (transitive) as when starting a falcon after its prey.

ravening fowl: birds of prey.

fames . . . sown and raised: rumours may be planted and encouraged.

132 *Mucianus*: see Tacitus, *Histories*, 2. 80, for his spreading a rumour that troops would be posted to the harsh duties of Germany.

cunningly: see Caesar, *De bello civili*, 1. 6 (where, however, the rumour is attributed to Pompey, not Caesar himself).

133 *Livia*: see Tacitus, *Annals*, 1. 5.

conceal: this had recently happened twice, in 1566 and 1574.

133 *Janizaries*: Turkish soldiers who formed the Sultan's guard, noted for their devotion.

Themistocles: see Plutarch, 'Life' of Themistocles.

the actions: political acts.

APPENDIX III

147 *Some . . . children*: as did Tiberius, according to Suetonius, 'Tiberius', 62.

149 *the cause of a benefit conferred*: cf. Seneca, *De beneficiis*, a lengthy discussion of benefits or gifts and their repayment as a sign of gratitude.

Circe's transformations: cf. Homer, *Odyssey*, 10. 133–574, 12. 8–150.

Paris . . . beauty . . . wisdom and power: alluding to the fable of Paris, made to choose between three goddesses, who preferred Aphrodite (Venus), rejecting Hera (Juno) and Athena (Minerva). Cf. Homer, *Iliad*, 24. 25 ff.; Apollodorus, *The Library of Greek Mythology* trans. R. Hard (Oxford, 1997), 146, 248.

Alexander . . . sleep and lust . . . earnests of death: cf. Plutarch, 'Life' of Alexander, 31. 5, and *Advancement of Learning* (TOA 159–60).

None . . . clemency: see Seneca, *De clementia*, 1. 2. 2.

150 *man is a god . . . not a wolf*: cf. the Latin proverb *homo homini lupus*, first found in Plautus, *Asinaria* 495, and the variant, 'Man unto man is either a god or a wolf', found in Erasmus, *Adagia*, Montaigne, *Essais*, and in many other Renaissance texts.

Fortitude: cf. Bacon's early device, *Of Tribute: or, giving that which is due*, the first speech, in 'Praise of the Worthiest Virtue, Fortitude' (TOA 22–9).

Fortitude . . . the iron age: according to a traditional scheme, the world began with a first age of gold, followed by ages of silver, brass, and (the present) iron. Cf. Hesiod, *Works and Days*, 109–201; Ovid, *Metamorphoses*, 1. 89 ff.

151 *To abstain . . . loss of it*: the Latin is more sharply turned, as if quoting traditional *sententiae*: 'Ista *Non uti ut non appetas; Non appetere ut non timeas*; pusillanimi sunt et diffidentis' (*Works*, i. 697).

152 *What art . . . art*: in the sense of an *ars*, an acquired skill. Cf. 'Of Studies, p. 114: 'they teach not their own use . . . that is a wisdom . . . above them.'

153 *If you are wise . . . are wise*: A saying ascribed to Theophrastus, found in Diogenes Laertius and in Plutarch (Bacon's probable source).

object of pursuit . . . distasteful and wearisome: cf. Ovid, *Amores*, 1. 9. 46, *Qui nolet fieri desidiosus, amet*: 'If you want a cure for slackness, fall in love!'

154 *Suspicion discharges faith*: cf. the Italian proverb, *sospetto licenza fede*.

A SELECTION OF OXFORD WORLD'S CLASSICS

GEORGE ELIOT | Adam Bede
| Daniel Deronda
| Middlemarch
| The Mill on the Floss
| Silas Marner

ELIZABETH GASKELL | Cranford
| The Life of Charlotte Brontë
| Mary Barton
| North and South
| Wives and Daughters

THOMAS HARDY | Far from the Madding Crowd
| Jude the Obscure
| The Mayor of Casterbridge
| A Pair of Blue Eyes
| The Return of the Native
| Tess of the d'Urbervilles
| The Woodlanders

WALTER SCOTT | Ivanhoe
| Rob Roy
| Waverley

MARY SHELLEY | Frankenstein
| The Last Man

ROBERT LOUIS
STEVENSON | Kidnapped and Catriona
| The Strange Case of Dr Jekyll and
| Mr Hyde and Weir of Hermiston
| Treasure Island

BRAM STOKER | Dracula

WILLIAM MAKEPEACE
THACKERAY | Barry Lyndon
| Vanity Fair

OSCAR WILDE | Complete Shorter Fiction
| The Picture of Dorian Gray

The Oxford World's Classics Website

www.worldsclassics.co.uk

- Information about new titles
- Explore the full range of Oxford World's Classics
- Links to other literary sites and the main OUP webpage
- Imaginative competitions, with bookish prizes
- Peruse *Compass*, the Oxford World's Classics magazine
- Articles by editors
- Extracts from Introductions
- A forum for discussion and feedback on the series
- Special information for teachers and lecturers

www.worldsclassics.co.uk

American Literature

British and Irish Literature

Children's Literature

Classics and Ancient Literature

Colonial Literature

Eastern Literature

European Literature

History

Medieval Literature

Oxford English Drama

Poetry

Philosophy

Politics

Religion

The Oxford Shakespeare

A complete list of Oxford Paperbacks, including Oxford World's Classics, OPUS, Past Masters, Oxford Authors, Oxford Shakespeare, Oxford Drama, and Oxford Paperback Reference, is available in the UK from the Academic Division Publicity Department, Oxford University Press, Great Clarendon Street, Oxford OX2 6DP.

In the USA, complete lists are available from the Paperbacks Marketing Manager, Oxford University Press, 198 Madison Avenue, New York, NY 10016.

Oxford Paperbacks are available from all good bookshops. In case of difficulty, customers in the UK can order direct from Oxford University Press Bookshop, Freepost, 116 High Street, Oxford OX1 4BR, enclosing full payment. Please add 10 per cent of published price for postage and packing.